# THE GREATEST LIES IN HISTORY

ALEXANDER CANDUCI

To my beloved wife Teresa, whose unwavering
faith and support have given me the strength
and self-belief to pursue my dream.

# THE GREATEST LIES IN HISTORY

*Spin, doublespeak, buck-passing and official cover-ups that shaped the world*

ALEXANDER CANDUCI

PIER 9

# CONTENTS

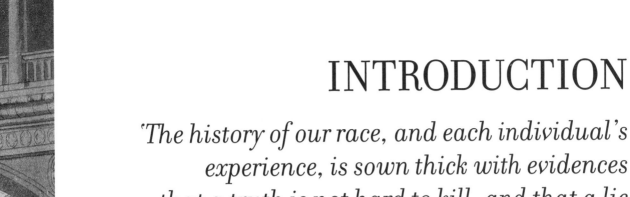

# INTRODUCTION

*'The history of our race, and each individual's experience, is sown thick with evidences that a truth is not hard to kill, and that a lie told well is immortal.'*

MARK TWAIN

Lies and the telling of them—we are all guilty to some extent. From small fibs about forgetting to take out the trash, to big lies about cheating on a spouse; whether we are driven by the best of intentions or the worst of motives, lying seems to come naturally to many *Homo sapiens*—a built-in genetic flaw or a highly evolved protective mechanism in our species, depending on who you ask about it. What is clear, however, is that in 40,000 years of lying, we've become pretty good at it.

It doesn't take much to discover that many pinnacles of human achievement, just as much as our worst moments in history, are inextricably bound with whoppers; that deceptions have played a major part in shaping the course of history and the destiny of nations. Lies have been used to justify wars, to acquire weapons, slaves, fire, food, gold, land, livestock and industrial secrets. Lies have been told to impose the dreams, ideology or religion of one person, or group of people, on the rest of humankind. Lies have allowed some to ascend to the peak of power, wealth and influence—and damn the rest.

This book is about those lies and their consequences.

With the history of the world liberally sprinkled with wars, persecutions and suffering caused by the pursuit of power, most reasonable people today would reject deception and manipulation as acceptable means to achieve social or national goals. Yet many governments continue to use precisely these tactics when the stakes are high enough, or when leaders feel the need to convince their nations to follow them into war. This book examines specific episodes in history to identify the reasons why politicians, religious leaders and others have supported some of the most outrageous lies ever told to justify war, repression, persecution and ambition.

In order to reduce their power and that of their papal supporters, the Knights Templar were cast as heretics.

The lies that have been chosen are those that have had some lasting impact upon the world, whether it be the creation of an organisation that has influenced the growth of the modern world, such as the medieval Papacy, or the persecution of a group of people, such as the Jews in the twentieth century. They are lies that have caused enormous suffering, led to wars or crackdowns on human rights, or been used as templates for deception in another country or period. Some of these deceptions have been astonishingly long lived, while others were quickly debunked. What is important, however, is not how successful they were, but that they were attempted at all, and that they played a part in shaping the fate and fortune of our world.

The book is divided into four parts, each identifying a specific theme or type of deception used throughout history. The central theme of each part is illustrated by a number of chapters, arranged in chronological order, giving detailed accounts of grand deceptions along with the truth of what really happened.

Part One: Spin & Doublespeak identifies situations in which a ruler or government has sought to manipulate information in an attempt to cover up a defeat, justify a course of action, or retrospectively give credibility to shabby motives through the use of spin—that is, the obscuring of certain facts and the emphasising of others to create a false impression of a given situation.

Part Two: Passing the Buck catalogues a number of famous and not-so-famous events in history that have seen governments and officials pick on a group of people in order to blame them for a disaster that, rightly or wrongly, was initially attributed to those in power. It also includes groups that have been targeted for other reasons, such as greed or envy.

Part Three: Official Deceptions & Cover-ups provides examples in which governments have undertaken some grand deception and incorporated the propaganda into their official accounts of history, claiming the deception as fact. Whether it was expunging a ruler from the records, depicting a repressive period as being glorious, or claiming that certain people were not acting in an official capacity during a shameful period in history, it is recounted here.

Part Four: Acting Under False Pretences tells of events in which the real motives for a war or campaign of vilification have been replaced by a blatant lie, either conceived by the persons wanting to start the conflict, or by those who sought to turn an episode in history to their advantage. Also included here are events that were hijacked by a variety of disreputable persons under the pretence of good intentions.

Each chapter is divided into three sections. The first portion gives the official version of events: the story as it is known by most people, recounted in history books, or promoted by those responsible for inventing it at the time. Some of these stories are widely known, but others are not.

The second section of each chapter sets out the true account of events, and highlights where the official story is distorted. Sometimes both versions—the official and the actual—will be the same for some time before diverging; in cases where deception and propaganda have been used to overwrite every aspect of the events concerned, they will deviate from the start.

The final section of each chapter details the legacy of the lie or deception perpetrated. Some may have had a significant impact for only a generation or two while others have continued to reverberate throughout history. In either case, the effect of the lie had a profound effect on the societies in which they occurred.

Certain ancient lies, because of their very antiquity, may seem very distant to us nowadays. Yet their story is important because of the way that individual civilisations or nations have evolved during the centuries that followed the falsehood. And we can remind ourselves what this means by looking at more recent deceptions, such as Watergate, which continue to have a significant and observable effect on the lives of people who live in the world today.

The retelling of these lies, how they came about and what the truth actually is, continues to be of the greatest importance. As George Orwell reminds us in his terrifying novel *Nineteen Eighty-Four*, 'He who controls the present controls the past. He who controls the past controls the future.' History is not simply the impartial recounting of events that occurred yesterday, last year, or in times of yore. It is always selective because it is literally impossible to include every detail in an account of the past; and history is always shaped by the perspective of the teller—someone who must construct a narrative that includes certain facts and excludes others, a process that will always be open to criticism and disagreement.

What this book does is examine a number of key events in the history of the world that have been skewed in the telling from the start; it uncovers evidence that has been suppressed, explains why that happened and demonstrates how the accepted accounts of these events need to be rejected for a more sophisticated understanding of what really happened.

The importance of this exercise is not simply to right the wrongs of the past, or to present a revisionist view of history. It is to expose the unfortunate fact that those in power regularly use spin, deception and scapegoating to achieve their agendas, which they hope that people will blindly follow. 'Those who cannot remember the past are condemned to repeat it,' said the philosopher George Santayana, and every time some grotesque deception is exposed we promise ourselves that we will learn from it and never allow it to happen again. Yet memories are short and humanity's propensity for self-deception seems to know no limit. So maybe we should take counsel from the great Roman defender of liberty, Cicero, and recall his warning that, 'To be ignorant of what happened before you were born is to be ever a child. For what is man's lifetime unless the memory of past events is woven with those of earlier times?'

THE GREATEST LIES IN HISTORY
## PART ONE

# SPIN &
# DOUBLESPEAK

*'Commentary and opinion is not spin.*
*What spin is, is taking a set of circumstances*
*[...] and making it not what it is.'*

BILL O'REILLY,

AMERICAN POLITICAL COMMENTATOR

Members of the Fourth Crusade gaze down at the city of Constantinople.

# THE VICTOR'S VERSION OF THE BATTLE OF KADESH (1275 BC)

*'And the brothers of the king were all gathered in one place, two thousand and five hundred pairs of horse, and they came right on in force, the fury of their faces to the flaming of my face. Then, like Monthu in his might, I rushed on them apace, and I let them taste my hand in a twinkling moment's space. Then cried one unto his mate, "This is no man, this is he, this is Sutek, god of hate, with Baal in his blood; let us hasten, let us flee, let us save our souls from death, let us take to heel and try our lungs and breath."'*

**Pharaoh Rameses II**

*'It depends on what the meaning of the word "is" is.'*
**Bill Clinton**

### LIE

Rameses II single-handedly won the Battle of Kadesh.

### TRUTH

Rameses was lucky to get out of there alive!

### CHIEF PARTICIPANTS

Pharaoh Rameses II, ruler of Egypt
King Muwatalli II, ruler of the Hittites

### THE STORY SO FAR

Rameses II came to the throne of Egypt in 1279 BC, during which time Egypt was the master of an empire stretching from northern Sudan in the south all the way to Syria in the Middle East. After faltering during the previous dynasty, the Nineteenth Dynasty pharaohs were determined to restore the greatness of Egypt. Standing in their way was the kingdom of the Hittites in what is now modern Turkey. The key to stopping the Hittites from expanding into Syria, Lebanon and beyond was the fortified town of Kadesh. It was also the main strategic point to establish a base for Egyptian forces to penetrate deep into Hittite territory. It was only a matter of time before the two empires clashed over Kadesh …

Reliefs from the Great Temple at Abu Simbel depict the defeat of the Hittites.

————— ❧ ❧ —————

**B**eside the calm blue waters of the river Nile in Egypt sit the ruins of the once great Temple of Luxor, where enormous granite columns rise from the sand, and cold-eyed colossi stare out into the distance.

It is here that visitors, having braved a 3-km (2-mile) avenue of sphinxes from Karnak, suddenly face the massive pylon (gateway) of Rameses II, standing 24 m (79 ft) high. Six statues of Rameses once stood before the pylon, but only two seated ones remain today, silently testifying to the vanished power of the pharaoh. In the light of the morning sun, visitors can see that the pylon's outer face is decorated with carved images depicting a long forgotten battle. Ordered by Rameses to be placed in temples throughout Egypt, these pictures and their accompanying hieroglyph texts tell the story of the pharaoh's single-handed victory against the neighbouring Hittites, and his exploits during the Battle of Kadesh in 1275 BC.

What visitors may think they are seeing is an accurate account of the battle, preserved for posterity. But what they are really seeing is a monumental act of historical rewriting, driven by a wounded ego in a desperate attempt to save face after a near disaster. The inscriptions on the walls at Luxor are an enormous fabrication and history's first recorded attempt at putting a favourable spin on events by a leader.

They are an example of deviousness that has been attempted throughout history by princes, priests, politicians and presidents as they have sought to turn some situation to their advantage by deception, obfuscation and outright lying. All can be said to be following in the footsteps of one of recorded history's early pioneers—Rameses II.

## The Official Story—The Pharaoh who Came to the Rescue

According to Rameses ('he who was the majesty of Horus, the Mighty Bull, Beloved of Truth; King of Upper and Lower Egypt; Son of Re, given life forever'), the Hittite campaign began on the ninth day of the ninth month of the fifth year of his reign, just after the pharaoh's thirtieth birthday.

The pharaoh readied his army and marched north through Sinai and the land of Canaan. All trembled before him, for they were struck by fear, and the people would prostrate themselves before the pharaoh as his army marched through their territory. After many days, he and his army reached Usermare-Meriamon, the city of cedar, from where they went north to the town of Shabtuna, which was within striking distance of their objective—the city of Kadesh. It was here, at Shabtuna that two members of the local Shasu approached to speak to the pharaoh, saying, 'Our families, who are among the greatest of the Hittites, have instructed us to say to pharaoh:

"We will be your subjects, O Pharaoh, and we will abandon the king of Kheta, King Muwatalli; for he is currently in the land of Aleppo, to the north of Tunip, and he will not come south because he fears you." '

However, these Shasu were lying to Rameses, for they were the spies of King Muwatalli, and they had instructions to ensure that the Egyptians would be unprepared for battle when they approached Kadesh. Hearing their report, Rameses split up his forces: the division of Re forded the river Orontes to the south of Shabtuna; the division of Ptah was sent south of the city of Aranami; the division of Sutekh was instructed to continue marching along the main road; and Rameses himself crossed the river Orontes with the first division of Amon to march directly towards Kadesh.

Approaching the city, Rameses discovered that King Muwatalli was there, and had gathered all peoples from the ends of the sea to assist him. With him were the Naharin, Arvad, Mesa, Keshkesh, Kelekesh, Luka, Kezweden, Carchemish, Ekereth, Kode, and people from the land of Nuges, Mesheneth and Kadesh. He had summoned all their chiefs, and they brought with them men and chariots in such great numbers that no one had seen their like. They covered the mountains and the valleys; they were like locusts in their multitudes. King Muwatalli had stripped his land of silver and gold in order to bring them with him into battle. So Rameses sent an order, urgently recalling the rest of his army, which was marching south of Shabtuna.

Suddenly the Hittites issued forth from the southern side of Kadesh, and they tore through the division of Re, which was unable to draw up in time for battle. The pharaoh's infantry and chariots fled north to where Rameses was observing the battle. Very soon the forces of King Muwatalli had surrounded the pharaoh and the Amon division.

When the pharaoh saw this, he became enraged and became like Baal in his fury. He seized his weapons, dressed himself in his battle armour, took a horse and charged into the army of King Muwatalli and all his allies. Looking around, he found that he was alone, for his army had not followed, and 2500 enemy chariots surrounded him.

The pharaoh's rage knew no bounds; he was like Sutekh the Great in strength, smiting and slaying his enemies and hurling them headlong, one after another, into the waters of the Orontes. Acknowledging the pharaoh's great victory, King Muwatalli laid the capital of the Hittite Empire at Rameses' feet and relinquished his territorial claims to Kadesh.

This account of the battle closes with a final protestation by Rameses: 'I attacked the Kheta [Hittites] and their allies while I was alone, my infantry and my chariots having forsaken me. Not one among them stood to turn about. I swear, as Re loves me, as my father, Atum, favours me, that, as for every matter which I have stated, I did it in truth, in the presence of my infantry and my chariots.'

## The Truth–Rameses' Lucky Escape

Needless to say, the idea that one man, however strong, could overcome a force of thousands is decidedly fishy, making it necessary to discover what really happened and why the story was altered to put so much glory on Rameses himself. The truth, it emerges, is that the country's reputation was at stake, and Rameses could not afford to allow his military near-disaster to become widely known. An official, alternative version of events had to be broadcast as widely, and as confidently, as possible.

Egypt in the reign of Rameses II (1279–1213 BC) was already ancient; 1500 years had elapsed since the Pyramid Age, and the state had collapsed and been revived twice during the intervening years. At this point in its history, in a period known as the New Kingdom, Egypt was ruled by the Nineteenth Dynasty of pharaohs, who set about re-establishing Egyptian authority in the Middle East—authority that had been crumbling since the collapse of the Eighteenth Dynasty in 1292 BC. Rameses' father, Seti I, had put down a number of rebellions in Palestine and southern Syria, and had fought border skirmishes with the Hittites of Anatolia in an aggressive campaign to recover Egyptian power in her former provinces to the north. The Hittites were an ancient people located in modern-day Turkey who, by 1340 BC, had become one of the dominant powers of the Middle East, with extensive interests in Palestine and Syria. Seti achieved some victories over them, but failed to regain control of Syria or to hold on to captured territory.

> Kadesh or Qadesh (now known as Tall an-Nabi Mind) was an ancient city located on the Orontes River in what is now western Syria, about 24 km (15 miles) southwest of the modern city of Homs.

The Hittite king Muwatalli II, meanwhile, was determined to control Syria. To achieve this aim he needed to hold Kadesh—an impressive fortress city with the Orontes River providing a natural defensive structure—close to the northern border between modern-day Lebanon and Syria. So where Seti had failed, Rameses was determined to succeed.

In the fifth year of his reign, Rameses set out to capture Kadesh. Leading four divisions of chariots and infantry up through Gaza, Canaan, Galilee and Lebanon, the 20,000-strong army reached the River Orontes, near modern Homs in Syria. Rameses then sent three divisions of his army in different directions, while he himself crossed the river at the ford of Shabtuna, about 13 km (8 miles) south of Kadesh, with one division. Two captured Hittite spies gave Rameses false intelligence that Muwatalli was at Aleppo, so that it seemed to the pharaoh that he had only the local troops at Kadesh to defeat. He learned too late that 16,000 Hittites were in fact hiding behind the city.

An illustration of the Battle of Kadesh, based on the Egyptian accounts, showing Rameses II personally overthrowing his enemies.

Rameses urgently sent messengers to summon the remainder of his forces, but all too quickly the Hittites attacked. With their bronze weapons, the Egyptians stood little chance against the Hittites' superior iron weapons and three-man chariots. The Hittites ripped through Rameses' single division, which broke and fled in disorder, leaving the pharaoh and a small retinue of household chariots completely surrounded by the enemy and fighting for their lives.

So far so good. It's at this point, however, that Rameses' version of what happened goes seriously awry. Instead of Rameses defeating the Hittites single-handedly, and throwing their forces back in disarray, he was on the verge of defeat when he was saved by two factors.

## RAMESES AND THE BIBLE

Traditionally, it has been held that Rameses II was the pharaoh of the Bible's Exodus story. The main reason for this was the identification of a city in the Bible associated with Exodus—Ra'amses, known in ancient Egypt as Pi-Rameses.

From this it was assumed that the flight of the Israelites must have occurred in the reign of Rameses II, and it was possibly this city that the Israelites were forced to build. Yet the pharaoh of the Exodus is not given a name—he is simply called 'Pharaoh'. Modern scholars have sought to identify exactly who this pharaoh was, but without success, and there is a good reason for this—there is little historical evidence that supports the events described in Exodus. Indeed, there is stronger evidence in the Bible that places the events of Exodus earlier than the time of Rameses.

In 1 Kings 6:1, it is said that King Solomon began constructing his temple in Jerusalem in the fourth year of his reign, 480 years 'after the children of Israel had come out of the land of Egypt'; and since Solomon's reign is thought to have begun in 971 BC, that would place the events of Exodus in 1447 BC, some 160 years before Rameses came to the throne. Another consideration is that the name Moses is Egyptian in origin: it is actually a corruption of Ahmose, a name that was popular during the Seventeenth and Eighteenth dynasties, but which was no longer used by the time of Rameses.

Most likely, the Exodus story is a retelling of an Egyptian event—the abandonment of Egyptian monotheism towards the end of the Eighteenth Dynasty (c. 1336 BC). As the Israelite chroniclers of the Judaic monarchy sought to ground their story of the founding of their nation in something familiar, they chose the most famous pharaoh as the antagonist, casting him as a weak and pitiful ruler who turns out to be no match for the all-powerful Hebrew God, Yahweh.

First, a division of his infantry that were marching separately appeared and joined with the main army, preventing a complete rout. Second, the Hittite army didn't pursue the fleeing Egyptians, but instead started to pillage the Egyptian camp. The Hittite soldiers fought without pay, so they depended on whatever they were able to plunder in battle. This meant that they could become distracted, as happened here. The Hittites lost forward momentum as they ransacked the Egyptian tents and looted the bodies of Egyptians already killed. In their greed, they missed the opportunity to capture or kill Rameses II and the military nobility of Egypt.

> Rameses often compared himself with Baal, a god of storms and the skies whose worship in Egypt was established during the Eighteenth Dynasty.

The result of the battle was a technical victory for the Egyptians, as they were able to force the Hittites into retreat. However, it was also a strategic defeat, because Rameses was unable to complete the mission and capture Kadesh. Nowhere was there any sign of Rameses dictating his victory conditions, as is claimed by Egyptian sources.

On the contrary, as both armies were exhausted, their leaders agreed to an armistice. King Muwatalli allowed Rameses and his army to retreat, leaving Kadesh in Hittite hands. As the pharaoh started the long journey back to Egypt, Muwatalli moved south instead of north. He conquered the city of Kumidi, and continued south into Damascus, eventually occupying all of the former Egyptian province of Upi. Only then did he turn north toward Anatolia, leaving his brother Hattusili in command of the captured territory.

## The Myth of Rameses

The Battle of Kadesh is significant for being the first occasion in recorded history when we have more than one account of a major military encounter. Although the majority of surviving sources are Egyptian, there are enough Hittite texts to provide a more balanced picture of the events of almost 3300 years ago.

So, given that there were other observers at this battle, just why did Rameses create a fictional conclusion to the battle, claiming he single-handedly crushed the Hittites? To understand this we have to look at the person of Rameses himself.

Rameses was many things—builder, warrior, king and living god. But two things that defined Rameses above all others were his massive ego and his embarrassment at the humble origins of his family. His grandfather, Rameses I, was a minor Egyptian official who was in the right place at the right time to ascend the throne of Egypt and so become the first pharaoh of the Nineteenth Dynasty. Rameses II was keen to ensure that this humiliating past would be eclipsed by his actions, and that his deeds would also be more memorable than those of his successful father, Seti I.

Rameses II's reputation in Egypt was built upon three things: his longevity (he ruled for 66 years, dying at the ripe old age of 90), extensive building programs and his military campaigns. It is clear that Rameses wanted to leave his mark on the world, because he initiated one of the most ambitious and egotistical construction programs for generations. Not content with building new temples, monuments and cities for himself, he systematically erased the names of other pharaohs from public buildings and inserted his name in their stead, thus claiming the credit for erecting them as well. He placed statues of himself throughout the length and breadth of the land, in numbers far surpassing any of his predecessors, and in every imaginable location: temples, public squares, even out-of-the-way locations such as cliff-faces. No matter where you went, Rameses was watching. He was also the first of the pharaohs who dared to name a city after himself: Pi-Rameses Aanakhtu, 'House of Rameses, The Great-in-Victory'.

The mummified remains of Rameses II, discovered in 1881 in Deir el-Bahari, now at the Egyptian Museum, Cairo.

But it was in his capacity as a military leader that Rameses' greatness ultimately depended. And much of this fame was built upon the reputation he gained from his 'victory' at Kadesh. Although he won subsequent victories, none was celebrated on the scale of this, his first. This was understandable: he had been pharaoh for just over four years, and he was keen to prove that he was a military genius; after all, he had been given the rank of captain in the Egyptian army at the age of ten.

Yet the actual result of the battle was unacceptable to Rameses. It was at best a draw, at worst an embarrassing failure. So, to save face with his people, Rameses undertook the first attempt of a now well-recognised political tactic of putting spin on the events. And in much the same way that it is done today, Rameses began by controlling the sources of information and dominating the media with his message— in this case, the inscriptions carved onto the walls and columns of the temples.

So when Rameses returned to Egypt after the battle, in a show of things to come, he inscribed in dozens of his temples and buildings the details of his famous victory at Kadesh. Even more improbably, the inscriptions reported that it was the pharaoh himself who had won the day. They told how Rameses, abandoned by his armies, had hurled himself at the Hittites, smiting them with his weapons, and carving a bloody path through the thousands of enemy soldiers. The rivers ran with the blood of his foes, cast down in front of him. With no contrary sources of information, the ancient Egyptians believed what they were told.

Other leaders, before Rameses, had also claimed such improbable victories and events. After Pharaoh Thutmose III's campaign against the Mitanni of northern Syria in 1445 BC, for instance, he claimed that he thrashed the enemy, and that he went freely among their cities to pillage them while their craven nobles hid in caves. To historians, some details of this story seem unlikely, but there are no independent sources that say that the Mitanni nobles did not hide in the caves. In fact, all surviving records of Thutmose's campaign recount the same tale.

But with the Battle of Kadesh the situation is different. For the first time in history there are divergent sources that challenge the victor's account of the battle. They enable us to see that Rameses' claim of a single-handed victory at Kadesh was just an exercise in political spin, designed to fool a credulous populace and retain the trust of the Egyptian people. And it was a spectacular success.

## Legacies

The reputation built up by Rameses II lasted long after his death. While he was alive, the peace that he secured with the Hittites held firm. Even though he was unable to hold on to the territory he invaded during his 16-year campaign in the north, he retained Egypt's existing possessions and built up Egypt's military reputation to such an extent that it was not seriously challenged for the next 150 years.

This was all the more remarkable because the pharaohs who followed him were nowhere near as capable as he was. Only 23 years after his death, the dynasty foundered and was followed by a new dynasty (the Twentieth), in which a succession of nine pharaohs all took the name Rameses for the glory they felt it conferred. Similarly, many nobles sought to attach themselves to his fame by claiming descent from him, while his subjects gave him the fitting name, 'Sese' (the Vanquisher).

Yet during the following centuries, as Egyptian culture decayed and crumbled into the dust, Rameses II was gradually forgotten. Over time, when his monuments were covered by the sands of Egypt and people were no longer able to read his feats, he lived on only as the Pharaoh of the Exodus story in the Bible.

It was during the nineteenth century, as Europeans uncovered the secrets that the sands had buried for so long, that his exploits were again sounded. Once hieroglyphs could be understood, one name stood out among all others—Rameses.

Egyptologists found his name everywhere. They assumed that a good indication of Egypt's success was the amount of temple-building the pharaohs could afford to carry out, and on that basis they assumed that the reign of Rameses II was the most outstanding in Egyptian history. It was the sheer number of temples he apparently constructed, coupled with the great length of his reign and his military achievements as carved on the temple walls that led the Egyptologists of the nineteenth century to bestow upon Rameses the title 'the Great'.

Sutekh was originally the Egyptian god of wind and the desert storms, whose intercession was sought to grant the strength of the storms to his followers.

Of course, we now know that a good number of the temples and statues of Rameses were not built by him, and that he arranged to have them reattributed to him from the already existing works of previous pharaohs. And, as we have seen, his military prowess as documented in the Egyptian account of the Battle of Kadesh is not borne out by the evidence. Yet his spin on those events did convince many people of his greatness, so that even now he is considered one of the most important pharaohs of Ancient Egypt. If he were alive today, he would undoubtedly be pleased that this spin on the events at Kadesh was still paying dividends over 3000 years later.

His other legacy is that his manipulation of the facts of Kadesh was the first concrete example of government spin and propaganda in history. In fact, Rameses' attempt to control the fallout from the Kadesh incident is in many ways a textbook case of what numerous governments and rulers have done ever since.

Rameses ensured there were no competing sources of information that could contradict the official story. He then undertook a 'media' blitz so that only his version would be heard, and heard constantly. He broadcast his message throughout the country so that everyone would be informed. Finally, he framed the event from a nationalistic perspective so that it would elicit a patriotic response from all the citizenry. His victory, the propaganda implied, was one for the 'good guys', helping to keep Egypt free from those terrible Hittites and their foreign ways.

As the other stories in this book will show, this basic formula has subsequently been used by every type of government down the centuries—imperial, monarchical, dictatorial and even democratic. It would be naïve to assume that spin, manipulation and propaganda are solely the preserve of power-hungry autocrats, for there is plentiful evidence of manipulation of the truth by powerful individuals and groups in modern democratic societies. In their ambition to be re-elected, democratic governments regularly seek to control and manipulate all information about their decisions, and the history and consequences of their actions. Yet such actions show that they are merely the latest in a long line of imitators who walk in the shadow of the god-Pharaoh Rameses, whose stone eyes gaze impassively into the distance, and whose fame has lasted to the present.

# THE LITTLE LIE THAT BUILT THE ROMAN EMPIRE (27 BC)

*'May it be my privilege to have the happiness of establishing the commonwealth on a firm and stable basis and thus to enjoy the reward which I desire, but only if I may be called the architect of the best possible government; and bear with me the hope when I die, that the foundations which I have laid for its future government, will stand deep and secure.'*
**Emperor Augustus**

*'Occupants of public offices love power and are prone to abuse it.'*
**George Washington**

### LIE
Emperor Augustus was prepared to hand the Roman republic back to the senate.

### TRUTH
Augustus never had any intention of relinquishing power!

### CHIEF PARTICIPANTS
Emperor Caesar Augustus (Gaius Julius Octavianus), the first Roman emperor
Mark Antony (Marcus Antonius), ruler of half of the Roman world

### THE STORY SO FAR
Julius Caesar, dictator of Rome, was assassinated in 44 BC by members of the Roman senate, led by the republicans Marcus Brutus and Gaius Cassius Longinus. Caesar's great-nephew and chosen heir, Octavian, and Mark Antony, Caesar's right-hand man, defeated the murderers at Philippi (42 BC). With Marcus Lepidus, another former supporter of Julius Caesar, they had already joined to form a triumvirate that would rule the Roman world. Octavian was to rule in Western Europe, Mark Antony in the East, and Lepidus in North Africa. In 36 BC, however, Lepidus was forced into exile, leaving the Roman world divided between Octavian and Mark Antony. Antony's wife Cleopatra, Queen of Egypt, convinced him to declare war on Octavian. Octavian, eager to be sole master of Rome, fought and defeated Antony at the Battle of Actium in 31 BC. Antony committed suicide shortly after the battle. Within ten years, Octavian had taken on the title of 'Augustus' ('the Illustrious One') and the fate of the republic hung in the balance …

A bust of the young Octavian before he was transformed into Caesar Augustus.

The Emperor Augustus has been something of an enigma for historians, with many divided over the significance of his time as ruler of Rome. For the first 1500 years after his reign, he was initially worshipped, and then idolised, by the majority of educated people in Europe. By the mid-1700s, however, his reputation with historians had undergone a complete revision. The great English historian Edward Gibbon described him as 'the crafty tyrant', seeing him as a man who had risen to a position of power on the destruction of the virtues of the Roman republic. By the 1930s, Augustus' reputation had been redeemed, and he was once again admired as the man who had rescued Rome from potential catastrophe, and set her on the path to military and imperial glory. At the start of the twenty-first century, his reputation is again being re-evaluated, with the result that he now appears to be placed somewhere between those two extremes. Most consider him to be a sly, power-hungry political manipulator who, in the act of constraining Roman liberty, did what was needed to rescue Rome from the consequences of that very liberty—the chaos and disorders of a century of civil wars. Perhaps that is a reasonable view, but it should never be forgotten that his reign as Roman emperor was based upon a lie. The lie was that his extraordinary position as *Princeps*—First Citizen—was only a temporary measure intended to stabilise the Roman political system, and that he fully intended handing the reins of power back to the senate and people of Rome when his task was complete. This was never his real intention, and during the 45 years he guided the Roman state, the people gladly swallowed his lie as they willingly gave away their freedom and sovereign powers. His legacy was to stabilise the Roman state after the civil wars, and to provide the empire with the mechanisms it needed to survive, including laws and institutions that were passed on to Europe and the west.

## The Official Story—Octavian Attempts to Relinquish his Command

The senators who approached the senate house on the morning of 13 January 27 BC didn't expect this meeting to be any different from the countless others they had attended. After all, the man who was chief consul and head of the Roman world, Gaius Julius Caesar Octavianus (Octavian), had been in charge for 15 years, first as a member of the Triumvirate with Mark Antony and Lepidus, and then as consul for the four years after he defeated Antony at the Battle of Actium. He was making all executive decisions and nobody expected that to change. As the 600 senators gathered, chatting amiably about local events, they were unaware of the momentous event about to unfold.

Having called the senate to order, the 35-year-old Octavian rose to speak from the magistrates' bench, where the consuls sat during sessions of the senate. In respectful silence, the senators listened as Octavian announced in a clear voice that, effective immediately, he was abdicating all powers over Rome and the empire, obtained during the period of the Triumvirate, that were contrary to the laws of the republic. The only exceptions were those powers that were legally his in his role as consul for that year. The senators could hardly believe their ears, and many no doubt recalled the words of Mark Antony, who maintained that the one obstacle to restoring the republican system was Octavian himself. Perhaps Octavian had finally seen the justice of his old rival's arguments.

As the shock began to subside, voices were raised as more and more senators joined in a cacophony of objections. Why was he doing this? Did he not know that the gods would abandon Rome if he were to stand down? Why was he deserting Rome after all he had done to save the city from her enemies? Did Rome's safety no longer mean anything to him?

But Octavian was adamant—he would step down, and that decision was final. The senators became even more vociferous and, during the course of that morning, their ceaseless pleas wore him down. He acquiesced to their demands and accepted responsibility for the provinces that were not completely at peace and the legions stationed there. Although Octavian rejected outright the title of dictator, he did accept the suitably republican titles of Proconsul and *Imperator* ('Commander'), but insisted that he only be allowed to retain them for a period not exceeding ten years. To reflect his status as first among equals, he was awarded the title of *Princeps* ('First Citizen')—the most esteemed member of the senate.

At the end of the sitting for that day, Octavian got up and thanked the senate for its kindness, remarking that it was with a heavy heart he continued to hold these offices. He maintained his hope that wounds inflicted on the republic by the civil wars would be fully mended before his ten years in office had expired. He further hoped that the republic, restored to its former glory and virtue, would no longer require the risky appointment of a Roman magistrate whose power exceeded that of all other magistrates. For his obvious humility and foresight, the senate gave him one further honour. From then on, he was no longer to be known as Octavian, but as Augustus—'the Illustrious One'.

## The Truth—The Power and the Glory

The Emperor Augustus was a very astute politician. Throughout his career, he was determined to secure control of the Roman republic, and used every opportunity to promote his agenda. It was the republic's weakness that bred him, and because the republic was so enfeebled it could do nothing as he gradually dismantled it to create an empire with him as its head. There were two main reasons for his success. First, he possessed a true genius for exploiting situations as they arose. He would even alter his appearance to change people's perception of him. He was not a tall man—only reaching 1.7 m (5 ft 6 in)—yet at public appearances he would wear wooden platforms to boost his height so that he appeared taller and more formidable than he actually was.

Just months before he was assassinated, Julius Caesar, who had no living legitimate children, adopted Octavian (his great-nephew) as a son, and named him as his main beneficiary and heir. As a result, Octavian, who had been born Gaius Octavius Thurinus, changed his name to Gaius Julius Caesar Octavianus. When Julius Caesar was killed, the 19-year-old Octavian rushed to Rome to claim his inheritance, which included the Roman legions loyal to his great-uncle. In the political confusion that followed the death of Julius Caesar, during which Mark Antony was forced to flee from Rome, the determined Octavian took advantage of the situation and used his armies to occupy Rome so that he could gain an official command from either the senate or the people. Antony marched on Rome to punish him, but found that two of his legions had mutinied and placed their arms at the service of Octavian. It was little wonder that Antony was heard to mutter, 'You, boy, owe everything to a name', before he reluctantly joined forces with Octavian and Marcus Lepidus to form a triumvirate to rule the Roman world.

> Roman legates were high-ranking officers serving commanders of the Roman armies. Today's papal legates are the personal representatives of the Pope to foreign powers.

Octavian and Antony then took their armies to defeat Brutus and Cassius, the assassins of Julius Caesar. Within the year Octavian was back in Rome, and at the age of 20 he was elected consul of the Roman republic. But sharing power with two other men was not part of his plan, so when Lepidus unwisely picked a fight with him in 36 BC, Octavian accused him of planning a rebellion, and forced him into exile. Only four years later came a showdown with Antony, who had married Cleopatra, the queen of Egypt.

By 32 BC, Octavian and Antony were sole rulers of the Roman world, Octavian in the west and Antony in the east, with a simmering tension threatening to erupt between them. Things came to a head when the consul Sosius, a supporter of Antony, denounced Octavian, who was out of Rome at the time. Octavian quickly returned with an armed force, convened the senate and denounced Antony. With Octavian's loyal troops standing in the senate house, the senate acquiesced, whereupon Sosius and his fellow consul Ahenobarbus fled, followed by other senators who supported Antony. Octavian then seized Antony's will from the Vestal sanctuary in Rome and disclosed its contents to the remaining senators. The details shocked them. Antony

The Roman Forum was the centre of politics and religious ceremonies in ancient Rome.

declared that Cleopatra's children were to be given provinces of the empire and that he was to be buried in Alexandria, next to Cleopatra. It was obvious—or so Octavian claimed—that Antony was planning to divide the Roman world and put a foreign queen and her children in command of the eastern provinces.

So began the final act of the civil wars, during which the western provinces swore an oath of allegiance to Octavian personally. Antony was toppled at the Battle of Actium (31 BC), and committed suicide when Octavian invaded Egypt the following year. In consequence, Octavian became the virtual ruler of Rome and all its provinces. He had achieved all this, by the age of 32, through guile, luck, cunning and skill. He ruled the empire for the next 45 years, all the while building upon his reputation. During his reign, he consolidated his power by gaining control of the most important provinces together with their legions. Most importantly, he kept civil discord to a minimum, preventing anyone from rising to power in the way he himself had done thanks to the chaos of the civil wars.

Impressive as his skills were, they were not the principal cause of his rise to power. The second and more important reason why he was able gain mastery over the Roman world was his emasculation of the Roman senate.

## The Events of 13 January 27 BC

In 44 BC, a number of senators had plotted the assassination of Julius Caesar because they feared that he had ambitions to become king. Yet 17 years later they effectively handed all real power to his successor without a murmur. What had happened to the senate over that period to bring about such a state of affairs?

In republican Rome, the senate was the pre-eminent institution within the body politic. Even though it could not pass laws, it contained the most powerful and important individuals drawn from the most illustrious families, all of whom were well aware of their own history and authority. Resentful of excessive ambition, they were constantly intriguing to ensure that no individual had more power than the others. These families were severely affected by two events: first, the civil wars fought between Julius Caesar and the republicans, such as Pompey the Great (49–46 BC); and, second, by the proscriptions of the Triumvirate; this was the judicial murder of the opponents of Antony, Octavian and Lepidus throughout the Roman world. Very few senatorial families survived these events intact.

After the fall of Antony, Octavian undertook a review of the senate, and it was then that it became his cat's paw. He removed the few senators who were still actively opposed to him, and raised a whole new generation of families from the equestrian class to the senatorial class. These new senators, several hundred in number, owed their new position and rank to Augustus, and knew it. It is hardly surprising that they continued to support and reward their benefactor in whatever way they could, including their refusal of the stewardship of the republic when Octavian offered it to them on 13 January 27 BC.

It was a masterful piece of theatre on the part of Octavian. He had planned this moment well, informing key senators of the scheme and, more importantly, the role he expected them to play in it. So it was that when Octavian announced to the senate that he was relinquishing the powers he had assumed throughout his career, these chosen senators were the first on their feet, imploring him not to desert the republic. They overcame his feigned reluctance, and he responded to their shouts by agreeing to remain in public office. Those senators not in the know—the majority—could not believe their ears. However, when Octavian's supporters began their protests, they could see which way the wind was blowing and gradually joined the chorus. Octavian finally agreed to accept command of Gaul, Syria, Cyprus, Egypt and most of Spain, while the senate and people kept the rest. To allay fears that he might become a dictator, he ensured that he was offered these powers for a period of ten years only, during which time he could appoint legates to administer regions on his behalf.

As may be expected, however, Octavian's powers were reconfirmed for another ten years when the first decade elapsed, to conform with the legal fiction that the republic was still a living and vital entity. Once again, Octavian (now known as Augustus) maintained that he was standing down and handing the republic back to the senate and the people of Rome, only to be 'persuaded' by the senate that his task was not yet

## AUGUSTUS' DIVINE ROLE

As was the case with many rulers in ancient times, stories began to appear about Augustus' early life that showed him to have been divinely favoured by the gods. During the course of his reign, these stories would have been useful in ensuring that the people accepted him as the new head of state, along with the belief that his role was necessary for the welfare of Rome.

The stories were numerous and all remarkably similar. One recounted how his father rushed to the senate to announce his son's birth. When he informed those assembled of the hour of the boy's birth an astrologer cried out, 'The ruler of the world is now born'. Another story related how, as a boy, he was eating his lunch along the Appian Way when an eagle swooped down, took a crust from his hands, and soared away. It then gently returned to give back to Augustus what it had stolen.

A third story tells how a famous senator dreamed that several nobleman's sons were playing near the altar of Jupiter when the god appeared, summoned one of the boys, and placed an image of the goddess Rome into the folds of his gown. Then he dreamed that the same boy was sitting in the lap of the statue of Jupiter. The senator tried to have him removed, but the god told him no, the boy was being raised as the saviour of Rome. The following day, the senator encountered the future Augustus and, even though they had never met, pronounced him to be the boy in his dream.

complete. Even after his death, this fiction was maintained, as Edward Gibbon writes: 'The memory of this comedy, repeated several times during the life of Augustus, was preserved to the last ages of the empire, by the peculiar pomp with which the perpetual monarchs of Rome always solemnised the tenth years of their reign.'

Even though the senate had been effectively tamed, Augustus continued to take actions that would ensure the senate became only an assembly of administrators, whose role was simply to enforce his will. To reduce their prominence, he banned the publication of the Proceedings of the Senate, which his great-uncle Julius had instituted. He was careful, however, not to antagonise the senators, going to great lengths to pamper their pride through numerous, but meaningless, honours. Consuls continued to sit and hold office, and he selected senators to administer new offices such as the prefecture of the city, or the curatorships of aqueducts or of public works. He consulted the senate frequently and treated it with all due respect, even allowing provocative remarks to be made during his speeches. Augustus allowed senators some access to decision-making through the creation of a cabinet of sorts, consisting of the two presiding consuls, a selection of magistrates and fifteen senators chosen at random. But all power remained with him and, regardless of what he said in public, he was never going to relinquish it and restore the republic. He had always been addicted to power, and the truth of the matter was that, as the Roman historian Cassius Dio pointed out, 'nothing was done that did not please Caesar'.

## Legacies

The rule of Augustus stabilised the empire after the civil wars, and provided it with mechanisms that allowed it to survive, eventually passing its laws and institutions to later European states. The first impact of the reign of Augustus on the world came as a result of his longevity. By the time he died in 14 AD, the majority of Roman citizens had known no other system of government other than his principate and the senate's subservience to it. Had Augustus been a more principled statesman and actually resigned his commission as he promised he would do in 27 BC, it seems certain that the chaos of the late republic would have recurred, with new strongmen plunging the state into costly and debilitating civil wars.

Retaining the reins of power for over 40 years allowed Augustus to stabilise and in many ways improve the functioning of the Roman state. By virtue of Augustus' own experience in climbing to power, together with his persistence, discretion and good judgment, he turned the Roman state into a stable monarchy. As Professor Garrett Fagan writes, 'This system ... was far from flawless, but it provided the Roman Empire with a series of rulers who presided over the longest period of unity, peace, and prosperity that Western Europe, the Middle East and the North African seaboard have known in their entire recorded history.'

Many people have looked to the Roman Republic for inspiration, as it was the empire that bequeathed to Europe and the West the foundations of civil and religious institutions that have survived for 2000 years. Christianity, for example, would never have flourished without the emperor and the empire. The Catholic Church in particular absorbed much from the imperial system. In the time of the Emperor

The Triumvirate between Octavian, Antony and Lepidus is properly known as the Second Triumvirate. It was modelled on the First Triumvirate engineered between Julius Caesar, Pompey the Great and Crassus some 20 years before, but differed in that it was a formal legal agreement.

Diocletian, the empire was reorganised, grouping provinces into a new structure called dioceses, each with its vicarus (or vicar). Representatives of holders of supreme administrative power in the Roman world were termed legates. All these titles were adopted by the Christian Church during its slow absorption into the Roman power structures. The existence of the Pontifex Maximus—the Roman chief priest, a position occupied by the emperor—also facilitated the acceptance of the Pontiff, or Pope, as head of the Roman Catholic Church. This would never have come about without Augustus.

Augustus provided stability to Rome in many other ways as well. He created the numerous standing professional armies that were stationed at or near the frontiers, thus providing security to the empire from 'barbarians'. He ensured that the political settlement he created survived his death by developing and employing an imperial succession. All these factors created circumstances whereby the Roman world was blessed with an age of peace and prosperity that it was to enjoy for the next 200 years—the Pax Augusta, as it was known—until barbarian invasions began her slow and steady decline.

> Mark Antony was Julius Caesar's first cousin once removed, and was expected to be named as his heir.

For the modern world, the legacy of the transformation from a republic on the brink of collapse to a healthy and adaptive empire is profound. Rome left a legacy of standardised measurements, such as miles, feet and inches. The standard width of a modern-day train track is based on the standard width of Roman chariots used in the empire. Latin became the lingua franca of the west, with most modern European languages either having their origins in Latin, or, as in the case of English, being profoundly influenced by Latin. Rome also gave the world a standardised calendar that was to remain unchanged for 1500 years. Slightly modified, it is still in use throughout much of the world today.

The imperial system developed by Augustus has also played a role in framing the constitutions of many European countries and their former colonies. In the case of the United States, the founding fathers declared explicitly that they sought to bring about a new 'Augustan Age'. As lawyer Scott Horton points out:

*The new order of the Augustan age included a law of nations and a law of war. These were seen as essential tools to the creation of an Empire and to the assimilation of the newly incorporated peoples. They were seen as the foundation for the Pax Romana. When the American Founding Fathers turn to this classical phrase, they are making a proud claim—that the introduction of democracy in America would mark a new age for mankind—just as the Augustan age saw its law-based state as the natural next step in the evolution of humanity.*

A president who acts as head of state in partnership with a body that makes the laws, and another that reviews them, is a situation based upon the Roman imperial political system as introduced by Augustus. The Western world's reliance on the public administration of basic utilities, an extensive civil service, governmental obligations to our armed forces' veterans and formalised tax collection all have their origins in imperial Rome.

Finally, the refashioning of the Roman republic into an imperial system provided circumstances that allowed Roman law to be introduced across the provinces of the empire, delivering the basis for structures of jurisprudence that are now in place across half the globe. While the foundations of Roman law lay in the obsolete Roman republic, Augustus presented that law in a new form, repackaged for a world empire. According to American historian J. Rufus Fears, writing for the Heritage Foundation, by the early third century, Roman jurists like Ulpian had built upon the Augustan reforms to espouse an ideal that the laws of the empire were an extension of natural laws. In this view, all men are created equal and are treated equally before the law, and more importantly have rights under the law—rights to life, liberty and happiness. Their task in passing judgment was to interpret this natural law (*jus naturale*), and bring it to bear on the *jus gentium*, or the law of the people, as well as the *jus civile*, the law of the state. This system of Roman laws and principles is probably the most important legacy of the deception that Augustus perpetrated upon the sad and decaying Roman republic. And without that lie, Rome might easily have died, preventing her empire from passing its benefits on to posterity.

Mark Antony, Octavian's greatest rival. He, Octavian and Marcus Aemilius Lepidus formed the Second Triumvirate.

# THE HIJACKING OF THE FOURTH CRUSADE (1204)

*'We will build transports to carry four thousand five hundred horses, and nine thousand squires, and ships for four thousand five hundred knights, and twenty thousand sergeants of foot ... on condition that you pay us for each horse four marks, and for each man two marks. We undertake to keep, wheresoever we may be, for a year, reckoning from the day on which we sail from the port of Venice in the service of God and of Christendom. Now the sum total of the expenses above named amounts to 85,000 marks. And this will we do moreover. For the love of God, we will add to the fleet fifty armed galleys on condition that, so long as we act in company, of all conquests in land or money, whether at sea or on dry ground, we shall have the half, and you the other half.'*
**Enrico Dandolo, Doge of Venice**

*'God is on everyone's side ... and in the last analysis, he is on the side with plenty of money and large armies.'*
**Jean Anouilh**

### LIE

We're on our way to liberate Jerusalem.

### TRUTH

The leaders of the Fourth Crusade always intended to sack Constantinople!

### CHIEF PARTICIPANTS

Enrico Dandolo, Doge of Venice
Alexius IV Angelus, Emperor of Byzantium
Count Boniface of Montferrat, leader of the Fourth Crusade

### THE STORY SO FAR

After the First Crusade succeeded in wresting the Holy Land from Muslim control in 1099, the crusaders established various kingdoms in the Middle East, the most important being the Kingdom of Jerusalem. These kingdoms were not to last for long, however. In between bickering among themselves, their leaders spent most of their time fighting Muslim states to the east and raiding the Christian Byzantine Empire to the north. After Muslim armies captured part of the County of Edessa in 1144, the Second Crusade was launched, only to end in failure. This

*The Capture of Constantinople in 1204*, as painted in the sixteenth century by Jacopo Robusti Tintoretto.

was followed by a Third Crusade, launched after the fall of Jerusalem to Saladin, sultan of Egypt and Syria, in 1187, but it was not a success either. It was during these crusades that some Christian leaders began to believe that the Byzantines were betraying their cause to the Muslims, causing resentment in France, England and Italy. It was then that Pope Innocent III began preaching a new crusade, one that would attack the Muslims through Egypt. All they needed were ships, and Venice had plenty of those …

The massive walls of Constantinople, with its mighty towers, would have been a remarkable sight to peasant soldiers from the backwaters of rural Europe. They seemed to stretch to the horizon whichever way you looked. Many must surely have turned to fellow travellers in bewilderment and asked, 'Is this Jerusalem?'

One can only imagine their disappointment at being told that this was Constantinople, and that the people gathered along its walls were not Saracens but fellow Christians. Disappointment would have turned to confusion with the news that this was now the principal objective of the crusading armies. 'But what of our vows of pilgrimage?' they would have asked.

Many leaders of the Fourth Crusade did not care a fig about those vows, however, nor would they have been bothered about the feelings of the soldiers who would shortly be asked to lay down their lives. As they cast their covetous eyes over the beautiful city, thinking of the wealth that lay inside, the Venetian contingent must have been congratulating themselves on their skilful handling of the crusading knights. They had not only manipulated them into abandoning their quest to free the Holy Land, but had convinced them to take part in the capture of this most precious of prizes—Constantinople, the greatest city in all Christendom. In doing so, they had managed to conceal the fact that the capture of Constantinople had always been their aim. As a consequence of this deception, the power of the Byzantine Empire was crippled, an act that would eventually see eastern Europe fall under Islamic domination for 400 years.

## The Official Story—The Fourth Crusade Is Sidetracked

The failure of the Third Crusade meant that most of the princes of Europe temporarily lost any enthusiasm they might have had for further crusades. Busy fighting their own petty wars, they were not inclined to go on any extended trips to the Holy Land. England and France were locked in a struggle for territory, the Christian kings of Spain were fighting Muslim kingdoms in the south of the country, and Henry IV of Germany had only recently been crowned Holy Roman Emperor, following the death of his father during the Third Crusade. However, the arrival of a new occupant on the Throne of St Peter in 1198 was to change all that. Charismatic and energetic, Pope Innocent III was committed to the crusading movement and determined to reverse the failure of the Third Crusade. Innocent's call to arms stirred the nobility of France, where thousands responded to his representative, Fulk of Neuilly. In November 1199, the enterprise acquired an informal leader when, during a tournament near his castle in the Ardennes, Count Thibault of Champagne announced that he would take the Cross and go on Crusade. When Thibault became ill shortly afterwards, leadership of the Fourth Crusade passed to an Italian count, Boniface of Montferrat. Geoffrey of Villehardouin, an envoy appointed by the leading nobles, described the count as a man of commanding presence, experienced in warfare and, importantly, related to the Kings of Jerusalem.

Having identified Egypt as a weak point, the crusaders decided to land there and move on the Holy Land from the south. To get them to their destination they approached the Venetians, who agreed to convey 33,500 crusaders and 4500 horses. The Venetians required a full year to construct the large number of ships needed, and to find the sailors to man them. During this period they had to suspend most of the city's regular mercantile activities. The contract specified that the crusaders were to head straight for Cairo—then at the heart of the Muslim world—and that they were to set sail no later than 24 June 1202.

Regardless of what their leaders had planned, many crusaders did not make their way to Venice, but chose instead to depart from other Mediterranean ports. The result was that, by the time the bulk of the crusader army had gathered at Venice in late 1201, instead of the planned 33,500 troops, only 12,000 were present. Venice, meanwhile, had delivered on her part of the bargain. As promised, 50 war galleys, 150 large transports and 300 horse transports lay waiting at anchor—sufficient for three times the army that was ready to board. The Doge of Venice, the blind, 94-year-old Enrico Dandolo, insisted that the crusaders pay the full amount outstanding—85,000 silver marks. The crusaders could only scrape together about 51,000 marks, and that only when some of the leaders had sacrificed everything they possessed. The Venetians reacted with outrage. They had cut back their trading activities for a considerable time to prepare for this expedition and refused to let the crusaders depart on their ships until the full amount had been paid. Appeals made by the crusaders to a shared Christian unity and faith left the Doge unmoved. Eventually, and against all expectations, it was Dandolo who finally broke the deadlock by proposing that he should join the crusade and become one of its leaders. He also suggested that, as a first objective, they should attack the Christian port of Zara in Dalmatia, which the Venetians had lost to Hungary in 1186. The papal representative agreed, declaring that it was necessary to prevent the crusade's complete collapse, and when the leaders of the crusade reluctantly acquiesced, Dandolo took the Cross at a public ceremony in the Basilica of St Mark.

During the siege of Zara in November 1202, Alexius, the son of the dethroned Byzantine emperor, Isaac II, contacted the crusaders and offered them a number of enticements if they would move against Constantinople and overthrow the reigning emperor, Alexius III. These included the submission of the Orthodox Church to Rome, the payment of any outstanding sums owed to the Venetians, and an undertaking to pay for the Egyptian campaign and to provide 10,000 Byzantine soldiers to join it. Even though the leading crusaders agreed to the plan because of their dire financial predicament, many in the lower ranks refused to participate in an enterprise that they regarded as being contrary to their vows. Those who remained joined the imperial claimant at the island of Corfu, and a fleet of 60 war galleys, 100 horse transports and 50 large transports duly arrived beneath the walls of Constantinople in late June 1203. One month later the city fell to the crusaders and their Venetian allies.

## The Truth—Destination Constantinople

Of all the peoples living around the Mediterranean basin, the Venetians were among the most interesting. Isolated as a result of their location, they were haughty, devious and incredibly suspicious. They had never been a particularly religious people, having defied the Pope on numerous occasions throughout their history. It would be fair to say that they were much more interested in money than religion. So there are good reasons to be sceptical about the Venetians' claim that they were simply trying to make the best of a bad deal with the crusaders after they had built all the ships that had been ordered. In fact, at no point were they ever interested in going to the Holy Land. The hijacking of the Fourth Crusade by the Venetians and the attack on Constantinople were undertaken with just one purpose in mind—that of looting the city's treasures and seizing Byzantine territory. While the Venetians may have masqueraded as devout Christians answering the Pope's call, the reality was quite different.

> Venice was originally established as a Byzantine administrative centre in the aftermath of the Lombard invasions of northern and central Italy in the 560s.

The fabled wealth of Constantinople was the talk of Europe, largely as a result of stories told by returning crusaders, and the Venetians had become obsessed with the idea of sacking the imperial city. Believing the Greek-speaking inhabitants to be effeminate, the Venetians were looking for any opportunity to take advantage of their supposed weakness. But there were other factors at play as well.

The crusaders entering a devastated Constantinople.

Venice at this time was ruled by one of the most remarkable figures of the Middle Ages—Enrico Dandolo, the 94-year-old blind Doge of Venice—who was involved in a series of events that started Venice on its quest to destroy the Byzantine Empire. Rivalry between Venice and Constantinople went back decades, with the Byzantines particularly keen to reduce the influence of Venetians in their affairs. Their opportunity came in 1171, when they accused Venetians living in Constantinople of destroying the Genoese settlement in the suburb of Galata. Emperor Manuel I arrested all Venetian citizens throughout the empire and imprisoned them. The Venetians reacted with fury and raised a fleet to attack Constantinople, but the expedition was a disaster. Dandolo had joined the mission led by Doge Vitale Michiel during 1171–72, which ended with the Doge's humiliation and death in Venice at the hands of a murderous mob. The following year, Dandolo was selected to be ambassador to Constantinople as Venice attempted unsuccessfully to arrive at a diplomatic solution over its clash with Byzantium. It was during this period that he developed his hatred of the Byzantines, especially after the events of 1182. In that year, a coup occurred in Constantinople in which Greeks rose up and massacred practically every Latin inhabitant of the city, including women and children, the old and infirm, even the sick in the hospitals. Among the victims were large numbers of Venetian merchants. These events must have seemed fresh in Dandolo's mind when he became the 39th Doge of Venice on 1 January 1193.

The opportunity for Dandolo to take revenge arrived with the leaders of the Fourth Crusade. The French leadership came to the Venetians to negotiate for ships and provisions. They were led by Boniface of Montferrat who, contrary to official accounts, was in fact weak, self-serving, inexperienced, ignorant, arrogant and completely lacking in faith, scruples or remorse—a dangerous combination. Dandolo found it easy to manipulate him and the rest of the crusader leadership, as future events were to show. The Venetians, using their financial acumen, manoeuvred the crusaders into a situation where they owed them a large sum of money. When they couldn't pay, the Venetians offered the crusaders a way of discharging their debt, using booty gained from an attack on Zara. Pope Innocent was appalled when he discovered the agreement, decreeing that it was unconscionable for the crusader armies to attack a Christian city. The Pope's protests were ignored, however, and the crusaders were unable to get the Venetians to change their minds—though how hard they tried is questionable, since it seems that Boniface was sorely tempted by stories of the great wealth that lay within the city.

Part of the deal was that Dandolo would become the leader of the crusade—only he had no intention of sailing to Cairo, of supporting the now-doomed kingdom of Jerusalem, or of liberating the Holy Sepulchre. He had only one goal in mind: the overthrow of Constantinople itself. It was thus that the Venetians got their way and were able to perpetrate one of the greatest disasters in history.

## Byzantium in Turmoil

The Byzantine Empire was in a state of chaos at the end of the twelfth century. The days of her greatness were over, and there were two rival contenders for the imperial throne. One of these—prince Alexius, the son of the deposed emperor Isaac II—believed he could use the crusading army to further his ambitions. About 14 years old and therefore easily manipulated, Alexius escaped from Constantinople and appealed to the crusaders, promising many things, including a commitment to heal the schism between the Eastern and Western Churches if they would help him to depose his uncle, the usurper Alexius III. Doge Dandolo found the perfect tool in the young Alexius to help him achieve his goal of conquering Constantinople.

The crusaders, whose stated objective had been Egypt, took very little persuading to set their course for Constantinople. They appeared before the walls of the city in June 1203, proclaiming the young prince as Emperor Alexius IV, and commanding the people to depose his uncle. Alexius III, sunk in debauchery, took no effective measures to resist, and the siege of Constantinople began. On 17 July the crusaders and the Venetians took the city by storm, installing Alexius IV and his father Isaac II as co-emperors.

Discovering that the Venetians had manipulated him, Alexius IV now attempted to get the invaders—who were camped outside the city walls—to resume their journey by offering them money, but to no avail. The Venetians were not going anywhere, and they placed all sorts of conditions and demands on

> It was rumoured that Doge Enrico Dandolo had lost his eyesight at the hands of the Byzantines during an earlier visit to Constantinople.

their puppet emperor. When these could not be met, the Byzantines attempted to close the city against the crusaders. At the end of January 1204, the city's populace rose in revolt against Alexius IV, imprisoning him and his father. The elderly Isaac died soon afterwards, possibly from poison, and Alexius was strangled on 8 February, allowing the anti-western Alexius V Ducas to be installed as emperor. Using these events as a pretext, the crusaders decided to take the city for themselves. Although Pope Innocent III had commanded them not to attack, the clergy concealed the papal letters, and the crusaders readied themselves for the assault, while the Venetians attacked from the sea. The Byzantines could put up little resistance, and within a very short period of time the greatest city in Christendom was overrun and sacked.

That a Christian army—one that was supposed to liberate the Holy Land—had done this, is an act that Orthodox Christians have never been able to forgive. As in any pillaging of a city, numerous atrocities were committed, including the desecration of the High Altar of the great church of Hagia Sophia. The crusaders took three days to sack the city, during which time many ancient Roman and Greek works were either stolen or destroyed. Nuns were violated and Orthodox clergy were hunted down and massacred. All of the great treasures of Constantinople (excluding those that had been

The bronze horses looted from Constantinople are displayed inside the basilica in St Mark's Museum.

destroyed by the rampaging crusaders) were taken back to Venice. While the leaders of the crusade were excommunicated by the Pope, the Western Church wasted no time in introducing the Latin rite and Latin prelates into the Orthodox East, further antagonising the Eastern Church. The crusaders then installed one of their own—Baldwin, Count of Flanders—as emperor in Constantinople, where they remained in command until 1261. Doge Dandolo returned home triumphant. He had established an empire for Venice, carved from the remains of the Eastern Roman Empire, and was able to present his city with the title of 'Lords and Masters of a Quarter and a Half-quarter of the Roman Empire'.

# THE HORSES OF ST MARK'S

Visitors walking around the Piazza San Marco in Venice will, at some point, have their eyes drawn to the top of the basilica dedicated to the Patron Saint of Venice. There, high above the main doors, stand four bronze horses, magnificent and proud, poised as if ready to launch themselves into a full gallop. These are modern replicas, installed in the 1980s to save the originals from the effects of pollution after they had stood guard over the church for the better part of 600 years.

But for some 900 years before their installation in Venice, the bronze horses of St Mark's had graced the northern end of the Hippodrome of Constantine, built in the centre of Constantinople by the Roman Emperor Constantine himself. For almost a millennium they looked down upon the hustle and bustle of the city's social life, centred on the regular chariot races that were held there, with fans betting enormous sums on the blue or green teams.

All of this was lost during the sack of Constantinople. While the crusaders destroyed everything they could get their hands on, the more refined Venetians were eagerly stealing as much booty as they could carry off on their ships. One item that caught the personal fancy of Doge Dandolo, possibly seen during a previous visit, was the group of four horses that stood over the ancient hippodrome, so he ordered their removal to Venice.

Ironically, these horses also caught the attention of another conqueror, Napoleon, who took them to Paris in 1797 for the Arc de Triomphe, but they were returned to the façade of St Mark's in 1815.

Visitors today can climb a steep stairway to where the four replica horses stand on the basilica, and they can view the originals inside a room on the same upper level. Gazing on them, visitors are admiring one of the treasures that became a victim of the fall of the greatest city in all Christendom.

## Legacies

The sack of Constantinople crippled the power of the Byzantine Empire, which until then had been the main barrier preventing the forces of Islam from entering Europe by the most direct route, across the Dardanelles or the Bosphorus. Its conquest had calamitous consequences for the future of eastern Europe, a fact that was evident to many even at the time. As historian Robert Payne writes: 'Innocent III … was aghast at their actions. There came from him, in letter after letter, cries of helpless rage. How was it possible that anyone could be so unreasonable, so inept, and so absurd as to conquer Constantinople? Were not the Turks on the march, and was it not certain that Byzantium served as a bastion against them?'

With the conquest of Constantinople, the Byzantine Empire suffered a blow from which it never really recovered. Even though it survived for another 200 years after the Latin emperors were evicted in 1261, it would never again be a formidable power, shorn as it was of territory, naval power and money.

The immediate effect of the sack of 1204 was felt in the local area, since it left neighbouring Balkan states free to pursue a policy of conquest. This happened slowly, since the Latin empire still exercised some authority. However, the rate of Balkan expansion accelerated during the 1300s owing to a futile civil war that completely crippled what was left of the Byzantine Empire. The main short-term beneficiaries in the area were the Serbs, who were able to create the Serbian Empire and subjugate much of the Balkans. The legacy of this short-lived empire still haunts the region today. Much of the recent conflict and tension within the former Yugoslav republics stems from a dream of resurrecting the empire and restoring all the land of 'Greater Serbia'. This was certainly one of the contributing factors in the wars over Kosovo during the 1990s.

> ❧ ⌘ ❧
>
> In 2001, Pope John Paul II apologised for the Fourth Crusade's attack on Constantinople, and this was accepted by Bartholomew I, Patriarch of Constantinople in 2004.
>
> ❧ ⌘ ❧

But perhaps the major consequence of the disastrous Fourth Crusade was that Byzantium was no longer able to provide a bulwark against Ottoman Turkish expansion into Europe. Bypassing the failing Byzantine Empire, the Turks conquered bordering states one by one. The final death blow came to the dying Empire in 1453, when Turkish forces under Mehmed II took Constantinople. By 1499 they had completely occupied the Balkan Peninsula, which they were to rule for the next 400 years. 'There are few greater ironies in history', writes John Julius Norwich, 'than the fact that the fate of Eastern Christendom should have been sealed—and half of Europe condemned to some five hundred years of Moslem rule—by men who fought under the banner of the Cross.'

In the midst of all this loss and desolation, the crippling of Byzantium did have one lasting benefit for the world—a surge of new influences on the Renaissance. With Byzantium in its final decline, the Emperor John VIII and his Greek entourage visited Florence in 1448 in a last-ditch effort to get Western help to prevent the fall of Constantinople to the Ottoman Turks. No aid was forthcoming, since most in the West realised that the Byzantine Empire was doomed. However, the splendour of the Greek delegation greatly impressed the Florentines, and stimulated a surge of interest in Greek culture, history and ideas. Their initial visit was followed by the creation of a Greek settlement in Florence after the Ottoman capture of Constantinople in 1453. It was made up of artisans, philosophers and doctors, who brought with them many texts of antiquity that had been lost to the West for centuries. This influx increased in the 1460s after the fall of the Morea—part of the Peloponnese Peninsula in southern Greece. These events infused the Italian Renaissance with many new ideas, which then spread throughout Europe, later bringing about the birth of humanism, the beginnings of the nation-state and ideas that eventually triggered the Reformation.

Having created conditions that allowed the Ottomans to subjugate eastern Europe, the events of the Fourth Crusade continued to reverberate down the centuries, even into the twentieth century. The slow decline of the Ottoman Empire during the 1800s earned it the title 'The Sick Man of Europe'. This encouraged nationalist sentiments to rise in the Balkans, which culminated in revolt. Serbia gained its independence from the Ottomans in two uprisings, the first in 1804 and the second in 1815, although Turkish troops continued to occupy the capital Belgrade until 1867. Greece gained her independence in 1830 and other states followed soon after. Meanwhile, the major European powers were involved in either propping up the Ottoman state (Britain) or seeking to destroy it (Russia). Over the next 50 years this became one of the principal causes of World War I, as Balkan nationalism tore the fragile fabric of European peace apart. That the roots of World War I can be seen to extend back some 800 years into the distant past is a legacy bequeathed to the world by Venice and her blind, vengeful doge.

# WHEN MERRY ENGLAND WAS A POLICE STATE (1558–1603)

*'I have no desire to make windows into men's souls.'*
**Queen Elizabeth I**

*'Government's first duty is to protect the people, not run their lives.'*
**Ronald Reagan**

### LIE

Elizabeth I was England's greatest monarch.

### TRUTH

Elizabeth's religious settlement radicalised many citizens, resulting in religious and civil wars that would devastate England during the seventeenth century!

### CHIEF PARTICIPANTS

Elizabeth I, Queen of England
Matthew Parker, Archbishop of Canterbury
Sir Francis Walsingham, head of the unofficial secret service

### THE STORY SO FAR

Queen Elizabeth's father, Henry VIII, had decided that he needed a divorce from his first wife, Catherine of Aragon. The Pope refused to grant one, since this would have annoyed the Holy Roman Emperor, who was Catherine's nephew, and this might have led to armed conflict. Since Henry was desperate to obtain a legitimate male heir, having only a daughter, Mary, he broke away from Rome and declared himself head of the Church in England. Divorcing Catherine, he married Anne Boleyn, who bore him another daughter, Elizabeth. While Henry was determined to remove the Pope's influence in England, he still remained a Catholic in terms of his beliefs and religious practices. By his death in 1547, the effects of the Reformation that was sweeping across northern Europe had had little effect in England. Henry's son, Edward, by his third wife, introduced more radical reforms in religion, but these were not complete by his death in 1553. Having no heir, Edward was succeeded by his sister Mary, a staunch Catholic, who reintroduced Catholicism into England. She died in 1558, also without an heir, bringing Elizabeth to the throne of England …

A hand-coloured genealogical chart tracing Elizabeth I's ancestry back to Adam.

The opening scenes of the film *Elizabeth* (1998) say it all. Huddled and oppressed peasants cower in fear as fanatical Catholic bishops ride by. Devout and defiant Protestant protesters are burned at the stake for their beliefs, as Queen Mary—'Bloody Mary' as she would come to be known—goes slowly mad and dies. Meanwhile, Jesuit priests haunt the corridors of power as they further their treacherous plots. This is contrasted with actress Cate Blanchett's noble Virgin Queen (Elizabeth), proud of her nation, determined to stand against all who would cause her people harm. Viewers are treated to scenes at the royal court, with dancing, pageants, maids in waiting and elegant suitors. This is the traditional view of the Elizabethan era, a golden age for England when a benevolent monarch ruled a flourishing nation of contented people enjoying peace and religious moderation after years of Catholic bigotry.

The true picture is not quite so rosy. The England of Elizabeth I was an intolerant society, where the whims of the monarch determined what the people were to believe, how they were to worship and even what entertainment they could watch. It was a police state where anyone could be arrested and tortured on the flimsiest of charges. Suspects could be convicted in secret, with no indictments, no right of appeal, no juries and no witnesses. This was a country where royal censors pored over every line of plays, where religious authorities ensured conformity to a state-endorsed religion, and where spies and informants lurked everywhere, searching out all forms of dissent. Elizabeth's reign was to bring about 300 years of intolerance and persecution of Catholics. Her decision to keep the puritans repressed and out of the established church divided England into two camps, a situation that was to lead to a destructive civil war that would tear the kingdom apart a scant 35 years after her death.

## The Official Story—Good Queen Bess

It was a moment that the unwanted daughter of Anne Boleyn thought would never come. Until then, Elizabeth had spent her life in the shadow of the court. Cast aside by her father, forgotten by her half-brother's government, and later kept under constant surveillance during the reign of her half-sister Mary, she suddenly found herself Queen of England on 17 November 1558. Legend has it that she was reclining under an oak tree reading the Bible when the news reached her, and that she received it with a quotation from Psalm 118: 'This is the Lord's doing, and it is marvellous in our eyes'. Thankful though she was for the freedom and power she now possessed, she came to the throne at a difficult time. England was a poor, almost bankrupt country, torn apart by religious squabbles. Catholics and Protestants had fought for control of the country ever since her father, Henry VIII, had broken away from Rome.

The people were desperate for a permanent solution to the problem of a state religion. The Catholic old guard had been re-established under Mary, but many Protestant radicals started returning home with Elizabeth's ascension. Steering the nation between these two competing camps was to be Elizabeth's first important task.

The years following the death of her father had called for her to be clear-headed and watchful, and she remained so as Queen. It soon became apparent that Elizabeth was at least as politically astute as her father. She was devoted to her country in a way few monarchs have been before or since, fostering good government by selecting able men to aid her in ruling the country. To restore the religious balance in England, one of her first tasks was to re-establish Protestantism as the official state religion. With the Acts of Supremacy and Uniformity, she set up a reformed religion that would satisfy the majority of Protestants, yet retain enough ceremonials to avoid offending a majority of Catholics. This 'reformed Church of England' was quickly adopted by the majority of her subjects, and was soon cherished by all but the extremists, settling the divisive question of religion once and for all.

The main issue that Elizabeth would have to face for the remainder of her reign was the hostility of foreign Catholic powers in Europe, that were determined to reimpose Catholicism on England. Chief among these was Spain, whose king, Phillip II, was Elizabeth's most implacable opponent. In July 1588, Phillip launched the Spanish Armada, a fleet of 130 ships carrying over 30,000 men, with orders to invade England. A defiant Elizabeth rallied her troops at Tilbury. There, seated on a grey horse and dressed in white with a silver breastplate, she addressed her troops in a speech full of passion, indignation and stirring nationalism. 'I know I have the body but of a weak and feeble woman,' she declared, 'but I have the heart and stomach of a King, and of a King of England too! And I think it foul scorn that Spain or Parma or any prince of Europe should dare invade the borders of my realm.'

The invasion was thwarted by the skill of the English navy, assisted by the Dutch, and the Armada was blown up the northeast coast of England and around Scotland, where many ships were wrecked. This victory was the crowning glory of her reign in the eyes of her subjects, and it was during the 1590s that people began to talk of the 'Golden Age of Elizabeth'. This was the era of playwrights such as William Shakespeare, Christopher Marlowe and Ben Jonson; of Francis Drake, who became the first Englishman to circumnavigate the world; of Francis Bacon, who wrote influential philosophical and political works; an era when England began to colonise North America under Sir Walter Raleigh and Sir Humphrey Gilbert. When Elizabeth died at Richmond Palace on 24 March 1603, England was no longer the bankrupt, divided nation she had inherited, but one of the most powerful and prosperous countries in the world.

## The Truth—Supremacy and Uniformity

*The Faerie Queene*—the title of Edmund Spenser's poem dedicated to Elizabeth—conjures up images of a magical realm ruled over by a benevolent monarch. There is no doubt that the official history of Elizabeth's reign supports such a picture, but there is another side to the story. Historian William H. Prescott, described an Elizabeth who was: 'haughty, arrogant, coarse, and irascible; while with these fiercer qualities she mingled deep dissimulation and strange irresolution.'

This contradiction between the benevolent queen and the capricious tyrant was evident from the start, as reflected in the first major legislation of her reign—the Acts of Uniformity and Supremacy, both passed in 1559. Whatever later propaganda claimed, England at the ascension of Elizabeth was not a realm sharply divided between Catholic and Protestant. While there was fierce antagonism between Catholic and Protestant factions within the nobility and the clergy, the remainder of the nation was essentially Catholic, both by tradition and desire. A plebiscite would have confirmed this simple fact—the people were happy with the religion of their fathers and their fathers before them, and did not want any change to their forms of worship. The fact that there were peasant revolts against religious changes during the reigns of Henry VIII and Elizabeth, yet none during the reign of the Catholic 'Bloody Mary', speaks for itself. Religious conflict was confined to the upper echelons of society, since this was basically a political fight and not a religious one. As historian P.G. Maxwell-Stuart writes: 'The political establishment was determined to impose on the English people, whether they liked it or not, the forms of Protestant belief and worship which best suited the requirements of those same political classes.'

Although the people of England were not interested in changing the English church from Catholic to Protestant, the same could not be said for their new sovereign. Elizabeth, like her father, was a pragmatist. Embracing English Protestantism was a political move, not a religious one. She was raised a Protestant, and was little inclined to change her persuasion for one very practical reason: the Catholic church did not recognise her father's divorce, meaning that she was regarded as illegitimate, and so could not legally occupy the throne if the country were Catholic. If she supported the Protestant cause, however, her father's remarriage and her inheritance became legal. She therefore imposed upon England her vision of a reformed Catholicism, as legislated through the Acts of Supremacy and Uniformity.

There were 53 torture warrants issued during Elizabeth's reign.

The *Act of Supremacy* allowed Elizabeth to declare herself Supreme Governor of the Church of England. It also included the Oath of Supremacy, which compelled any person taking public or church office to swear allegiance to the monarch and not to the Pope. Failure to swear such allegiance was considered treasonous. By this Act, Elizabeth reclaimed control of the English Church, preventing ecclesiastical dissent.

Queen Elizabeth I in coronation robes, *circa* 1585–1590.

The Act of Uniformity was designed to specify one set of religious rules and regulations, as set out in the *Book of Common Prayer*. All other forms of worship, especially the traditional Roman Mass were banned, and everyone had to go to church once a week or be fined 12 pence—a significant amount for working people. For the first time in the history of England, there was now a legal obligation to attend church on Sunday.

By these actions, Elizabeth effectively set up a new arm of government, and shaped it according to her will. It legitimised her reign and created a new religious hierarchy that depended on her to preserve its supremacy. Distrustful of the prevalent Catholic mood in the country, but unwilling to go as far as many Protestant divines wanted her to go, she imposed a religious settlement that pleased no one but herself, and punished all who dissented.

According to Vatican archives, in 1533, Pope Clement VII had drafted a papal bull granting Henry VIII an annulment of his marriage to his first wife, Catherine of Aragon. However, owing to pressure from the Holy Roman Emperor Charles V, who had imprisoned Clement in 1527 and who was nephew to Catherine, the Pope was prevented from issuing the bull formally.

The changes Elizabeth introduced were for the most part deeply unpopular, and would remain so for a generation. In fact, the first version of the Act of Uniformity did not pass through the House of Lords, because the Catholic bishops and peers of the realm voted against it. To express their discontent, they altered much of the Bill, changed the litany to permit the belief in transubstantiation in the sacrament of Communion, and denied Elizabeth the title of Supreme Head of the Church, allowing her only to be Supreme Governor of the Church.

## The Elizabethan Police State

To ensure that the Acts were fully complied with, Elizabeth set up one of the world's most efficient police states. Most people would never associate the term 'police state' with the Golden Age of Elizabeth, but the common people enjoyed very few individual liberties, and members of groups deemed subversive or treasonous by the government had no liberties at all. The groups that felt the wrath of the Elizabethan police state most forcefully were the Catholics and the puritans. Both sought to change government religious policies and both were harshly repressed as a result.

Elizabeth's Catholic persecutions lasted for her entire reign. Shortly after she ascended the throne, the names and deeds of the Protestant martyrs—those executed by her sister, Mary—were widely publicised for political and propaganda purposes, effectively branding Catholicism a brutal and despotic religion. It was to the benefit of the new sovereign that her predecessor's reign should be blackened as much as possible. It is impossible to know the full extent of the oppression enforced by the Elizabethan police state, although in one brutal episode over 600 Catholics were executed for daring to restore the Catholic Mass in Durham in 1569, during the so-called 'Rising of the North'. What is certain, is that by the end of Elizabeth's reign, the number of Catholics in England had been reduced by death or exile from over 90 per cent to about 30 per cent of the total population. Thousands died in England, and tens of thousands of Catholics were killed in Ireland during repeated rebellions against English rule.

## SHAKESPEARE IN TUDOR ENGLAND

The Elizabethan police state even affected the lives of prominent figures such as William Shakespeare. Watched closely by the royal censors on the one hand, and by the religious establishment on the other, Shakespeare had to tread a fine line. The royal censors were always on the lookout for treasonable material, so anyone hoping to stay on the good side of the Queen and the court had to take great care. For example, the play *King Richard the Second* was examined by authorities because the plot involves the overthrow of a monarch who had become an enemy of the people.

Shakespeare's historical plays make an interesting study in the art of political propaganda. To justify the rise of the Tudor dynasty, Shakespeare had to present recent English history in such a way that the Tudors could clearly be seen as having a legitimate right to the throne. In doing so he had to justify the overthrow of the Plantagenets (Richard II), eulogise the Lancastrians (Henry IV to VI), and vilify the Yorkists (Richard III), showing how events had paved the way for the greatest dynasty of them all, the legitimate successors to the House of Lancaster, the Tudors. While the plays were principally intended as entertainment—for both the common people and the monarch—they were also, importantly, pieces of propaganda.

Elizabeth was an enthusiastic devotee of the theatre, so it was just common sense for the leading playwrights of the day to try and curry favour with the royal court by presenting certain events in recent history in a favourable light. Even after Elizabeth's death, when James I came to the throne, Shakespeare would have known that James was a descendant of Henry VII, and would have been wary of offending the Stuarts by criticising their royal ancestors—Lancastrian or Tudor.

Yet it was not only Catholics who were offended by Elizabeth's religious Settlement; so too were the more zealous Protestants, who were convinced that the Reformation had not gone far enough, and that obeying the Settlement was giving in to 'popery'. Although puritans were not as severely persecuted as Catholics, Elizabeth still regarded nonconformists with great suspicion, seeing the puritan movement as potentially dangerous to royal control of the Church. Indeed, they were vocal in their criticism of the structure and liturgy imposed by Elizabeth and her ministers, and of the pressure brought to bear on bishops of the Church of England to enforce uniformity via the *Book of Common Prayer.* Ministers who refused to conform were deprived of their living, and the government began to act against the nonconformists by suppressing meetings. Hundreds of individual nonconformists were fined for not attending Church of England services, and even puritan archbishops were not immune. Archbishop Grindal was summoned several times before the Court of Star Chamber—Elizabeth's secret court used to punish suspected traitors and malcontents—in order to pressure him to declare publicly that he had been wrong in his support of nonconformist meetings considered dangerous by Elizabeth.

Shakespeare's play *Hamlet,* first performed in Queen Elizabeth's reign in 1602, contains a description of a place where his father's spirit has to endure torments for the sins committed during his lifetime. This is very like the Catholic concept of purgatory, which although it is never called that in the play, shows how careful even Shakespeare had to be to avoid official scrutiny.

Puritan Members of Parliament were not safe from Elizabeth's paranoia either, as Peter Wentworth discovered in 1593 when he presented the ageing Queen with a petition asking her to name her heir. Her response to this request was to incarcerate Wentworth in the Tower of London, where he remained for four years until his death.

Elizabeth even tried to control what people thought and believed. Through her bishops, she instituted catechism classes, where young people throughout the realm were introduced to the basic teachings of the Church of England. All parents were legally required to send their children to these classes to ensure that the new generation would support the authorised state religion and the monarchy.

A police state cannot function on the whims of the ruler alone. It requires people to actually enforce the orders of government, and Elizabeth's England was no exception. On religious issues, the Archbishops of Canterbury were expected to carry out a program of enforcement. Inclined to be radical in their Protestant outlook, most Archbishops were more than happy to repress their fellow Protestant nonconformists. Ambitious and frightened of the monarch, they ensured that conformity to the church as established by law was enforced during Elizabeth's reign.

In secular affairs, Elizabeth was served by loyal ministers who could be relied upon to do her bidding. To ensure the effectiveness of the police state, she put Sir Francis

Walsingham in command of an army of spies and informers. Cold, calculating and a fanatical Protestant, Walsingham was the perfect man for the job. He employed double agents to identify individuals within England who might be harbouring a secret desire to overthrow the monarch. His greatest success was in uncovering plots to remove Elizabeth and replace her with Mary, Queen of Scots. Yet most of Walsingham's paid informants were debtors seeking a way out of prison, which meant that their information was often of dubious value. In foreign affairs, Walsingham had an extensive network of spies supplying him with news of schemes being hatched in the various Catholic courts of Europe, as well as informants planted within groups of English Catholics exiled abroad.

Last, but not least, a police state needs men to do its dirty work. While many were willing and able to offer their services, the most infamous was Richard Topcliffe. A Member of Parliament, this notorious priest-hunter, torturer and rapist was under the direct command of Walsingham, and acted with the approval of Elizabeth herself. Topcliffe nurtured a singular loathing for the Catholic Church, and participated in the examination and torture of large numbers of Catholic priests and laity. He acquired notoriety as an efficient and brutal torturer, boasting that his own devices and techniques were more effective than any official methods, even going so far as to employ torture when no torture warrants had been issued. He set up a torture chamber at his home in London, and was involved in hanging, drawing and quartering Catholic recusants who had been sentenced to death. Topcliffe's victims included the Jesuit priest and poet Robert Southwell, who was tortured repeatedly in a vain attempt to get him to reveal information about other Jesuits in the country. He even interrogated the famous playwright Ben Jonson during an investigation into the content of one of Jonson's plays, *The Isle of Dogs*.

## Legacies

In trying to navigate a course between Catholicism on the one hand, and the more extreme forms of Protestant puritanism, Elizabeth instituted a police state in which she tried to repress both. While she was able to remove the Catholic threat, the simmering discord between the established Church of England and the nonconformist Protestant middle class was set to explode into civil war within 35 years of her death. Her decision to halt the Reformation in England at a point where the church was neither fully Catholic nor fully Protestant meant that the instability created would eventually force a confrontation between high and low church factions. This did not happen during her reign, but her distant cousin Charles I would not be so lucky. His support for the established church infuriated the puritans, while his weakness emboldened them. Determined to sweep away the last vestiges of popery in the House of God, they condemned the British

Isles to a devastating war and political turmoil that lasted from 1638 until 1688. This period included the execution of the monarch, the establishment of a republic run by a nonconformist military junta, and the disestablishment of the official church.

With the benefit of hindsight, it can be said that Elizabeth's police state was one factor that led England towards becoming a constitutional monarchy and parliamentary democracy. When the less popular Stuart kings wielded powers instituted by Elizabeth, it led to their undoing because their opponents had developed more effective forms of resistance and were determined to end the monarch's arbitrary powers, particularly the ability to reign without summoning parliament. They achieved their goal with the final overthrow of the Stuart kings in the Glorious Revolution of 1688.

Religious pluralism in Western societies also had its beginnings in the overthrow of James II in 1688. Circumstances in which all citizens are legally forced to go to a specified form of worship could simply not be sustained in the long term. The supremacy of the Church of England, as established by law, came to an end in 1688, when nonconformists were permitted to gather together and worship in places of their own choosing.

> Some prominent lawyers believe that a number of nineteenth-century laws could actually prevent a Catholic from becoming Prime Minister of Great Britain, and that former Prime Minister Tony Blair's conversion could have provoked a conflict with his role in appointing Anglican bishops.

Some shadows cast by the Elizabethan age took longer to dispel. While royal power and religious authority gradually eroded, the persecution of Catholics continued for centuries. Forbidden to enter parliament, hold public office, celebrate Mass or pray together; forbidden even to bequeath land and houses to their offspring, Catholics were a repressed class in England until astonishingly recently. There were attempts to redress this situation, but all were doomed to failure due to a latent anti-Catholic bias in the community, as well as within the Church of England. In 1780, for example, Londoners rioted because they were concerned about Catholics in the United Kingdom being offered a Catholic Relief Bill in exchange for help in repressing the revolt in the North American colonies. Catholic churches were burned and the Bank of England was attacked in some of the worst rioting London has ever seen. It was only in 1829 that the majority of anti-Catholic legislation was repealed with the *Catholic Relief Act*, although even at the beginning of the twenty-first century it is illegal for a monarch of Great Britain or their spouse to be a Catholic. While there is no barrier for politicians, former Prime Minister Tony Blair waited until he had relinquished office in 2007 before converting to the Catholic faith of his wife and family.

Elizabeth and her Parliament. Given Elizabeth's notorious temper, her relationship with the Parliament was surprisingly good; she exercised her veto in relation to only 70 out of 506 bills.

# WHAT HAPPENED TO THE PRISONERS OF THE BASTILLE? (1789)

*'I was stripped of my clothes, covered with rags half rotten, chained hand and foot and then thrown into a dungeon with a few handfuls of straw.'*
**Henry Masers De Latude**

*'Believe only half of what you see and nothing that you hear.'*
**Dinah Maria Craik**

### LIE

The Bastille prison in Paris was a hell on Earth, where hundreds of freedom-loving citizens were kept prisoner by a cruel and repressive monarch.

### TRUTH

There were only seven inmates in the Bastille, two of them insane!

### CHIEF PARTICIPANTS

Camille Desmoulins, a leading revolutionary
Bernard-René de Launay, the governor of the Bastille prison
Louis XVI, King of France

### THE STORY SO FAR

King Louis XVI inherited a ticking bomb when he came to the throne in 1774. He was an absolute monarch married to the unpopular Austrian Marie Antoinette, and ruled a resentful, powerless aristocracy that constantly yearned for the days when their ancestors regularly made and toppled kings. The government was perpetually short of money because the nobility and clergy refused to pay taxes, that burden falling unequally on the middle classes and the peasants. The middle classes were acutely aware that their financial contributions did not translate into political power and they were looking for ways to change the situation. By 1789, events were coming to a head. French intervention in the American War of Independence had placed the state heavily in debt. Unable to find the funds to discharge this debt, the government lurched from crisis to crisis. Famine gripped the countryside, prices skyrocketed and the king was persuaded that the only solution was to summon the French parliament, which had last met in 1614 …

A depiction of the dungeon of the Bastille at the moment the prisoners were freed by revolutionaries.

The three things most people would probably mention if asked about the French Revolution are Marie Antoinette, the guillotine and the Bastille. Of the three, the fall of the Bastille probably lingers most in the mind. The story of how the ordinary people of Paris rose up to liberate fellow citizens enduring a living hell, simply because they had offended their despotic king in a quest for liberty, fraternity and equality, has been handed down from generation to generation.

This description of the fall of the Bastille spread across the whole of France within a matter of days. Periodicals and journals appeared on the streets of Paris, recounting eyewitness accounts of 'cells [...] thrown open to set free innocent victims and venerable old men who were amazed to behold the light of day'.

Stirring though the story undoubtedly is, it is a complete fiction. The rioting protestors did not discover hundreds of political prisoners languishing within the walls of a fiendish prison, but only a few men who were either criminals or mad. Eager to ensure that their actions were not in vain, however, the revolutionaries created a story that gave their deeds a heroic aspect—a story that would eventually carry the revolution to its bloody apogee in the Reign of Terror.

## The Official Story—Symbol of a Despotic Regime

For as long as people could remember, the Bastille had cast its shadow over the less fashionable part of Paris, where it loomed menacingly over the poor quarter of Faubourg St Antoine. Built as a fortress during the Hundred Years' War (1337–1453) against the detested English, it had later become a state prison. In about 1630, Cardinal Richelieu, chief minister of Louis XIII, decided it would make a perfect place to incarcerate important prisoners of state and from then on it acquired a sinister reputation. An air of secrecy descended on the prison and anyone unfortunate enough to be held there. Locals spoke of it in whispers, telling tales of men who would go in and never come out again, buried alive within its dungeons. They spoke of the use of new, scientific methods of torture, of men confined in tiny spaces, of minds and bodies broken after years of torment.

This fear always lurked in the minds of Parisians, and it gave an added sense of urgency to events of July 1789. The Estates-General (the French Parliament) that Louis XVI had called into being had turned against him. Meeting in Paris in June, it judged itself a sovereign power, became the National Assembly, and demanded reforms. The tense situation became critical on 11 July, when the king, acting on the advice of the more conservative aristocratic members of the royal council, exiled his reformist finance minister, Jacques Necker.

The people of Paris, who regarded Necker as the man who could save France from ruin and famine, decided that this was the beginning of a royal counter-offensive against the National Assembly, and openly revolted. Members of the military joined an excited, 6000-strong mob led by Camille Desmoulins in a successful attack on royal troops stationed in the city. News of events spread rapidly, and soon there was a mob of almost 50,000 Parisians roaming the streets in search of bread and guns.

A cache of 30,000 muskets and some cannons was soon discovered, but the crowd lacked the gunpowder necessary to make use of them. When rumours spread that 250 barrels of gunpowder were stored in the Bastille, the crowd descended upon this last bastion of royal authority. On 14 July they laid siege to the prison, and opened negotiations for the release of the gunpowder and the fort's cannons.

By midday, the crowd grew impatient and pushed its way into the courtyard of the Bastille. The governor of the prison, Bernard-René de Launay, frightened and desperate, attempted to negotiate, but the crowd accused him of stalling for time. Shots were fired, and in the confusion that followed a pitched battle began, which ended with the surrender of the royal guards, the capture of de Launay, and his death at the hands of the angry mob.

The leaders of the mob then proceeded to open the cells, allowing a sad collection of scrawny and emaciated old men, many with waist-length beards and frail, pale bodies to emerge blinking into the light. Once the prison had been emptied of its inhabitants, the contents were removed and paraded before the crowd. These included iron corsets and masks, and torture wheels with the skeletal remains of victims still locked in their metal shackles and chains.

The prison was gradually demolished in the months and years that followed, but it lived on in memory as a potent symbol of the power of the people. Just as the Bastille had been toppled, so too would the king, his harlot queen and the country's detested aristocrats.

## The Truth—A Hell on Earth?

The images are certainly evocative, but this romantic tale conceals a more mundane reality, which is that most of the prisoners who found their way into the Bastille were aristocrats who had conspired against the Crown, or Protestants and Catholics who had fallen foul of other state or religious authorities. Other prisoners included writers whose works were considered seditious, such as the philosopher Voltaire, and deviants who were incarcerated by order of the king at the request of their family, such as the notorious Marquis de Sade. Since it was generally members of the upper classes who found themselves in the Bastille, the prison had a capacity of around 50 inmates at most. This meant that conditions were nowhere near as bad as in many other prisons in operation at that time, and certainly nothing like the gulags and concentration camps of the twentieth century.

By the reign of Louis XVI, the lower levels of the Bastille were no longer in use, and those that remained were in reasonable shape for their time. Each prisoner was allotted a sum of money every day—the amount varying according to rank—to provide for their basic nutritional needs. Instead of the narrow, coffin-like cells of popular imagination, most were around 5 metres by 5 metres (16 feet) and furnished with a bed and curtains, a table and chairs, and a stove or fireplace. Most prisoners were allowed to bring in their own possessions, including pets, books and clothes. Prisoners of higher social rank were allowed to take walks in the garden courtyard and on the towers.

Food was also provided on a class basis. Although those of the lower classes generally received either gruel or soup, with the occasional portions of ham added, they also regularly received bread, wine and cheese. For those of a higher social standing, the fare was much better. The historian Jean-François Marmontel recorded that on one occasion during his brief incarceration he was fed 'an excellent soup, a succulent side of beef, a thigh of boiled chicken oozing with grease, a little dish of fried, marinated artichokes or of spinach; really fine Cressane pears, fresh grapes, a bottle of old Burgundy and the best Moka coffee'.

The more privileged inmates also received supplies such as alcohol and tobacco, and card games were permitted for those sharing a cell. While conditions for poorer prisoners were anything but luxurious, the prison was still nowhere near as inadequate as subsequent propaganda made it out to be. In fact, many of the poorer prisoners were probably healthier and arguably better fed than they would have been on the outside.

The Bastille's bad reputation was based in large part on the memoirs of writers who were held there. Their feelings of injustice at having been taken and locked up for expressing their opinions meant that all the comforts provided were of little importance compared to the unfairness of their imprisonment. It was this sense of anger and injury that led them to exaggerate conditions in the prison. An old mattress was transformed into one that was eaten by worms, and adequate clothing became moth-eaten and crawling with parasites.

The routines of prison life were an additional burden for these well-bred and creative children of the Enlightenment. Everyday events like being accompanied by guards during a walk around the yard, having items like scissors confiscated, and being forced to mix with men they regarded as morally depraved, meant that they felt themselves to be brutalised and dehumanised by authorities determined to extinguish their creative spark.

Their memoirs were therefore often written in an attempt to exact revenge on a system that they regarded as having treated them very badly. Books such as Simon-Nicolas-Henri Linguet's *Memoirs of the Bastille* and Louis Pierre Manuel's *The Bastille*

*Revealed* were eagerly devoured by a public both repelled and fascinated by the lurid tales they told. It was stories like these that fed the fires of indignation raging through Paris during the crucial year of 1789, and that were used by leaders of the revolution as propaganda in their struggle.

## The Propaganda Revolution

The events in Paris on 14 July 1789, were the culmination of months, even years, of turmoil. The French crown was burdened with crippling long-term debts, which had recently increased considerably as a result of aid given to the Continental Congress of the Thirteen Colonies during the American War of Independence. France had decided to support the Americans in their fight for independence from British rule, but this came at a price they could ill afford.

The mob that stormed the Bastille is said to have included men, women, children … and an actor dressed as a Cyclops.

During the reigns of Louis XV and Louis XVI, several ministers had unsuccessfully proposed revisions to the tax system to include nobles among those who paid taxes. To get around the financial troubles he had inherited, Louis XVI assigned a moderate minister of finance to deal with the crisis, and on 8 August 1788 agreed to call together the Estates-General for May 1789. When the Estates-General gathered in Versailles on 5 May, it became clear that the Third Estate, representing the emerging middle class, was seeking radical changes, and all efforts by ministers to focus solely on taxes failed. On 28 May, the Third Estate went ahead and gave itself the power to make laws. Three weeks later it voted a radical measure, describing itself as the National Assembly, representing not the Estates, but the 'People'.

## THE MARQUIS DE SADE

One of the Bastille's more colourful prisoners between the years 1784 and 1789 was the notorious Marquis de Sade, made infamous by his sexual and physical abuse of young men and women, and by his writings espousing radical libertinism, unfettered by religion or morality of any sort.

Although revolutionary propagandists made much of the anti-royalists supposedly held in the Bastille, de Sade was the sort of malefactor for whom the prison was really used. And, contrary to popular descriptions of the vile conditions endured by prisoners languishing in the Bastille's dungeons, de Sade's experience of the prison was anything but austere.

As a member of the aristocracy, he was entitled to many special considerations during his stay. He was allowed a desk and a wardrobe, a large number of shirts, silk breeches, coats and dressing gowns, four family portraits, tapestries for the walls of his cell and velvet cushions and pillows. He had three fragrances—rosewater, orange water and eau de Cologne—for his personal needs, as well as candles and oil lamps so that he could read selections from his ample library at night. When his eyes deteriorated, he was allowed visits by an oculist to help him see better.

On 2 July 1789, de Sade shouted through a window of the Bastille 'They are killing the prisoners here!', for which he was removed to the insane asylum at Charenton. He was given his freedom in 1790, and was elected to the National Convention under the name 'Citizen Sade'. However, his aristocratic background caused difficulties for him, which were not helped by his open opposition to the Terror. In 1792, he was again sent to prison and later condemned to death, but his date with Madame Guillotine was delayed by chance on the day before by Robespierre's fall. Declared insane in 1803, he lived to the ripe old age of 74, dying in 1814 in the asylum at Charenton.

The Marquis de Sade in prison.

With events spiralling out of control, Louis XVI shut down the assembly, but it simply moved to the king's tennis court. There it resumed deliberations and swore the 'Tennis Court Oath', agreeing not to break up until it had given France a constitution. By 27 June, the army began to appear in large numbers around Paris and Versailles, which made the people of Paris very nervous. When Louis XVI sacked his reformist finance minister, the people believed that these events were a prelude to a royal crackdown, which propelled Paris into revolution.

The actual events of 'Bastille Day' are shrouded in myth, and have been much embellished by later storytelling. The reality is that on 14 July, the rebels, consisting of the common people of Paris, together with actors, writers and Parisian guardsmen, stormed the Bastille prison, believing that it contained gunpowder and anti-royalist prisoners.

The battle for the Bastille commenced when the crowd began to push forward; in the confusion, someone fired a musket, and each side assumed that the other was responsible. The drawbridge to the inner courtyard was lowered by some of the revolutionaries, but the crowd believed the governor had ordered it to be dropped to lure them inside so they could be mowed down by the cannons arrayed within. As a result, when the crowd later captured him they showed him no mercy.

When the doors of the Bastille were thrown open, a mere seven inmates emerged—four forgers who had been tried by a court of law and found guilty; two lunatics, one of whom believed himself to be Julius Caesar; and a dangerous sexual offender, the Comte de Solages. So where were all of the prisoners who had fallen victim to the brutal and repressive regime of Louis XVI? They simply didn't exist.

This was not what the young revolutionaries wanted the country to hear, however. If the reality of the Bastille failed to serve their purpose, then a new reality would have to be created. The revolutionary leadership therefore invented prisoners to liberate, and published tales of their deliverance as widely as possible. The unsavory characters that emerged from the Bastille forced Revolutionary apologists to manufacture one out of thin air—the comte de Lorges. This creation had been unjustly incarcerated and locked in a damp cell under solitary confinement for forty years, before being released on July 14 to his complete and utter bemusement. To emphasise the poor man's sufferings, he was consistently described as malnourished with the longest white beard imaginable, and his scrawny arms outstretched in appreciation to his rescuers.

To add colour, the revolutionaries took medieval suits of armour from the fortress and paraded them as iron corsets used to crush unfortunate prisoners. Toothed components from an old printing press were described as a wheel of torture, and when skeletal remains were exhumed from within the prison they were immediately declared to be those of prisoners who had died in their cells, forgotten by their guards and left chained to the walls. In fact, they were more than likely to have been the remains of guards who had died some centuries before and been buried within the fortress, but that didn't stop them from being used as bit players in the unfolding drama.

The remains were duly removed with great ceremony, and treated to a service conducted in honour of their memory. Everything that occurred was carefully reworked for maximum effect, with the aim of both demonising the Bastille—and through it the tyrannical monarchy—and of sanctifying the people who were at the forefront of rebuilding the nation.

## Legacies

The storming of the Bastille was a key event in the unfolding of the French Revolution. Its fall demonstrated the weakness of the king in the face of determined opposition. This weakness was again vividly demonstrated when the king was forced back to Paris on 27 July to accept a poorly made tricolour cockade, presented to him with hostile shouts of 'long live the nation'. As propaganda about the Bastille became widely known, it was Louis who was held accountable for all the prison's supposed evils.

Events in Paris inspired further uprisings throughout France. In rural areas, the populace became even more radical, with many peasants burning title deeds and pillaging the manors of their landlords. Anarchy loomed, helped along by the National Assembly, which abolished feudalism and indiscriminately removed both the land-holding rights of the nobility and the tithes gathered by the clergy. Eventually they declared a single chamber for their parliament and announced the confiscation of church property to ease their financial crisis.

As the country lurched from crisis to crisis, a constant refrain was heard repeatedly—the need to return to the values and the inspiration of those first glorious days of the revolution. When parts of the army revolted in protest over the National Assembly sitting beyond the year for which they had been elected, they were accused of being counter-revolutionaries who sought to undo the good achieved when the Bastille had been stormed.

Convinced that he was not going to survive the chaos, the king tried to flee secretly with his family in June 1791. Dressed as servants, their intention was to get to the royalist stronghold at Montmédy, but their flight failed when the king was recognised and the whole party captured at Varennes. Taken back to Paris, Louis was regarded with even greater suspicion as being duplicitous and treacherous, and was forced to accept a new constitution in September 1791 making France a constitutional monarchy.

In an effort to harness forces unleashed by the storming of the Bastille, the National Assembly, under the influence of two political factions, the Girondins and Jacobins, sought to create a new world order by exporting the revolution to other countries in Europe. In 1792, France, under the leadership of the Girondin politician Jacques Pierre Brissot, declared war on Austria, prompting Prussia to join the Austrian side a few weeks later. The war went badly at first. The French army lacked discipline and materials and was easily routed, allowing the Austrians and Prussians to invade. At the same time, there was an acute food shortage due to a mediocre harvest as well as the Legislative Assembly's agricultural policies.

Prices skyrocketed and the people began to attack stores and depots. Convinced that the famine was a royal plot to help the invading foreign armies, a mob stormed the royal palace in Paris and arrested the king in August 1792. One month later, the Assembly abolished the monarchy and declared a republic. The King was executed on 21 January 1793 on the orders of the National Convention and the heir to the throne, the seven-year-old Louis XVII, was thrown into a cell where he died three years later. The famously beautiful Marie Antoinette followed her husband to the guillotine on 16 October 1793.

When prices continued to rise, poor labourers and radical Jacobins rioted, and the Jacobins, under the pretext of thwarting suspected counter-revolutionary activities, seized power through a parliamentary coup. Up to this point, when events had gone badly, Parisians would blame so-called counter-revolutionaries, and then take to the streets in riots in which they sought to re-create the atmosphere and civic pride that had accompanied the fall of the Bastille. If the government attempted to control grain prices, if famine spread, or if a favourite of the mob was killed or arrested, Paris was always ready to rise up in protest, usually at the instigation of agitators who would inevitably invoke the events of 14 July 1789. This time, however, the National Convention had learned its lesson.

∼❧❀❦❀∽

The Jacobins were a radical group in the National Convention, who were determined to eradicate all vestiges of the old order—the *ancien régime*. Under the leadership of Robespierre, they instituted the Reign of Terror, which lasted from 5 September 1793 until 27 July 1794. Today their name is a byword for political extremism.

∼❧❀❦❀∽

During 1793, the Committee of Public Safety came under the control of the ruthless Maximilien Robespierre, a lawyer who was elected to the National Assembly in 1789. The Jacobins unleashed the Reign of Terror, which Robespierre oversaw as the virtual dictator of France. Some 17,000 people died, many under the guillotine. They included some of Robespierre's former friends, such as fellow Jacobin Georges Danton. The slightest hint of counter-revolutionary thought or activity was enough to place anyone under suspicion, and those trials that were conducted were often mere shams. Among the Terror's principal victims were those who had begun the revolution in the first place. Robespierre grasped the fact that unless violence was controlled by the government, it would eventually destroy the government. But in the end he went too far, and was finally overthrown when other members of the National Convention turned against him, fearful for their own lives. Robespierre tried to commit suicide by shooting himself, but survived, only to be guillotined without trial the following day.

The modern world has been indelibly shaped by the ideas and ideals of the French Revolution. Although profoundly influenced by its American forerunner, the French example had far greater impact on the world at large. It was the French Revolution that gave birth to democracy as many now understand it, promoting the structures and style of the presidential system of government found outside the British Commonwealth's Westminster system.

Revolutionaries all over the world in the nineteenth and twentieth centuries would look back at the French experience as an inspiration for their own endeavours. The Russian Revolution, for example, was directly inspired by the events of 1789. As Lenin declared, 'we need the real, nation-wide terror which reinvigorates the country and through which the great French Revolution achieved glory'.

The rise of European nationalism and its attendant horrors in World War I also stem from the revolution. Members of ethnic minorities, originally part of larger empires, saw in the French Revolution an example to be emulated in their yearning for freedom and a nation-state of their own. In many respects, it was their quest for liberty that destabilised Europe to such an extent that it exploded into war in 1914.

# THE FORCED MIGRATION OF THE AMERICAN INDIANS (1830)

*'It will be my sincere and constant desire to observe toward the Indian tribes within our limits a just and liberal policy and to give that humane and considerate attention to their rights and their wants which is consistent with the habits of our Government and the feelings of our people.'*
**President Andrew Jackson**

*'Violence can only be concealed by a lie, and the lie can only be maintained by violence. Any man who has once proclaimed violence as his method is inevitably forced to take the lie as his principle.'*
**Alexander Solzhenitsyn**

### LIE

The westward migration of the Cherokee and other American Indians was peaceful and voluntary.

### TRUTH

President Andrew Jackson was brutal in his treatment of the American Indians!

### CHIEF PARTICIPANTS

Andrew Jackson, seventh President of the United States of America
Martin Van Buren, eighth President of the United States of America

### THE STORY SO FAR

After the 13 colonies of the United States declared their independence from Great Britain in 1776, they quickly began the process of consolidation, establishing a federal government and state legislatures. Although the newly born United States was conceived as one nation, there were peoples living within its boundaries who regarded themselves as separate nations—the American Indians. Many Indians had been granted territories that they could self-govern outside the state legislatures in which they lived. However, an ever-increasing demand for land by white settlers meant that the Indian territories were slowly being reduced by illegal encroachments, often with the connivance of state bodies. By the 1820s, many white politicians favoured a scheme to move the Indian tribes westward

Andrew Jackson was the dominant player in American politics in the 1820s and 1830s.

73

across the Mississippi River onto land that was not likely to be brought into the Union in the foreseeable future. This would enable them to seize land currently owned, occupied and cultivated by the Indians. The Indians, of course, had no desire to go anywhere …

To many children growing up in the mid-twentieth century, Westerns were standard fare at Saturday matinee performances in local cinemas. The plots were often virtually identical. In John Ford's *Stagecoach*, for example, Apache Indians attack the coach and are only beaten off at the last minute, thanks to the timely arrival of the gallant US Cavalry. The Indians were almost always the villains in these epics, and while children may not have questioned the stereotype, some adults might have wondered why the Indians were always attacking the settlers.

In movies, that was simply what Indians did, but in real life they were motivated by a burning anger—anger at the encroachment of the white man onto their lands, and anger at forced relocations farther and farther west throughout the nineteenth century.

The forced resettlements began in the 1820s and 1830s, despite the fact that official transcripts of government policy, especially plans outlined by President Andrew Jackson, took pains to emphasise the peaceful and voluntary nature of the relocations. Report after report declared that the relocations were going well, and that the Indians, apart from a few malcontents, were happy in their new situation.

The reality could not have been further removed from the picture presented in sanitised accounts prepared for domestic consumption by white legislators. Talk of peaceful relocations was a lie. Jackson's program was murderous, extreme and the cause of much suffering for the Indians concerned. His policy may have opened up the boundless natural resources of North America for exploitation, providing a basis for America's future prosperity, but it came at the cost of the lives and happiness of thousands of men, women and children displaced by his unyielding strategy to exclude them from the southeastern states.

## The Official Story—Voluntary Indian Migration

The hardy frontier families were becoming agitated. Vast tracts of forest and rolling grassland beckoned these adventurous and ambitious settlers, but the trouble was that it was legally occupied by Indians.

By the 1820s, the problem with Indian tribes living on the eastern side of the Mississippi was clear for all to see. The pressure from white settlers and land speculators, who continually harassed Indians by stealing their livestock, burning their villages and squatting on their land, was causing conflict, suffering and deaths on both sides. The discovery of gold on Cherokee land in what is now modern-day Georgia only worsened a situation that was nearing its flash point.

After pleading by southern states such as Alabama, Georgia, Tennessee, Mississippi and the Carolinas, President Andrew Jackson agreed that something needed to be done to provide a permanent solution to the problem. This he did by setting aside a region west of the Mississippi River for the Indian tribes. In an address to Congress in 1829 he declared: 'This emigration should be voluntary, for it would be as cruel as unjust to compel the aborigines to abandon the graves of their fathers and seek a home in a distant land. But they should be distinctly informed that if they remain within the limits of the states they must be subject to their laws.'

Safe within their own territory across the Mississippi the Indians might slowly be introduced to the benefits of white civilisation, as well as being sheltered from predatory and unscrupulous frontiersmen. Any who chose to remain on their ancestral lands would be treated as every other citizen, and would 'ere long become merged in the mass of our population'. The Indian Removal Bill was duly passed in 1830.

The main tribes involved in the migration were the people of the Cherokee, Creek, Choctaw, Chickasaw and Seminole nations. To these groups, President Jackson promised a generous and reasonable swap for their ancestral lands, and a guarantee of self-government free from interference by white men. Claiming not to be an Indian-hater, he maintained that once the Indians were west of the Mississippi, their culture would not be undermined and they would not be forced into extinction by an increasingly mercenary white population. Because most white Americans believed that their nation would never extend beyond the Mississippi, the Indians would be out of harm's way in their new province.

Ratification of the removal treaties began almost at once, with the focus on the great southern tribes, although several weaker tribes of the north were included as well. During the period of the Jackson administration, the government ratified approximately 70 individual treaties, covering some 46,000 Indians.

Importantly, and true to Jackson's word, the *Removal Act* did not explicitly compel the Indians to leave their land. Because many Indians didn't possess the means or provisions for the long journey west of the Mississippi, the Act specified that the federal government would help by providing food and transportation. However, during the course of the migrations, Jackson's fears about the Indians who remained on their lands were realised. For the most part, those staying behind found themselves dispossessed and treated like second-class citizens. If any Indians ventured to return to their old homes they were met with open hostility from now-resident settlers and newly established state authorities.

When the Cherokee nation went to the Supreme Court to fight a series of laws enacted by the state of Georgia to force their removal, Jackson pleaded with tribal elders and chiefs to negotiate a federal treaty and avoid the potential for escalating violence. 'Think then of these things,' he said. 'Shut your ears to bad counsels. Look at your condition as it now is, and then consider what it will be if you follow the advice I give you.' They agreed, and began the march west, so that by 1838 fewer than 2000 remained in Georgia.

It was with some pride, therefore, that President Martin Van Buren, Jackson's successor, confirmed to Congress that 'the measures authorised by Congress in the last session [...] have had the happiest effect', and that 'the Cherokees have migrated without apparent reluctance' across the Mississippi and onto their new lands in what was to become modern-day Oklahoma and Kansas.

## The Truth—The Real Andrew Jackson

Despite professing to have the best interests of the Indian tribes at heart, President Jackson was really far more interested in keeping his political constituents happy. These were the tough, blunt and sturdy folk of the southern and western frontiers, and it was for their benefit, and because of their desire for Indian land, that the Indian Removal Bill was first conceived.

Jackson's constituents had great faith in their man, since he had already proved his worth to them over a number of years. Standing nearly 1.85 m (6 ft 1 in) tall, he had a mane of red hair that had turned grey with age. His face and hands bore the scars of sword slashes given to him by a British Redcoat after the young Andrew had refused to clean the soldier's boots. The scars ran deeper than the flesh, however, marking him as a man who was as tough as nails and not one to be swayed by doe-eyed sentimentality. He could be a devoted friend, but an implacable enemy.

It was Major General Andrew Jackson who had repelled the British at New Orleans in 1815. He had also fought against the Indians in the Battle of Horseshoe Creek in Alabama the year before, when the Creek Indians lost nine million hectares (22 million acres) of land in southern Georgia and central Alabama. He captured more territory in 1818 when, using the Seminoles' habit of providing refuge for fugitive slaves as an excuse, he invaded Spanish Florida and waged war against them. Jackson's campaign was murderous, leading to the wholesale destruction of homes, the death of thousands and the capture of their chief. The Seminoles were then forced to abandon their lands and travel west towards territory not yet considered desirable by white settlers.

Jackson also had his eye on Cherokee territory in what is now Georgia, and his supporters knew that he would do whatever it took to gain it. When the southern states began to pressure the federal government during the early 1820s to implement forced Indian removal policies, they realised that they had to get their man into the Oval Office.

Tah-Chee was a Cherokee leader who fought against the forced removal of Indians.

TAH-CHEE

## A. CHEROKEE CHIEF

Philadelphia Published by F. C. Biddle

Entered according to act of Congress in the year 1837 by F. C. Biddle in the Clerks Office of the District Court of the Eastern District of P.a

They did this in the 1828 election, when voters in Alabama, Mississippi, Georgia and Tennessee provided Jackson with the large popular mandate needed to effect radical changes in the settlement of Indians on federal territory. Upon election to the presidency of the United States, Jackson made it clear through statements made by his Secretary of War, and by his own announcements to Congress, that he, 'would no longer protect the Indians against the southern states who wanted their land.'

Although Jackson promised peaceful removal, the reality was to be quite different. Those who knew him best, especially those who knew him as 'Old Hickory', understood that his portrayal of Indian relocation as a voluntary migration was a fiction designed to obscure a harsh reality. Whatever the cost, it was always clear that Jackson was going to do everything in his power to facilitate dreams of expanding white hegemony over the eastern United States. As Jackson himself declared, 'what good man would prefer a country covered with forests and ranged by a few thousand savages to our extensive Republic, studded with cities, towns, and prosperous farms [...] and filled with all the blessings of liberty, civilisation, and religion?'

## OLD HICKORY

The War of 1812 against Britain established Andrew Jackson's reputation as a national hero, a status that was due in no small part to his decisive victory over the British at the Battle of New Orleans on 8 January 1815.

During this engagement, Jackson's 4000 soldiers and militiamen faced some 10,000 British troops. The British used their usual tactic of marching in regular formation across an open field, but Jackson had concealed 16 heavy cannons behind a row of cotton bales and used them to cut down the advancing British. When the battle was over, the British had suffered more than 2000 casualties to Jackson's 13 dead and 58 injured or missing. Jackson emerged from this encounter with a reputation as a battle-hardened commander, popular with his troops, but more importantly, as a leader who knew how to win.

It was during this conflict that Jackson gained the sobriquet 'Old Hickory'. He had been instructed to deliver his Tennessee militia to Natchez, Mississippi, but when he arrived he was ordered to disperse his troops because they were no longer required. Jackson rejected the order and marched the troops back to Tennessee. Discipline was harsh for the men during the marches, but they grudgingly grew to respect Jackson's determination and authority, remarking that he was as tough as old hickory. It was a name that stuck, and one that he bore with pride, believing it to sum up an unflinching and unbending approach to adversity.

Although Jackson had no qualms about his proposed course of action, the same could not be said for the rest of Congress. It was bitterly divided over the issue, which many saw as an unconscionable attack on the principles of liberty and justice that had been enshrined in the Constitution. In the end, however, the president prevailed, and Congress passed the bill into law by the narrowest of margins.

Jackson had now obtained the legal authority he needed to relocate Indian tribes from the eastern side of the Mississippi to the western. For the Indians, this was a poor exchange since it involved them leaving land that was already settled for untamed territory. Although the government promised that it would 'forever secure and guarantee' this land to them and their 'heirs or successors', and provide compensation for the improvements upon their eastern lands, this never happened. It didn't matter much what the Indians thought, however, since any who refused to obey the injunction to move were forced from their homes by state militiamen.

Jackson naturally took full credit for the removal of the tribes, claiming that the threat posed by the Indians to God-fearing settlers and frontiersmen was over. Citizens of the republic were now free to use the land to spread civilisation and God's Holy writ. This view was resoundingly endorsed by Jackson's fellow countrymen, who re-elected him for a second term in 1833. Jackson claimed that he was removing the Indians for their own good, and his fellow citizens took him at his word. Very few knew or cared about the devastating effects these changes were to have on Indian society and their way of life.

## The 'Trail of Tears'

The plight of the Indians is tragically demonstrated by the fate of the Cherokee who, regardless of official propaganda, were not willing to move. They had originally been guaranteed ownership of their tribal lands in Georgia, Alabama and Mississippi by George Washington himself in 1794. They had also won the right to be recognised as a sovereign people. The Cherokee were among the most Westernised of the American Indians, having adopted many of the ways and lifestyles of the colonists. They embraced the laws of the United States, had started using the settler's farming techniques, and were cultivating orchards and gardens. Schools and Westernised education had been introduced, they engaged in trade and manufacturing, had converted to Christianity, owned African slaves, and had even developed a written constitution.

Regardless of their 'advancement', however, the Cherokee had seen their lands diminished over time from 130,000 square km (50,000 square miles) in 1800, to 39,000 square km (15,000 square miles) by 1828. Nevertheless, they stubbornly refused to sell their territory to the United States or to Georgia, so the state government responded by seizing their property and compelling them to move to another location. When

Andrew Jackson referred to Martin Van Buren, his successor as president, as 'a true man with no guile'.

the Georgia legislature extended its authority over all of their territory, the Cherokee knew their independence was under threat.

When the *Indian Removal Act* came into force, the Cherokee took a defiant stance. They appealed to the federal government in 1830, stating that, 'We are not willing to remove, and if we could be brought to this extremity, it would be, not by argument [...] but only because we cannot endure to be deprived of our national and individual rights, and subjected to a process of intolerable oppression.' They were stirring words, but Jackson was deaf to the pleas.

The one thing that gave the Cherokee some hope was criticism of government policy coming from the eastern states. They began legal proceedings in the hope that it would force the *Removal Act* to be revoked. Their first action in the Supreme Court was thrown out on the grounds that the Indians were a 'domestic dependent nation', and therefore not eligible to bring any actions against the federal government.

A second attempt was more successful. A Vermont missionary filed a suit in the Supreme Court against the state of Georgia, the substance of which was whether the Cherokee, who lived in Georgia, were beneficiaries of the state's laws and regulations, the same as any other citizens. To the consternation of Jackson's supporters, the court declared that the Cherokee nation was not a 'foreign state' as written in the Constitution. The Cherokee were the legal owners of the land they occupied. Because the intent of the *Indian Removal Act* was to deprive the Cherokee of their land and to expand the laws of Georgia over Cherokee land, the Supreme Court stated that 'all these laws [including the *Indian Removal Act*] are averred to be null and void because repugnant to treaties in full force, to the Constitution of the United States, and to the Act of Congress of 1802'.

The Cherokee leadership was jubilant that an independent judiciary was capable of placing a brake on the abuse of power by the executive branch, just as those who had framed the Constitution had intended. But their joy was to be short-lived. The state of Georgia rejected the court's verdict, and an infuriated President Jackson declined to implement the judgment. Having spent so much time and effort bringing about the eviction of the Indians, he was not about to let a court decision get in his way. Being constitutionally unable to cancel the relevant laws itself, the Supreme Court's hands were tied, so martial law was declared to enforce the expulsion of the Cherokee.

The Jackson administration exerted maximum pressure on the Cherokee leadership, and in 1835 approached members of the tribe with an offer to which they finally agreed. The Treaty of New Echota signed away all Cherokee lands in Georgia for a total amount of US$5 million, and stipulated that the Cherokee were to move across the Mississippi River. However, because the chief of the Cherokee was not one of the signatories, the majority of the tribe declared the treaty illegitimate. Once again they took their case to the Supreme Court and once again they lost. All hope was finally extinguished when the senate, after a lengthy debate, ratified the treaty by a majority of one.

When Martin Van Buren became President of the United States in 1838, the majority of the Cherokee had still not started their migration, so he sent in 7000 troops to force them into makeshift camps at bayonet point. The Cherokee were not permitted to collect their possessions, and as they departed their homes were ransacked. Conditions within the camps were atrocious, with the result that the Indians were plagued by dysentery and a range of other illnesses, many of them dying as a result. From these temporary camps, the Cherokee were organised into groups and forced to march from Georgia to Oklahoma in what became known in Cherokee folklore as the 'Trail of Tears'. During these forced marches, more than 4000 people, one-quarter of those who departed their ancestral homes, died of disease, starvation and hypothermia.

> Although the USA had obtained land west of the Mississippi through the Louisiana Purchase of 1803, its purpose was not to expand US territory, but to create a buffer zone in order to prevent France and Spain from building their power on the nation's western flank.

## Legacies

The forced removal of the Indians of the southeast had a number of consequences. Most important was its impact on the fate of the independent nations of the American Indians. Prior to Jackson's presidency, there had been intermittent conflict between expanding white communities along the eastern seaboard and the native Americans who dominated the interior. However, it had been the position of all previous administrations from George Washington onwards to support the idea of independent Indian nations, and through protection and interaction to gradually 'civilise' them.

The position of federal governments through to the presidency of John Quincy Adams had been to prevent the removal of the Indians from lands they had been granted. A comparison of Adams' protective instincts towards the Indians—such as his refusal to implement a controversial treaty negotiated by Georgia, removing the Creek Indians—with Jackson's record of conquest, both by arms and treaty, shows a clear shift in policy towards the native tribes. The effect of their sanctioned removal by the federal government was to formally institutionalise the notion that the Indians were never going to be the equals of whites, and that maintaining treaties with them was simply a waste of time and effort.

> It is estimated that by 1824 the Cherokee owned over 1200 black slaves.

As the wisdom of George Washington was replaced by the greed of Andrew Jackson and his supporters, the realisation that the Indians were occupying valuable land meant that they were never going to be safe. The rapid expansion of the United States constantly strained boundaries established to keep the two races apart. Inevitably, the notion of a permanent Indian frontier was abandoned and the few Indians that remained were either killed, herded into small communities living on land of no economic value, or swamped by the increasingly homogeneous culture that surrounded them.

Seeing little value in trying to civilise the natives, many Americans were amazed by Portuguese and Spanish approaches to Indians living in South America. Not only did they attempt to fully integrate Indians into the communities that had settled there, but they also allowed them full membership of the Catholic Church, as demanded by Dominican and Franciscan missionaries. Even worse, they began to marry and produce 'half-caste' children with their Indian partners. Having no desire to interbreed with the natives, and thus dilute their heritage as God's chosen people, Americans sought to kill or relocate those they regarded as socially and spiritually inferior. It was Jackson's legacy to remove the Indians from sight, a policy that very nearly succeeded in condemning them to oblivion for ever.

A second consequence of the forced migration was that it exacerbated a sectional conflict that had been brewing in the infant United States since the War of Independence. The heavily industrialised North increasingly saw its interests as diametrically opposed to those of the slave-owning South, and both groups sought to turn every circumstance to their advantage. With the *Indian Removal Act*—which was split along clear North–South lines—Georgia saw an opportunity to extend the southern way of life into new regions, with ever-increasing numbers of plantations and the expansion of slavery. Many of the other southern states also saw the potential for slowing their political decline through the acquisition of more land, counteracting the North's rapidly expanding population and industrial output. These gradually growing tensions would come to dominate the next 20 years in America as the two regions drifted slowly apart while their mutual antipathy increased. It would end in a descent into madness with the outbreak of civil war in 1861.

Apologists of the forced removal of the American Indians prefer to claim that the policy's most significant legacy was that it opened up the enormous resources of the continent, providing the basis for America's future prosperity and greatness. The settlers now had access to fertile lands bordering the Mississippi, perfect for growing crops and raising cattle. There were also forests enough to satisfy demands for timber, fresh water in abundance, and the fish and game needed to feed an expanding population. Gold, precious metals and a range of other natural resources were discovered on former Indian lands, all of which helped to fuel the growth of industry, particularly in the North. A rapidly increasing population forced people to move farther and farther from population centres in search of land. Factories and mills all experienced a boom in the 1830s as a result of the acquisition of the Indian territories, which totalled some 10 million hectares (25 million acres) in the southeast alone. This was the bedrock upon which the future greatness of the United States was built—but a future that was bought at the expense of the continent's original inhabitants.

# FRANCE'S LEGITIMATE WARTIME GOVERNMENT (1940–1944)

*'Faced by the [...] disintegration of a government in thrall to the enemy [...] I, General de Gaulle, a French soldier and military leader, realise that I now speak for France. In the name of France, I make the following solemn declaration: It is the bounden duty of all Frenchmen who still bear arms to continue the struggle.'*
**Charles de Gaulle**

*'Better a noble lie than a miserable truth.'*
**Robertson Davies**

### LIE

The Vichy regime, formed in 1940, was illegitimate and did not represent France.

### TRUTH

The Vichy regime was the official government of France!

### CHIEF PARTICIPANTS

Charles de Gaulle, leader of the French Resistance
Henri Philippe Pétain, World War I hero and leader of the Vichy state

### THE STORY SO FAR

By the 1930s, the Third Republic of France was in a state of chaos, riven by feuding factions. Mediocre non-entities became government leaders and the French state became directionless, just as Germany was re-arming under the malign influence of the Nazi Party led by Hitler. But the danger posed by Germany was not taken seriously. French socialists were dedicated to pacifism and appeasement, while the Catholic parties had fascist sympathies, seeing fascism as the only bulwark against communism. France's military was kept below strength and under-resourced as 1939 approached …

General Charles de Gaulle reviewing Free French Forces during Bastille Day in London, 1942.

It was a trial that made French history. In 1997, Maurice Papon, a former French civil servant in the Vichy regime who had become treasurer of the Gaullist party, was put on trial for war crimes. In his role as General Secretary in charge of Jewish Affairs in Bordeaux, he was accused of personally ordering the arrest and deportation of 1560 Jews to Drancy deportation camp, including children and the elderly, often in inhumane conditions.

During the trial, Olivier Guichard, a former minister responsible for the economic development of the provinces under President de Gaulle was called as a defence witness. When asked if Papon's wartime collaboration with the Vichy regime was known, he responded: 'at the Liberation, de Gaulle had a strong desire to liberate the country. That's why he invented the story that the Vichy Regime did not exist in reality and the other myth that we won the war. De Gaulle was trying to avoid having to try the majority of the French people. His reasoning was that you couldn't incriminate people on behalf of a state that simply did not exist!' The courtroom was stunned into silence. But there was more. 'Of course, all the Prime Ministers under the General were previously in the public service of Vichy. But since Vichy was illegitimate, it was as though it had not been.'

There it was, finally out in the open—the real reason for the post-war declaration made by de Gaulle that the Vichy regime was illegitimate and did not represent France; that 'France' somehow resided in London, and that the only French citizens on the continent were a part of the Resistance. De Gaulle had invented a deliberate fiction for the sake of post-war national unity. The truth was that the Vichy regime was the official government of France, recognised by many countries, including the United States, and that many of the leading collaborators became members of the Resistance when it seemed that the Vichy regime was doomed. The legacy of this deception was to bury wartime atrocities and accusations of collaboration for half a century in the hope that history would forget, but even today it is the cause of violent debates.

## The Official Story—France in London

Death came to the French Third Republic in the shape of the German Wehrmacht and Luftwaffe on 10 May 1940. The German blitzkrieg was fast, brutal and completely unexpected and, as a result, it took only a few weeks for Allied resistance to be resoundingly crushed. Between 27 May and 4 June, over 338,000 men were evacuated from the beaches at Dunkirk, and on 14 June the German army marched triumphantly into Paris. Two days later, on 16 June, the Third Republic of France ceased to exist, as 569 of France's 649 deputies voted Marshal Henri Philippe Pétain full and extraordinary powers to save the country from certain defeat. The next day, Marshal Pétain announced the intention of his newly formed government to negotiate an armistice with the German occupiers.

Under the terms of the armistice, signed in the very same railway carriage in which Germany had been forced to sign the armistice of 1918, the French army was disarmed and demobilised. The country would be divided into two zones, with Germany occupying about 60 per cent of the country, comprising the whole of the Atlantic and Channel coasts, together with the richest parts of France in the west, north and east. The unoccupied 'free zone' lay in the south, and it was here that a semi-independent French government would be allowed. This was established by 84-year-old Marshal Pétain in the health resort town of Vichy, which became its administrative centre. Paris remained the capital for the entire country, and the new political order would be known as the *L'État Français*, the French State, rather than the French Republic. Pétain was granted legislative, judicial, administrative, executive and diplomatic powers, as well as the title of 'Head of the French State'. The laws maintained by Vichy were valid for both occupied and unoccupied zones, so long as they didn't countermand German directives. And so the Vichy state was born.

But waiting in the wings was the last hope of all true French patriots. In May 1940, Colonel Charles de Gaulle had been promoted to the rank of Brigadier General after two successful armoured engagements against the advancing Germans, and was subsequently recalled to become a member of the French cabinet. As the French defences were overwhelmed, he argued vehemently against surrendering to the Germans. This view was shared by Paul Reynaud, President of the Republic, so it was with his blessing that de Gaulle made a dramatic escape to England, from where he witnessed the collapse of the French government. He consequently made London his base of operations, and from there called upon all Frenchmen to take up arms against the foreign occupation and the illegitimate puppet government that had been installed after the unlawful dissolution of the Third Republic. Thousands responded to his call, with the result that the famous French Resistance was born.

De Gaulle established a government in exile in London with himself as its leader, noting that he was the last remaining member of the legitimate Reynaud government able to exercise power, and claiming that the ascension of Pétain was an unconstitutional coup. He maintained that France no longer existed politically in any real sense on the Continent, and that its only legitimate structures resided with him and his followers. The rest of the French people were cut off from the physical and historical nation. He then created the Free French Forces, instrumental in liberating France in 1944–45 and numbering 400,000 by D-Day. It was therefore de Gaulle and his Free French Forces—and, by extension, France—that defeated Germany along with the rest of the Allies. When de Gaulle landed at Bayeux in Normandy, he was greeted by ecstatic crowds shouting 'Long Live the Republic and de Gaulle'. After his triumphant entry into Paris in August 1944, members of the puppet regime, including Pétain, were put on trial for collaborating with the Germans. Many were executed; Pétain himself had his death sentence commuted to life imprisonment because of his advanced age (he was nearly 90) and outstanding military record in World War I.

De Gaulle accordingly brought the real French government back with him, and after the war he became president of the new republic, just as he had promised to all those who awaited his return. The final act in this story occurred in 1953, when the French National Assembly passed a general amnesty law to pardon anyone who had worked for the Vichy government. It didn't matter what they had done, since it was de Gaulle's France—the 'real' France—that had triumphed.

## The Truth—Recognition of Vichy

The French have coined a phrase to describe this period of their history, which includes the Vichy years, the Resistance and the reconstruction under de Gaulle; they call it *la boue* (the mud), a name that tacitly acknowledges that this period was dark and dirty, staining everyone associated with it.

De Gaulle's revisionist treatment of the immediate past was not a new idea for the French. After the fall of Napoleon in 1815, the newly returned government of King Louis XVIII proposed political amnesia for opinions expressed before the restoration. The result was that royalists, republicans and Bonapartists all worked together, as if the previous 25 years had never happened. This ensured administrative, military and religious continuity between the empire and the restored monarchy. With de Gaulle, however, the whole notion that he promoted, both in exile and later when he was elected President of the Republic, was a desperate attempt to wipe out a shameful history and refashion it to suit a new France. In this refashioned history, the entire population had heroically resisted the invading Germans, 'France' had somehow resided with de Gaulle in London for the duration of the war, and the creation of the Vichy regime had been illegal. It was a fiction, but one gratefully accepted by that part of the French population who had stood idly by and done nothing, and especially by the numerous Vichy functionaries who had actively implemented the policies of the regime.

The first of de Gaulle's deceptions was the declaration of Vichy's illegitimacy. This had been his position as early as 18 June 1940, when he broadcast a famous appeal to the French people to reject the Vichy government, and has been the view of all French governments since the war. The former French Prime Minister Pierre Messmer laid out the familiar argument in 1998: 'From the moment the government of Vichy signed the armistice, it was illegitimate. An illegitimate government does not represent France, nor can it engage France.' But this was not the position the world, or indeed the French population itself, had taken at the time.

The vote that gave Pétain full powers under the Constitution was legal, and the revision to the Constitution was accepted by the two chambers of government (the senate and the national assembly), in accordance with the law as it then stood. In the emergency then facing the French, those elected representatives of the Third Republic who were left took it upon themselves to try and save the country. To this end they voted to give Pétain almost dictatorial powers. Pétain, a hero of World War I, became a symbol of hope for his dejected and beleaguered countrymen, including the thousands who clogged the roads as they tried to escape the advancing German armies. To them, Pétain was France's saviour. Ordinary men and women wept for joy when he passed by, and the French Catholic hierarchy gave him their complete and unanimous support. He was convinced that the government of France should not leave French soil, and this was the opinion of the majority in both official and political circles. By the time the armistice was signed and enforced, writes journalist and author Roger Cohen: 'Pétain's authority was accepted inside France and throughout practically the whole of the vast French Empire [...] for as soon as the news of the formation of a government under Pétain reached the colonies, with very few exceptions their authorities, both military and civilian, came into line [...] By a tacit but nation-wide plebiscite he was entrusted with the task of taking France out of the war.'

It was also the case that the Vichy regime was widely accepted abroad as the legitimate government of France. Until August 1945, the regime's credentials were acknowledged as lawful by the United States and many other countries, among them Canada and Australia. Even the United Kingdom maintained unofficial contacts with Vichy for a time, at least until it became apparent that they intended full collaboration with the Germans. The USSR also withdrew their recognition when Vichy supported the German invasion of the Soviet Union in 1941. It is therefore evident that the majority of people inside France, and a majority of national governments, even among those opposed to Germany, recognised the existence and legality of the new French state. But not so Charles de Gaulle and his followers.

De Gaulle served as president of the provisional government of the French Republic from September 1944 until his resignation in January 1946. Though his influence was profoundly felt in the years that followed, he would not hold another official post until he helped to found the Fifth Republic in 1958 and became its first president.

De Gaulle's claim that he represented the true spirit of France was dealt a sharp blow by the lack of enthusiasm that greeted his rallying calls, broadcast from London. The idea that these broadcasts played a critical role in galvanising resistance to the Germans and French collaborators was another post-war myth. In reality, there was initially little support for de Gaulle's appeals, either in France or the French overseas territories, although Equatorial Africa and the French Cameroons were notable exceptions. And even though the British supported de Gaulle and provided him with vital resources to continue the fight, the relationship was often strained.

Across the Atlantic, the Americans were deeply suspicious of de Gaulle and his ambitions, with Roosevelt calling him an 'apprentice dictator'. It wasn't until the Allied conquest of North Africa that things started to turn around, and de Gaulle was able to position himself as the single, acknowledged leader of both the external Free French Forces and the Resistance movement inside France. But even then, the Allies did not take him or his forces as seriously as he would have liked. They doubted his ability to rally enough support in occupied France or in Vichy, and were contemptuous of French preparations for any military operations they were called on to undertake. In fact, the Allies had so little faith in de Gaulle that they didn't even tell him of the plans for D-Day until the eve of the invasion—a humiliating experience for the man who considered himself the official face of the French government in exile, and who claimed to be the only true representative of the French nation. Even so, the situation was nevertheless changing within France itself.

> Pétain was hailed as a national hero during his command of the French Second Army during the Battle of Verdun, which halted the German advance in 1916.

## From Collaboration to Resistance

It soon became obvious to everyone that the Third Reich could not resist intervening in the affairs of Vichy. They began to make specific demands, and when the regime complied it had the effect of increasing resistance within France. As the war gradually turned in the Allies' favour, this also aided de Gaulle in his efforts to recruit fighters for the Free French Forces. After all, everyone wants to be on the winning side, which is why so many within France supported Pétain and the Vichy regime in 1940. But any notion that all, or even most, of the French nation resisted the German occupation was another post-war myth concocted to help bury the divisions of the past.

It has been estimated that of France's wartime population, only about 1 per cent actively fought in the Resistance, while about the same number were actively engaged in

# CATHOLIC SUPPORT FOR VICHY

One group that was happy to see the arrival of Pétain and the Vichy State was the Catholic Church; indeed, they became Vichy's greatest supporter. The Catholic Church had never concealed its dislike of the French republics, because of their birth in the French Revolution, their displacement of the Catholic hierarchy and their generally anti-Catholic sentiments. The Third Republic (1870–1940), though not as fanatical as the First Republic, was still filled with left-wing, anti-clerical republicans, eager to reduce what they saw as the Catholic threat. It was for this reason that bishops, clergy and most of the Catholic laity were pleased when the Third Republic fell, to be replaced by a regime that rejected its liberal, secular traditions in favour of an authoritarian and paternalist Catholic society. The new French motto, 'Work, Family, and Fatherland' reflected the Church's own leanings; 'these three words are our own', declared Cardinal Gerlier, 'Pétain is France and France is Pétain'.

After the fall of France, the French bishops decided that supporting the new national government was the correct course of action, particularly since it was pro-Catholic. Their faith in Pétain as 'the incarnation of suffering France' was sadly misplaced, however. When Pétain introduced various anti-Semitic laws in October 1940, the church became worried, but only a small number of spirited French bishops voiced their concern. The objections of the Protestants was significantly louder, and they began to take steps to help fleeing Jewish fugitives.

Things began to change in July 1942, when over 12,000 Parisian Jews were arrested and detained. The Catholic hierarchy was horrified and they wrote a protest to Pétain under the signature of the Archbishop of Paris. When more arrests followed in August, this time in Vichy itself, the response was more forceful. The senior clergy openly revolted against the Vichy state and Cardinal Gerlier personally rescued 84 children who were on their way to Drancy, placing them under the protection of the Church. As the Church withdrew its support from the government, the arrests and deportations were cancelled. As a result, a much smaller proportion of Jews was deported from France than from any other occupied country, mainly thanks to a belated change of heart by the Catholic Church.

pro-Nazi activities. The remaining 98 per cent either passively or openly supported the leadership and policies of Pétain and the Vichy administration, including the Catholic Church. This is a far cry from the standard claims of widespread support for the Resistance, especially in 1940–41. It would take something major to shake the widespread support

Marshal Pétain shaking hands with Adolf Hitler after the fall of France, October 1940.

enjoyed by Vichy, and that turned out to be the German invasion of Russia, which began on 22 June 1941. Until then, the Resistance had been largely ineffective, but once the German–Russian pact was broken the Communist Party, which until then had supported the Nazi push to eliminate the Resistance, put its full weight behind the anti-Vichy forces instead. Their militants joined Resistance operations, bringing with them the advantages of a large and robust underground movement. France now descended into a type of civil war, with right-wing Vichy supporters in a constant battle with what became a left-wing resistance movement. This development caught everyone by surprise, especially de Gaulle, though he moved quickly to use it to his advantage.

Over time, as the Resistance became more effective, important figures in the Vichy regime began to switch sides. Many managed to keep their affiliations with both groups for a number of years, however, until it became clear that the Germans were going to lose and that Vichy was doomed. At that point they cut all ties with Vichy and became fully fledged Resistance fighters, working tirelessly for the liberation of France. The standard story told by many Vichy officials at the end of the war was that they were double agents, working for the Resistance while only pretending to serve the Nazis and the Vichy regime.

A classic case is that of François Mitterrand, President of the Fifth Republic, leader of the left and celebrated hero of the Resistance. He revealed in his autobiography that he was a keen supporter of General Franco and the fascists in the Spanish Civil War, and that when France was split after her defeat, he chose Pétain and worked for the Vichy regime as a civil servant. 'Before he died', writes prize-winning author Erna Paris, 'Mitterrand avowed publicly what the French had "known" for fifty years: that the lines between the Resistance and the Collaboration were often fluid and that some people remained […] loyal to both sides. He himself had joined the Resistance late—in 1943—then distinguished himself in action; at the same time he had continued his connection with his ultra-rightist friends from Vichy.'

Even Maurice Papon, convicted for crimes against humanity so many years later, was protected by the myth of the Resistance that de Gaulle fostered. One minister recalled de Gaulle declaring that Papon had rendered great service to his representative in Bordeaux at the time of the liberation. When de Gaulle returned to France, Papon, Mitterrand, and many others who had offered their services to the pro-Nazi regime joined in shouting 'Vive la Republique'. France had won, and everyone could be proud of the role they had played in the fight against tyranny and injustice.

## Legacies

It is clear that de Gaulle's post-war lie was necessary. In a country devastated by war, the last thing anyone wanted was the spectre of civil war as different factions tore each other, and the country, apart in futile recriminations and revenge. Unity was to be the catchcry of the new republic in the wake of the collapse of Vichy and the retreat of the German armies. Of course that didn't mean that everyone could start their life anew and escape punishment for misdeeds and collaboration. After the liberation, when de Gaulle had established a provisional government, some 120,000 senior officials and leading functionaries of the Vichy regime were brought to trial. Of these, 1500 were sentenced to death, including Pétain, though he escaped death by firing squad on the orders of de Gaulle. The courts established for these trials did not always follow legal procedure in cases involving prominent figures, however. Prime Minister Pierre Laval, for example, was silenced during his trial and subsequently sentenced to death without being allowed to defend himself. He took poison before his execution, but was resuscitated in time to be taken out and shot.

And then there were the unofficial executions of collaborators, estimated at 10,000 or more before de Gaulle took control of the judicial process. The post-war reckoning could not go on forever, and de Gaulle was determined that it would not. The government soon declared a period of amnesty, during which many Vichy representatives came forward to declare themselves. Many others who had been convicted were paroled and given official pardons. In declaring the amnesty, de Gaulle justified his decision by invoking the illegitimate nature of the Vichy government. But one important consequence of this is that it absolved many Vichy officials of crimes committed in the name of the regime. As a result, many continued serving the French state, either as police, or as members of various French governments over the following 30 years or so.

A further consequence of all this is that France has still not come to grips with the actions of its citizens during World War II, a problem that has been exacerbated by the voluntary amnesia induced by de Gaulle and his successors. They overlooked as many accusations of collaboration and wartime atrocities—especially involving the Jews—as they could for nearly 50 years in the hope that history would forget. But inconvenient facts have a way of resurfacing as the children of victims begin searching for answers and for the individuals responsible.

Silence about the fate of the Jews in Vichy was nearly absolute. For many years, the so-called Jewish 'deportees' were described as members of the Resistance, never as Jews. In the days after the war, the French government issued death certificates to any Jews who had not survived the Holocaust. Apart from stating where they died and the date, all bore the inscription 'Died for France'—ironically, the country that had abandoned them to their fate. As the truth slowly emerged it sparked a furious debate in France, and one that rages to this day. Although it is widely accepted that the Vichy government collaborated in the implementation of the Holocaust, those on the left and right wings of politics cannot agree on how extensive the cooperation was. The trials of prominent Vichy collaborators in the 1980s and 1990s was a first attempt to bring justice to those who could no longer speak for themselves. While there was some hope that the nation was at last starting to own up to what actually happened during the war, the Papon saga showed that in many ways it was, as a commentator in *USA Today* wrote, a 'final sign of indifference, contempt and provocation with regard to all victims of the Holocaust.'

After his trial, Pétain was imprisoned in a fortress on the Île d'Yeu, a tiny island off the western coast of France. He died and was buried there in 1951, aged 95.

It would take until 2009 for the French Council of State to officially recognise the role played by the Vichy regime in the deportation of the Jews during the occupation. Yet even such a positive move was dogged by debates about the apparent 'victimisation' of history, where the victims rather than the victors write about such events. Questions about the legitimacy of Vichy still cause heated discussions between the supporters of the French republics and their opponents. Also recently subjected to critical scrutiny are heroes of the Resistance, and any role they may have played as collaborators. Even Pablo Picasso has been dragged into the debate, with artist David Harkins claiming that 'for Picasso to survive the way he did in Paris and for him to continue working the way he did during the German occupation of that city, he must have received help and support from high-ups inside the Nazi regime'. In other words, he must have been a collaborator. Others claim that he was undoubtedly part of the Resistance; journalist Senay Boztas wrote Journalist Senay Boztas of *The Independent* wrote in 2007 that Picasso gave uncompromising support to the Resistance activist Robert Desnos, prior to his arrest and deportation to Auschwitz by the Gestapo. No matter where you look, it seems that everyone—hero or villain—was tainted by contact with the Vichy Regime, except for de Gaulle himself. He was spared the need for compromise by his self-imposed exile.

In conclusion, the act of de-legitimising the Vichy state allowed many people to avoid responsibility for actions committed by what was, in fact, a legitimate and duly recognised state, and thereby avoid having to face up to a shameful past. This lies at the heart of many debates in French society, and is the reason why so many people in France reject the idea that their country in any way assisted the Nazis in carrying out the Final Solution. They are also resentful of those who continually seek to revisit a painful past in an effort to redress old wrongs. For many, the headline on the cover of *Le Point* Magazine on 1 November 1997 said it all: 'Vichy, the Resistance, the Algerian war […] France is sick from memory'.

# PASSING
# THE BUCK

*'The man who can smile when things go wrong has thought of someone else he can blame it on.'*

ROBERT BLOCH

Photographs of Russian radicals and revolutionaries from the papers of the Okhranka, or Tsarist Secret Police.

# ROME BURNS AND NERO POINTS THE FINGER (64 AD)

*'While I yet live, may fire consume the Earth!'*
**Emperor Nero**

*'It's not whether you win or lose, it's how you place the blame.'*
**Oscar Wilde**

### LIE

The Great Fire of Rome was started by the Christians.

### TRUTH

The fire was probably an accident!

### CHIEF PARTICIPANTS

Nero Claudius Caesar, Emperor of Rome
Poppaea Sabina, Nero's mistress and later his wife

### THE STORY SO FAR

Nero became Emperor of Rome in 54 AD, at the age of sixteen, after his mother, Agrippina, had the old emperor, Claudius, poisoned. The last of the Julio-Claudians, a dynasty that had begun with the Emperor Augustus 70 years previously, Nero was a depraved and debauched young man. He became addicted to absolute power, murdered members of his family and abused his position as emperor. His popularity plummeted during the course of his reign, reaching a low point in 64 AD. During this period, a new cult had established itself in Rome, one dedicated to the worship of a man who was claimed to be the incarnate son of the one, true God. Accused of being secretive, distrustful and unpatriotic, members of the cult were rapidly gaining a reputation for barbarity, inhuman acts and seeking the destruction of Rome herself. They were the Christians, and very soon they would face martyrdom in the Circus Maximus after an event that devastated the capital—the Great Fire of Rome …

A restored fresco from Nero's residence, the Domus Aurea, or Golden House, in the Roman Forum.

~᷾ ᷾ ᷾ ᷾᷾

Visitors walking through the old centre of Roman power, the Forum, are confronted by the monuments of antiquity: enormous columns supporting the vaults of temples dedicated to long-demoted gods, all of them crumbling from the effects of time, rain and man-made pollution. While many of the buildings created by the pride of the Roman emperors are there on view, one building modern visitors won't be able to see is the Domus Aurea—the Golden House of Nero. This enormous villa was created by Nero as a luxurious venue for his lavish parties. It comprised a succession of pavilions and a lengthy wing containing living and reception rooms, all set in an enormous landscaped park with an artificial lake at its centre, and a colossal statue of the emperor himself, testifying to his power and glory. Built in the aftermath of the Great Fire of Rome in 64 AD, it was part of Nero's grandiose plans for a new Rome, which he envisioned rising from the ashes of the old. Yet, within 40 years of its construction, Nero's Golden House had been either built over or altered, and stripped of its marble, jewels and ivory. The site of the Golden House was filled in and used as foundations for the Baths of Trajan, with the Baths of Titus and the Temple of Venus and Roma also being built on the site. The lake was drained and covered by the Colosseum, and the statue's head was replaced with that of the god Sol. What little remains of the villa today lies under the ruins of the Baths of Trajan.

Although little survives of Nero's architectural masterpiece, one thing he devised has endured through the centuries, though not in the way that he intended. Unlike the Golden House, which took years to plan and construct, Nero's most enduring legacy derives from a plan that was hastily put together to deflect a growing chorus of accusation and anger that was aimed at him. He devised a lie to blame an innocent group of people—the Christians— for the devastating fire that swept through Rome in 64 AD, in order to take the heat off himself. The lie was a success in that the people of Rome duly blamed the Christians for starting the Great Fire, with the result that they turned on them and many were killed. Tragic though these events were, they proved to be the glue that bound the Christian community more tightly together in its adversity.

## The Official Story—The Christians Burned Down Rome

According to the Roman senator and historian Tacitus, writing some 50 years after the event, the fire began on the hot summer's night of 18 July 64 AD, in shops surrounding the southeastern end of Rome's largest hippodrome, the Circus Maximus. Because the majority of Romans lived in wooden houses, the fire spread rapidly through the city, where it continued to burn for five days. By the time it had been extinguished, it had razed four of Rome's fourteen districts and severely damaged seven others. Many important buildings were destroyed, including Nero's palace, the Temple of Jupiter Stator and the hearth where the sacred fire was kept burning in the Temple of Vesta. The people of Rome were devastated and looked to their emperor for help.

When the fire started, Nero was taking his ease at Antium, a resort town on the coast some 50 km (31 miles) south of the capital. Leading Romans built magnificent seaside villas there, and the early emperors were frequent visitors to the town. Interrupting him from his daydreams and debaucheries, news of the fire roused Nero to act in a manner befitting the chief magistrate of the Roman world. He hurried back to the capital in order to coordinate efforts to extinguish the fire and provide disaster relief for the population, with funds paid out of his own treasury. Once the fire was doused, Nero opened his palaces to survivors whose houses had been destroyed and ensured that food and other essentials were distributed.

Once the fear and shock had worn off, people started looking around for someone to blame. It was widely known that Nero had grand plans for the reconstruction of Rome, so rumours began to circulate around the city that it was the emperor himself who had ordered Rome to be burned to the ground. Alarmed by the growing hostility of the people and desperate to retain their loyalty, he looked for a scapegoat, at which point his gaze fell upon a new sect called the Christians. Tacitus records what happened next:

> *Therefore, to put an end to the rumour [that he had burned Rome], Nero created a diversion and subjected to the most extraordinary tortures those hated for their abominations by the common people called Christians. The originator of this name [was] Christ, who, during the reign of Tiberius had been executed by sentence of the procurator Pontius Pilate. Repressed for the time being, the deadly superstition broke out again not only in Judea, the original source of the evil, but also in the city [Rome], where all things horrible or shameful in the world collect and become popular. So an arrest was made of all who confessed; then on the basis of their information, an immense multitude was convicted, not so much of the crime of arson as for hatred of the human race.*
>
> *Mockery of every sort was added to their deaths. Covered with the skins of beasts, they were torn by dogs and perished, or were nailed to crosses, or were doomed to the flames. These served to illuminate the night when daylight failed. Nero had thrown open the gardens for the spectacle, and was exhibiting a show in the circus, while he mingled with the people in the dress of a charioteer or drove about in a chariot. Hence, even for criminals who deserved extreme and exemplary punishment there arose a feeling of compassion; for it was not, as it seemed, for the public good, but to glut one man's cruelty, that they were being punished.*

Eventually, satisfied that the evildoers had been amply punished, and seeing a new Rome start to rise from the ashes of the old, the people once again got on with their lives. Nero continued to rule as before, although within four years his armies would be in revolt, with several of his generals seeking to end his life and seize his throne.

## The Truth—How Did the Fire Start?

The Rome of 64 AD was not as it is portrayed in the movies. Visitors to the great city expecting to see wide streets, vast marble temples and a passing parade of senators, imperial guards and slaves would have been disappointed. While there had been a large building program underway since the time of the Emperor Augustus, most of Rome was a jumble of wooden terraced houses squashed cheek by jowl along narrow, winding streets. Fires were quite common in Rome, with as many as 100 minor blazes breaking out every day. Why, then, was arson suspected in the case of the 64 AD fire, and why was Nero the suspected arsonist?

According to Tacitus, the only way that the fire could have spread from timber houses in the slum areas to the marble residences of the two aristocratic orders—the senators and the equestrians—was if it had been deliberately lit and then spread by one or more arsonists. Tacitus also observed that even though the fire was driven by a south-easterly wind, it was seen advancing both southward, up the Aventine Hill, and northward, up the Palatine Hill, something he interpreted as being further evidence of arson.

However, it is now possible to account for the behaviour of the fire as described by Tacitus. Archaeological and scientific evidence has been uncovered indicating that the fire was very hot and moving at great speed. As it gathered pace, it would easily have reached temperatures of over 550°C (1022°F), consuming everything in its path and causing masonry to collapse. Furthermore, it seems that the sheer length of the fire front would have caused many updrafts, regardless of prevailing winds. This could explain two fire fronts moving southward and northward simultaneously.

Although, as now seems likely, the fire and subsequent firestorm were accidental, at the time many believed that the fire had been deliberately lit. This was due in part to the nature of the fire, and also to a desire felt by many people to find someone to blame for any misfortune. The citizens of ancient Rome were no different to modern humans in their

In ancient Rome, magistrates had to handle all matters related to their office personally. For the emperor, who was the ultimate magistrate in the empire, every petition, decision and arbitration had to be dealt with by him directly. The workload of the emperors was vast, with no time for trivialities.

search for some sense of certainty in a haphazard and often apparently malign world. For many, there are no real accidents. Everything happens for a reason and someone is always to blame. When word spread around Rome that the fire had been purposely lit, Nero became the prime suspect.

Nero did not, according to contemporary accounts, cut a particularly prepossessing figure. The Roman historian Suetonius described him as being of average height with a pustular and malodorous body. Considered pretty, rather than handsome, with light blond hair and weak blue eyes, he had a thick neck, potbelly and spindly legs. While the emperor's looks might not have inspired confidence, his actions were those of a man with few moral scruples. He slept with his mother and later had her murdered; roamed the streets with cronies, beating and murdering citizens; seduced boys as well as married women; raped a Vestal Virgin; killed numerous members of his family, including his first wife; and wasted huge sums of money on extravagant projects. It was small wonder, then, that the empire finally rose up in revolt and overthrew him.

Nero saw himself as a genius in music, acting, chariot racing and poetry. He was obsessively interested in all the arts, particularly theatre and architecture, and produced grandiose plans for a redesigned capital. It was these latter schemes that gave rise to suspicions that Nero might have had a hand in the Great Fire. The historian Dio Cassius believed that Nero had always had a wish to see Rome destroyed in the way that Troy had been destroyed—by fire. Suspicions were strengthened when Nero unveiled plans for rebuilding the city: plans that included taking over a large part of its centre, then occupied by working-class and middle-class citizens' houses, for his new palace. As anger and suspicion grew, Nero discovered that his usual methods for appeasing a restless citizenry—free bread and circuses—were not working. He needed to find someone else to blame for the disaster, a scapegoat that would placate his discontented and potentially rebellious people.

## Why the Christians?

For Romans who knew the story, Jesus was a minor Jewish prophet who had been executed in the distant province of Judea some 30 years earlier. The obscure Jewish breakaway sect established by Jesus' followers—the Christians—had barely been in existence for a generation, with most of its small membership drawn from the lower classes.

The person responsible for bringing the Christians to Nero's attention appears to have been his mistress, Poppaea Sabina, regarded as the most beautiful woman of her day. She has been blamed for some of the worst of Nero's behaviour, including the murder of his mother Agrippina and his wife Octavia so that they could be married.

The traditional image of Nero playing the lyre as Rome burns.

After Nero and Poppaea were married in 62 AD, Poppaea apparently encouraged Nero to attack the Christians after the Great Fire. She is known to have had Jewish sympathies and was possibly a Jewish convert, and it was around this time that Jewish-Christian relations were undergoing a difficult transformation, with a number of early Christians put to death under orders of the Jewish authorities.

The Christians were not helped by popular misunderstandings of their teachings. In an attempt to find 'evidence' against these evildoers, Nero publicised their various 'crimes', including cannibalism (eating the flesh of Christ and drinking His blood) and disloyalty to the state (gathering together in secret, refusing military service and declining to worship the Roman gods). The Romans could not understand a belief in only one god. They were a religious people, but they had many gods who were consulted frequently concerning every important decision made by individuals and the state. It made no difference to the Roman state who you worshipped, as long as the deity was sanctioned by Rome, and more importantly, that the worship was conducted openly.

For many pious Romans, however, the strongest proof of Christian guilt was their belief that the world was about to end, and that it would be annihilated by fire. The Christians prayed for the day that their saviour would return in glory, descending from the skies to lay low the City of the Seven Hills (Rome) and purge it with a cleansing fire. Talk such as this was perfect for Nero's purposes, and he broadcast the fiction that it was the fanatical Christians who had started the fire in an attempt to fulfil their apocalyptic visions. General acceptance of this story was to lead to the deaths of many Christians, including the apostle Peter, who was crucified upside down on Vatican Hill

In Nero's inimitable style, the giant statue of himself he had raised in Rome was called the Colossus Neronis.

sometime between 64 and 67 AD, and possibly the apostle Paul; according to the historian Eusebius of Caesarea, Paul was beheaded in Rome in 67 AD.

## Legacies

Nero's urgent need for a scapegoat led to the first of many persecutions of Christians in the Roman empire, culminating in the 'Great Persecution' under the emperors Diocletian and Galerius (284–311 AD). But rather than destroying the early Christian community, these persecutions played an important role in shaping it. Joining together with ever greater conviction in the face of adversity, Christians not only survived persecution under Nero and subsequent emperors, but also went on ultimately to inherit the empire.

Persecution by the Romans had a profound effect on the Christian faithful, hardening their opposition to the pagan Roman administration. Their antipathy is strikingly expressed in the vivid imagery of the Book of Revelation, which seems to identify evil and the works of Satan with Rome and her empire. The Whore of Babylon, the source where evil arose according to Revelations, is portrayed as being clad all in imperial purple, with the following words upon her forehead: 'Mystery, Babylon the Great, the Mother of Harlots and Abominations of the Earth'. The Whore can be seen as representing the Emperor of Rome sitting atop a beast with seven heads. According to Revelations, 'The seven heads are seven mountains', a statement that can be interpreted as a reference to Rome, which has always been known as the city of seven hills. To reinforce the suggestion that this powerful imagery relates to the persecution of the faithful, the author of Revelations specifically states that the Whore was drunk with the blood of the saints, and with the blood of the martyrs of Jesus. At the same time, the author promises that Babylon the Great will fall, and all will see the smoke of her burning, for God will have His vengeance upon her to account for all the blood of the prophets, the saints and of all who were slain upon the Earth.

This imagery, and the promise of divine retribution, sustained the persecuted Christians and bonded them into a cohesive whole. The Christian writer Tertullian, in about 200 AD, declared that 'the blood of martyrs is the seed of the Church', and there is some truth to that statement. Stories of persecutions and martyrdom were used to gain new converts and to sustain the faith and conviction of surviving Christians.

## NERO'S FIDDLING

One of the most enduring myths in history is that of a wild-eyed Nero 'fiddling'—that is, playing the lyre—while all about him Rome is consumed by flames. This myth had its origins in contradictory accounts of Nero's whereabouts during those fateful few days of 64 AD. The most reliable accounts have the emperor located some kilometres from Rome at the time of the fire, but there are a number of other stories. One has Nero watching from his palace on the Palatine Hill, singing and playing a lyre; another has Nero watching from the Tower of Maecenas on the Esquiline Hill; and a third has him singing and playing the lyre on a private indoor stage. These stories all have an element of truth about them, because Nero considered himself to be a maestro of the lyre. But they owe far more to the idea that Nero either didn't care about the fate of Rome, or that he was actually the mastermind of the fire, and was happy to see the slums go up in smoke. The historian Tacitus, writing a few decades after the Great Fire, explicitly contradicts these stories, which indicates that they were already widely accepted by Romans hostile to Nero.

During the near collapse of the Empire during the third century, many new pagan cults flourished as Romans sought certainty in a world plunged into chaos. A rise in the number of Christians during these years was no doubt related to the Church's explanation for the chaos—that the world was being punished because of the worship of false gods.

The survival of Christianity cannot be attributed simply to the martyrs and their sufferings, however. The persecuted group was good at avoiding the attention of Roman authorities, while at the same time replicating Roman command structures. By the time Constantine became interested in the Christian faith in about 313 AD, the Church was a highly organised and disciplined organisation, well able to exploit

Constantine's desire for stability and unity in an empire that had grown increasingly divided. Constantine needed a unifying state religion, and in Christianity he saw structures in place that would provide this foundation, as well as support for the idea of one empire, one emperor, one faith. He therefore favoured the new religion, flattered and charmed its religious hierarchy and began merging the Christian chain of command with the power structures of the state.

Once this happened, the days of pagan dominance were numbered, and in 380 AD Emperor Theodosius I declared Christianity the official religion of the Roman state. Over time, the decay of the Empire in the West saw a collapse of Roman political control, and a concomitant rise in the power of the Christian Church, the only institution with access to power structures capable of exercising control in an increasingly fragmented and anarchic society. The result was that, in a little over three centuries, a persecuted Christian minority inherited one of the world's greatest empires, transforming itself into what was to be the most powerful institution in Europe for the next 1000 years—the Catholic Church.

It was the Church that kept alight the few remaining embers of civilisation as the West descended into the period of the Dark Ages. As medieval historian Sir Richard Southern writes:

> The fall of the Roman Empire left a mental and spiritual as well as a political ruin which it took centuries to repair. The collapse was a long and complicated business, but in the West it was complete by the end of the seventh century. It was then that the work of rebuilding began. The dominating ideal in the rebuilding was that the unitary authority of the Empire should be replaced by the unitary authority of the papacy.

The Church not only preserved many texts of antiquity from the onslaught of pagan barbarians, it also kept intact Roman laws and institutions, which were ultimately adopted by those very invaders. The Church also began the lengthy process of converting pagan invaders, such as the Ostrogoths and the Visigoths, to Christianity, which more than anything else was the key to preserving the shattered remains of the old empire. The barbarians, overawed by the solemnity, rituals and antiquity of the Romans, began to imitate them, flattering themselves that they were the inheritors of the Roman ideal. They raised the successor of Peter to the heights of spiritual greatness and ensured the dominance of Christianity throughout the Middle Ages.

Had it not been for Nero's desperate lie, and the persecution that followed, it is doubtful whether Christianity would have risen to the position it now occupies. While its influence may be in decline today, it still plays an important role in the lives of people in many nations around the world.

# KING RICHARD III—VICTIM OF A SMEAR CAMPAIGN (1483–1509)

*'The usurper King Richard III then ascended the throne of the slaughtered children whose protector he was himself. Richard was born at Fotheringhay in Northamptonshire, retained within his mother's womb for two years and emerging with teeth and hair to his shoulders.'*

**John Rous (1486)**

*'I just do not understand how people can become so upset over the fate of a couple of snivelling brats. After all, what impact did they have on the constitution?'*

**Helen Maud Cam**

### LIE

Richard III killed his nephews to secure the throne of England.

### TRUTH

Henry VII killed the remaining heirs of the House of York!

### CHIEF PARTICIPANTS

Richard III, King of England (1483–85)
Henry Tudor; later Henry VII, King of England (1485–1509)
William Shakespeare

### THE STORY SO FAR

Since the 1450s, England had been convulsed by the Wars of the Roses, a civil war between the noble houses of Lancaster and York. Its origins lay with King Edward III, who reigned for a long time (1327–77) and had many children. Edward's eldest grandson became Richard II, who was overthrown in 1399 by his cousin, Henry of Lancaster, who became Henry IV. But there was someone else who had a better claim to the throne—Richard of Conisburgh, son of Edmund of Langley, First Duke of York and grandson of Edward III. Tension between the houses of York and Lancaster erupted into civil war 50 years later, when Henry VI had a nervous breakdown. The House of York eventually won, when Edward of York became King Edward IV in 1461, defeating his Lancastrian rivals and killing Henry VI and his son in 1471. Edward himself had two sons

The enigmatic and much-maligned Richard III, the last English king to die in battle.

who were still quite young when he died in 1483. After Edward IV's death, his brother, Richard of Gloucester, became Protector of the Realm for his nephews, the princes Edward and Richard. Acting quickly, he had their guardian arrested and transferred to Pontefract Castle in Yorkshire; he also transferred the two young princes to the Tower of London, apparently for their own protection …

Members of the audience settle back into their seats as the curtain rises. There, confronting them from the stage, is a bent and misshapen man, with an expression on his face to match the distortions of his body. Thrusting his features at the audience he hisses the famous lines, in envy and bitterness: 'Now is the winter of our discontent made glorious summer by this sun of York [...] but I, that am not shaped for sportive tricks [...] that am [...] deformed, unfinish'd, sent before my time into this breathing world, scarce half made up [...] therefore, since I cannot prove a lover, to entertain these fair well-spoken days, I am determined to prove a villain and hate the idle pleasures of these days.' It is a scene that electrified audiences in the late 1590s, when the play was first performed, and continues to do so today, as it depicts the rise and deserved fall of that most wretched of English kings, Richard III.

However, the image created by William Shakespeare's immortal words reflect a lie, a distortion of the truth behind this most enigmatic of English kings. Of all the accusations hurled against him, one charge above all has been used to blacken his reputation for all posterity: the murder of his two young nephews after he had secured them in the Tower of London. Based on what we now know of Richard III, the politics of the time and the circumstances under which subsequent chroniclers wrote of those years, the accusation of murder turns out to be one of the most successful lies ever perpetrated in the history of England.

## The Official Story—The Death of the Princes

In 1483, things were looking good for Edward IV, by the Grace of God, King of England and France, and Lord of Ireland. Forty-one years old and married to Elizabeth Woodville, with children including two healthy male heirs, he had given his realm a decade of peace and prosperity, the first real peace it had known since the Wars of the Roses, a dynastic civil war, had started in 1455. Well liked by his people, he was an astute and flourishing entrepreneur, investing heavily in a number of corporations within the City of London. By the time Easter came around, he was enjoying himself heartily, indulging his passions for good food and good wine.

Unfortunately, as a result of his indulgent lifestyle, Edward had become immensely fat and prematurely aged, and by Good Friday he was suffering from a bad case of indigestion brought on, it was said, by an excess of fruit and vegetables. A day or two later he caught a chill while fishing, and soon afterwards suffered what seemed to be a stroke. The King's failing health was a dilemma, since his eldest son, also named Edward, was only a child of twelve and therefore incapable of ruling the realm on his own. Minority rule had been a problem in England in the past. The last time it had occurred was when the seven-year-old Henry VI was crowned in 1429. Dominated by powerful courtiers during his youth, he had not been able to rule England effectively, thereby bringing about the Wars of the Roses. Fearful of this happening again, Edward quickly made some amendments to his will, the most important being to name his brother Richard, Duke of Gloucester, as

It has long been asserted that Edward IV could not have been his father's son. A blond giant of a man, he bore no resemblance to his father, and seems to have been conceived at a time when his father was on campaign in France. His supposed father has been identified as an English archer named Blaybourne, stationed at the garrison at Rouen, where his mother was staying. If true, this would mean that the current royal house of Windsor has no legitimate bloodline claim to the throne of England.

Protector of the Realm after his death. Edward IV died on 9 April 1483, and his eldest son duly inherited the throne, becoming Edward V of England.

At the time of his father's death, the young Edward V was staying at Ludlow Castle, where he was nominally President of the Council of Wales and the Marches. When he heard of his sudden elevation to the throne, he gathered his entourage and headed to the capital. He was intercepted on the way by his uncle Richard, who escorted him to London. After a ceremonial procession to St Paul's Cathedral, Richard established Edward in the Tower of London, then a royal residence as well as a prison. The coronation was to take place on 22 June 1483, and Edward's mother Elizabeth was persuaded to allow her other son, Richard, Duke of York, to join his elder brother in the Tower as preparations were made for the coronation.

Less than three months later, Richard of Gloucester convened a meeting of the Regency Council. There, Robert Stillington, Bishop of Bath and Wells, offered proof that Edward IV had contracted a secret marriage to Lady Eleanor Talbot in 1461, and was still alive when Edward married Elizabeth Woodville in 1464. The Council declared this a clear case of bigamy, nullified the second marriage and made all the children of that marriage illegitimate. Parliament then passed the *Titulus Regius Act*, declaring young Edward and Richard to be illegitimate, thus removing them from the line of succession. Richard of Gloucester then had himself crowned King Richard III of England on 6 July, and nothing more was heard of the two young princes.

No one knew what happened to the boys, and any solution to the mystery had to wait until after Richard's death, at the Battle of Bosworth Field in 1485, when Henry Tudor became king as Henry VII. It was during Henry's reign that a man named James Tyrrell was arrested for treason. Under questioning, Tyrrell admitted to killing the two young princes on orders from their uncle, Richard III. According to his testimony, Richard sent a messenger to Robert Brackenbury, Constable of the Tower, with orders to murder the two princes. Brackenbury flatly refused to perform the deed, so Richard sent Tyrrell to Brackenbury with a new order, to hand over the keys to the Tower to Tyrrell for one night. This time Brackenbury did as instructed. Tyrrell and two other men killed the boys that night by smothering them with pillows. They then buried their remains at the foot of the stairs, although they were subsequently moved.

## The Truth—A Tarnished Reputation

There have been few people in English history whose reputation has been quite so successfully blackened as that of Richard III. Shakespeare painted him as the wickedest villain, capable of any infamy. In Shakespeare's play, Richard is depicted as a deformed hunchback; a monster who murders his nephews and butchers friends and enemies until he is finally stopped by a true Englishman—Henry Tudor—who ends his reign of terror and ushers in a new era of freedom and prosperity. As the popularity of the play amply demonstrates, this makes for good theatre, even if it is totally unreliable as history. As historians today know all too well, the play is full of historical inaccuracies; even the depiction of Richard as a hunchback is a fiction, taken by Shakespeare from an unreliable history written by Sir Thomas More, chancellor to the second member of the Tudor dynasty, Henry VIII. In those unenlightened days, physical deformities were often taken as evidence of an evil character, and Shakespeare exploits this detail to its fullest effect.

What confuses the issue is that Shakespeare's *Richard III* has a considerable aura of historical authenticity by virtue of being broadly based on real events, and real characters, of the time. The final phase of the Wars of the Roses did begin with the death of Edward IV. His son, Edward V, was to have been crowned, but because he was too young to rule his uncle, Richard, Duke of Gloucester, was made Protector. And Richard did briefly rule as King Richard III, before being killed in battle against Henry Tudor in 1485.

We also know that the young Edward V's mother, Elizabeth Woodville, detested Richard and called for a Regency Council to run the country instead. Richard retaliated by approaching parliament to determine whether Edward IV had been

An illustration based on Shakespeare's *Richard III*, depicting Richard being haunted by the princes.

legally married to Elizabeth Woodville. Parliament declared young Prince Edward and his brother illegitimate after a mystery priest—believed to have been the Bishop of Bath and Wells—presented evidence that Edward IV had contracted to marry Lady Eleanor Talbot before he married Elizabeth Woodville. Edward's marriage to Elizabeth was therefore considered invalid, and Prince Edward was not the true heir to the throne. Richard of Gloucester, Edward IV's only surviving brother, then claimed the throne for himself, after having placed his nephews, the uncrowned king and his younger brother, in the Tower of London. The facts up to this point are not in dispute.

However, there has never been a single shred of hard evidence that Richard III then ordered his nephews to be killed. After Richard was defeated by Henry VII, no one came forward with evidence concerning the death of the boys, until some 15 years later, when an old Yorkist sympathiser in prison on other charges apparently confessed under torture to having killed the boys on Richard's orders.

So what did happen to the boys? The English royal succession follows a royal bloodline of legitimate offspring, with the result that an illegitimate child of a monarch can never succeed to the throne, except by force. Once parliament had decided that Edward IV had been bigamously married to the Queen consort, Elizabeth Woodville, young Prince Edward was instantly debarred from the throne. Richard therefore had nothing to fear from him, and no reason to have him killed. He had the princes locked in the Tower, where they could remain for the rest of their lives if necessary. The Woodvilles were certainly Richard's resolute enemies, and could be expected to pursue Edward's claims. However, Richard was in a position of strength, and there was in any case no getting around the fact that Edward had been declared ineligible to occupy the throne by parliament. In fact, Elizabeth Woodville was reconciled to Richard in 1484, and such a reconciliation seems highly unlikely if she had held Richard responsible for the deaths of her two sons.

It is therefore hardly surprising that other culprits have been suggested, perhaps none more plausible than Henry Tudor, or, as he is better known, King Henry VII. After all, he was of a different family, and had more to fear from heirs of the House of York than Richard III. When Henry moved against Richard, he justified his rebellion by declaring that Richard had usurped the throne from the rightful king, Edward V. And when Richard was killed at the Battle of Bosworth Field in 1485, Henry's first action was to declare himself king, rather than waiting to see if the princes were still alive. If the children had been alive, they would have been rivals, so Henry had a good reason to want them dead. In short, of the two monarchs—Richard III and Henry VII—it was the latter who had the stronger motive for despatching the princes in the Tower.

## Just Who was Illegitimate?

The marriage of Edward IV and Elizabeth Woodville caused a crisis when it occurred, not only because it took place secretly, but also because it sabotaged all hopes that Edward would marry a French princess. Edward was also a notorious womaniser. So, while it is not outside the realm of possibility that Edward IV was contracted to marry Lady Eleanor Talbot—with the result that his children by Elizabeth Woodville were illegitimate according to English law at the time—the accusation nevertheless remains unlikely. There was another charge of illegitimacy, however, and one that provided a much stronger reason for Richard to assume the throne.

## BONES UNDER THE TOWER

In the years that followed Henry VII's coronation, barely a thought was given to the fate of the royal youths who had vanished in the Tower of London. However, in 1674, workers renovating the White Tower—part of the Tower of London—unearthed a box located under a staircase leading to the chapel. Inside it were the remains of two small human skeletons and some animal bones. The workmen thought little of it, and discarded the bones on a rubbish heap. Some time later, however, they were retrieved by someone who thought that they might be the bones of the two princes. They were accordingly gathered up and placed in an urn, which Charles II ordered to be reburied in Westminster Abbey.

The bones remained undisturbed in the Abbey until 1933, when the urn was exhumed and the bones examined. The results were inconclusive. No one could agree on the ages of the children at the times of their deaths, or even whether they had belonged to boys or girls. All that could be said for certain was that one skeleton was bigger than the other. Part of the problem was that many bones were missing, including part of the smaller jawbone and all of the teeth from the larger one. After being examined, the bones were replaced in the urn and returned to their vault under the Abbey.

Suggestions that Edward IV was himself illegitimate had been circulating for years. His brother George, Duke of Clarence, hinted at the possibility three years before when Edward had him charged and executed for treason. And Shakespeare himself repeats the claim in his play *Richard III*, when Richard urges the Duke of Buckingham to spread this rumour about his royal brother:

*Tell them, when that my mother went with child*
*Of that unsatiate Edward, noble York*
*My princely father then had wars in France*
*And, by just computation of the time,*
*Found that the issue was not his begot.*

The 'unsatiate Edward' referred to here is Edward IV, who was well known for his many mistresses. But the main point that Richard is making is that his mother was unfaithful to his father, 'noble York', who was campaigning with his armies in France when Edward was conceived.

Richard would have been aware of the rumours about his brother's illegitimacy, but wouldn't have dared to say anything while he was alive and King of England. After Edward's death, however, Richard would have been acutely aware that his brother's children had no real claim to the throne, as a result of their father's illegitimacy, whereas he, as the only surviving legitimate son of his father, would be the natural successor to the throne of England. He therefore needed to remove Edward's two sons and install himself as king in order to ensure the true blood succession of the House of York and the Plantagenet dynasty, which stretched back to Henry II (1154–89). To this end, he probably arranged for an obedient prelate to confirm the accusation that Edward had been contracted to marry Lady Eleanor Talbot, thereby making the young princes ineligible to succeed their father. But there is no firm or convincing evidence that he went on to have them murdered.

Contrary to Shakespeare's portrayal of Richard III as a tyrannical, scheming monster, contemporary evidence shows him to have been a devout man and a competent administrator. However, he was childless and unpopular, and he made many enemies, who eventually united under the leadership of Henry Tudor.

Henry was the son of Edmund Tudor, a half-brother of King Henry VI (their mother had remarried after the death of her first husband, Henry V). And Henry's mother was the formidable Lady Margaret Beaufort, great-granddaughter of John of Gaunt, the powerful Duke of Lancaster, whose eldest son had seized the English throne as Henry IV (1399–1413). Henry Tudor therefore had strong blood ties to the royal family on all sides, but no enforceable claim to the throne. He inherited the title Earl of Richmond from his father, and could claim descent from the House of Lancaster through his mother. To strengthen his position even further, he pledged to marry Edward IV's eldest daughter, Elizabeth, thereby linking himself to the House of York.

Henry was being named as a desirable alternative to Richard III soon after the latter ascended the throne. In August 1485, Henry landed in England with a small army with which he went on to win his only encounter with Richard, at Bosworth

> *Henry VII's mother, Lady Margaret Beaufort, was the great-granddaughter of the formidable John of Gaunt, third son of Edward III. Her great-grandmother had been Katherine Swynford, whose four children by Gaunt were all born out of wedlock. Although Gaunt married Swynford after the death of his wife, and had their children legitimised, they were nonetheless officially barred from ever claiming the throne—something that Henry VII retrospectively overturned after coming to the throne.*

Field. But there was still much to be done, as can be seen in the effort that Henry put into promoting the idea that the warring houses of York and Lancaster were finally united in the House of Tudor. This is symbolised by the Tudor rose, which contains both the white rose of York and the red rose of Lancaster. Less admirably, Henry also began a campaign of vilification against Richard III to justify what was essentially his taking of the crown by right of conquest.

This tradition continued under the next Tudor monarch, Henry VIII, and even under Elizabeth I, whose approval Shakespeare was doubtless seeking when he depicted Richard III as a remorseless villain. In taking this line, Shakespeare followed the authority of Sir Thomas More, humanist scholar and Lord Chancellor under Henry VIII. Thomas More played a significant role in blackening Richard's reputation. A loyal servant of the King, More did what he could to help stabilise the Tudor dynasty, and reviling Richard served that purpose admirably.

## Legacies

With the fall of Richard III, the Wars of the Roses ended, bringing to a close a period of political chaos and social disturbance that had plagued feudal England. In the words of Winston Churchill: 'Richard's death [...] ended the Plantagenet line. For over three hundred years this strong race of warrior and statesmen kings, whose gifts and vices were upon the highest scale, whose sense of authority and Empire had been persistently maintained, now vanished from the fortunes of the Island. The Plantagenets and the proud, exclusive nobility which their system evolved had torn themselves to pieces.'

Following the Wars of the Roses, the feudal power of the nobles quickly waned while that of the merchant classes increased. The obvious beneficiaries of this change were the new Tudor kings, who exploited the failing strength of a nobility no longer able to muster large standing armies, to create a strong, centralised monarchy. After putting down a number of rebellions by pretenders claiming Plantagenet blood, they were determined to ensure that such circumstances should never occur again. They thwarted any attempt to create an organised opposition by the few remaining Plantagenet heirs, who now had no direct line to the throne, by undermining them and playing one off against the other.

A major legacy of the overthrow of the House of York was that the new Tudor rulers were able to change England dramatically over the following century and a quarter. The reign of Henry VII has been identified by historians as the time when medieval England ended, and movement towards the Renaissance began. The Tudors steered the realm towards a period of greatness, changing England from an

impoverished state into a potent nation that, in the centuries following, would extend its power over a large part of the world. Fiercely independent, they were always on the lookout for challenges to their authority from both inside and outside the realm, which is why it was perhaps inevitable that there would be a confrontation with the Church, and the Pope in particular. The creation of an independent Church of England by Henry VIII would become a key factor in helping England achieve its greatness under his daughter, Elizabeth I; another was Henry's decision to strengthen the country's navy.

It would be in Elizabeth's reign that the legacy of Richard III's downfall would be seen most clearly, for it was during this period that England left its medieval past convincingly behind. The Elizabethan age is often held up as the pinnacle of the English Renaissance. It was a time that saw the flowering of English drama and poetry; it also saw the expansion of the universities as institutions no longer focused solely on the training of future clergymen. The numerous lay scholars and well-informed gentleman sons of the new aristocracy who emerged from the halls of academe were to be the bedrock upon which Elizabeth built her success. She was the shining example of a new culture sweeping the land, having gathered about her some of the ablest minds of her generation, among them William Cecil, Francis Walsingham, Nicholas Bacon, Roger Ascham and Robert Dudley, the Earl of Leicester.

This was a period when the theatre thrived, with authors such as William Shakespeare, Ben Jonson, Christopher Marlowe and Thomas Kyd, among others, breaking new ground with their plays. It was an era of growth and discovery abroad, with England challenging the might of Spain in the waters of the New World and encouraging her captains to win fame and fortune in any daring enterprise they sought to pursue. Elizabeth encouraged the discovery of new ways to the East, and in 1600 granted a charter to the Honourable East India Company, which was to provide the foundations for Britain's growing power and influence in India. At home, the Protestant Reformation had accomplished its goal, with most citizens believing that England's future stability and success depended on rooting out superstitious Catholic influences. By the time of Elizabeth's death in 1603, the Church of England was a very different organisation from the uncertain body of earlier years. Confident in its role, it was less disposed to seek the middle ground between Catholics and puritans. England's future prosperity and influence had its genesis in the reign of Elizabeth I.

The Yorkish princes Edward and Richard in the Tower of London, which was both a royal residence and a prison.

# THE FORGERY THAT 'PROVED' A JEWISH CONSPIRACY (1905)

*'Three hundred Zionists, each of whom knows all the others, govern the fate of the European continent.'*
**Gamal Abdel Nasser**

*'The tools of conquest do not necessarily come with bombs, and explosions, and fallout. There are weapons that are simply thoughts, ideas, prejudices, to be found only in the minds of men. For the record, prejudices can kill and suspicion can destroy. A thoughtless, frightened search for a scapegoat has a fallout all its own for the children yet unborn.'*
**Rod Serling**

## LIE

Jewish leaders gather together in a cemetery every 100 years to plan the conquest of the world, as recorded in *The Protocols of the Elders of Zion*.

## TRUTH

*The Protocols of the Elders of Zion* were created by Russian secret police to promote anti-Semitism and crush potential revolutionaries!

## CHIEF PARTICIPANTS

Hermann Goedsche, an anti-Semitic German writer
Sergei Nilus, a Russian religious writer and self-described mystic

## THE STORY SO FAR

By the 1860s, Russian society was in ferment, with small revolutionary groups agitating for social change and the overthrow of their repressive rulers, the Tsars. Numerous attempts were made on the life of Tsar Alexander II, until one finally succeeded in 1881. Ironically, the assassins not only killed the country's most progressive ruler, a man who had brought about genuine reform, but they ensured that power would go to men who would put the brakes on further change. Alexander II was succeeded in turn by his son, Alexander III, and his grandson, Nicholas II, who were both ruthless in using the Russian secret police to ferret out hidden conspiracies. Because one of the 1881 conspirators was

An anti-Bolshevik poster from 1917 depicting Trotsky as a Jewish devil.

Jewish, and because many revolutionary groups attracted Jewish intellectuals, the secret police sought to limit the appeal of such groups by creating anti-Semitic propaganda. They spread rumours that all such revolutionary groups were tools in a vast Jewish conspiracy aimed at destroying the Tsar, the Orthodox Church and the Russian state. To back up their claims, they announced that they had discovered incontrovertible proof of the existence of such a treasonous plot ...

Type the correct words or phrases into any internet search engine, and you will be presented with thousands of websites that allege a worldwide conspiracy: one that aims to eliminate all nationalities and religions, upset the foundations of the world's social order, overthrow its executive and judicial systems, and create a world government. Its tactics allegedly involve controlling the world's media, publishing propaganda through the reputable press agencies, using gold to spark riots and other disturbances, and seducing people by catering to their lusts. All of this is revealed in a mysterious document written over 100 years ago, entitled *The Protocols of the Elders of Zion*, which catalogues secret Jewish plans for world domination.

Although the *Protocols* are clearly a literary forgery, ever since they first appeared in 1903 they have been used in attempts to blame the Jews for almost all the ills of the modern world; everything from the rise of communism to the destruction of the World Trade Center towers in New York. They were one of the main pieces of 'evidence' used by the Nazis to justify anti-Semitic acts during the 1930s and 1940s, and even today they are used by fanatical propagandists in support of a range of causes. The appeal of the *Protocols* seems to confirm a deep-seated human need for explanations for the many apparently random and unconnected events that occur in the world. If such events can be seen to be part of an organised scheme, however unlikely, they become explicable.

## The Official Story—The Master Plan

Russia was in turmoil during the opening years of the twentieth century, and by 1905 events were coming to a head. Russian armed forces had lost a war with Japan, an enemy they had never taken seriously; a peaceful gathering of workers and their families was attacked outside the Winter Palace in St Petersburg by government troops; and the country was on the verge of exploding into revolution. Out of this chaos emerged a very strange book. Its author was Sergei Nilus, a Russian religious writer and self-proclaimed mystic who had recently converted to Orthodox Christianity. The title of his book was *The Great within the Small and Antichrist, An Imminent Political*

*Possibility: Notes of an Orthodox Believer,* and its last chapter presents details of a secret Jewish plot to destroy the governments of the world and replace them with a Jewish-controlled world government.

This final chapter describes how a group of high-ranking Zionists controls all major decisions made in the world, and reproduces the document—*The Protocols of the Elders of Zion*—that allegedly sets out their aims and procedures. According to Nilus, the *Protocols* was produced at the First Zionist Congress, held in Basel, Switzerland in 1897. Because of the complexity of their plans, members of the Zionist Congress wrote an instruction manual for all newly recruited members, describing their goals and ambitions, and the ways and means by which they would control the world, deceiving all non-Jewish nations into following their orders.

The methods to be used to control people and their governments are described in meticulous detail. They would allegedly involve the use of alcohol and pornography to corrupt non-Jews; the propagation of ideas such as socialism and Marxism to destroy Western governments; the creation of a world government and the abolition of all religions in order to establish a new world order; the use of economic depressions; the undermining of banking and financial systems; and the destruction of world money markets. Finally, Jewish 'elders' would come to control all the world's media and financial institutions, having replaced established social structures and political systems with one supported by mass manipulation and state-authored misinformation campaigns. Even when the conquest was complete, gentile populations would not realise what had happened since the Jewish elders would continue to remain hidden, manipulating affairs from behind the scenes by means of their control of fiscal policy.

Nilus distributed a number of editions of the *Protocols* in Russia, claiming that the chaos of the times was a result of this Jewish conspiracy. While early editions were in Russian, translations soon appeared all across Europe, spread by refugees in the aftermath of the Russian Revolution of 1917. Copies reached the United States around 1920, where they were enthusiastically embraced by many, including the powerful industrialist Henry Ford. By the time of Nilus' death in 1929, millions of copies of the *Protocols* had been printed and disseminated.

An English translation of the *Protocols* by Victor Marsden, a fiercely anti-Bolshevik correspondent for the *Morning Post* in London, revealed the Jewish plot in even greater detail. His version claimed to show how King Solomon and other learned Jews of Antiquity had worked out a scheme for the peaceful conquest of the world by Zion as early as 929 BC. Key stages in history allegedly manipulated as the result of this Jewish master plan were identified, stretching from ancient Greece at the time of Pericles to Russia under the Tsars. England and Germany were next, he warned ominously.

## The Truth—The Origins of the *Protocols*

Any reader with even a rudimentary knowledge of world history can easily spot the inaccuracies in Marsden's expanded edition of the *Protocols*. But facts and accuracy were never the point of the exercise. The *Protocols* were actually the work of the Tsarist secret police, the Okhranka, which produced them with the aim of blaming the Jews for Russia's problems in the late nineteenth century. The imagery and vocabulary of the text draw on long-standing anti-Semitic traditions that have their origin in the folklore and superstitions of medieval Europe. These include accusations that Jews used the blood of Christian children for the Feast of Passover and that they poisoned wells, spreading the Black Death. Fantastic beliefs like these appear to have been held by ignorant villagers throughout Europe, together with beliefs in secret rabbinical meetings where plots were hatched to conquer and eradicate Christians.

The text of the *Protocols* has a complex history. In 1868, Hermann Goedsche, a German anti-Semite, published a book entitled *Biarritz* under the pseudonym Sir John Retcliffe. In one of its chapters, entitled 'The Jewish Cemetery in Prague and the Council of Representatives of the Twelve Tribes of Israel', Goedsche creates a fictional secret rabbinical faction that gathers in a cemetery at midnight every 100 years to plan the schedule for the great Jewish conspiracy. The idea of such a gathering was probably a distorted echo of the meeting of rabbis and other learned laymen summoned by Napoleon in 1807 to advise the Assembly of Jewish Notables. Even at the time, many believed that Napoleon's convention was merely an officially sanctioned version of a secret international Jewish assembly. Goedsche's book also borrowed heavily from many other sources, including an 1864 pamphlet entitled *Dialogues in Hell between Machiavelli and Montesquieu*, by the French satirist Maurice Joly. This attacked the political ambitions of Napoleon III, using the literary device of a debate between damned conspirators in Hell. In Goedsche's book, the conspiracy is planned in a cemetery, rather than Hell, and the main characters are Jewish.

> Western anti-Semitism began in the clash of Hellenistic and Judaic cultures in the fourth century BC. Hecataeus of Abdera, a Greek philosopher, was an early example, declaring Judaism to be an unwelcoming and misanthropic religion.

Goedsche's text was translated into Russian in 1872, and in 1891 the Russian secret police circulated an extract from the chapter describing the meeting of the fictional rabbinical council under the title 'The Rabbi's Speech'. Not only did the secret police use this text to create a climate of anti-Jewish hysteria, they also used it to try to convince Tsar Nicholas II of the reality of the Jewish threat. This was a time when the position of the Tsar was weak, and the government was plagued by numerous radical groups, the leadership of which contained many Jewish intellectuals.

The goal of the secret police was to discredit such radical groups by stirring up latent anti-Semitism, making it harder for them to recruit ordinary Russians as members.

When *The Protocols of the Elders of Zion* first appeared in the Russian newspaper *Znamya* ('The Banner') in 1903, there was considerable debate about its origins. It was first said to be the work of a Masonic–Jewish conspiracy, but when Sergei Nilus republished the text in the final chapter of his book on the coming of the Antichrist, he claimed that it was the creation of the First Zionist Congress, held in Basel, Switzerland, in 1897. When Nilus was reminded that the First Zionist Congress had been a public and open meeting, attended by many non-Jews, he had to retract his initial claim. But he was soon back, this time insisting that the *Protocols* was the work of the 'Elders of Zion' in their meetings of 1902–03. Yet again this created problems, since Nilus had previously declared that he had obtained his copy in 1901. Despite all the doubts and obvious lies surrounding the origins of the *Protocols*, and the strong evidence that exists for its being a forgery, even today there are those who believe that the *Protocols* is a true account of the First Zionist Congress.

## The Great Jewish Conspiracy?

Another idea that came out of Russia in the 1920s was the allegation that Jews were responsible for Bolshevism, the Russian Revolution and communism. This was given prominence by a pamphlet called *The Jewish Bolshevism*, which first appeared in Russia, and spread quickly to the West. The notion that communism was part of a Jewish conspiracy aimed at world domination subsequently caused global interest in the *Protocols*.

Amazingly, this idea is still believed today, although there is patently a difference between claiming that some Bolshevik leaders were Jews and that the whole communist movement was a Jewish plot. As journalist and historian Paul Johnson points out:

> *It was simply assumed that, since the Jews were among the principal instigators of Bolshevism, they must be among its principal beneficiaries. The all-important distinction between the great mass of Jews, who were observant, assimilationist or Zionist, and the specific group of non-Jewish Jews who had actually helped to create the revolution, was not understood at all.*

In fact, it is hardly surprising that the idea of ending the Tsarist regime was attractive to members of the Jewish intelligentsia, since many non-Russian nations had been ruthlessly repressed in the Russian Empire. Many others rebelled against such injustice, which accounts for the fact that non-Russians—notably Latvians, Poles and Georgians—were disproportionately represented in the communist party leadership. This fact was also seized upon by the Tsarist secret police, which used both anti-

Semitism and xenophobia as weapons against the Bolsheviks. As things turned out, it mattered little that some of the leaders of the revolution—among them Trotsky, Kamenev and Zinoviev—were of Jewish origin. The man who turned Russian communism into the monster it became was a graduate from an Orthodox Christian seminary: Joseph Stalin. If, as a communist, he was secretly part of the conspiracy, why did he engineer the deaths of nearly all of the Bolshevik leaders in the 1930s, including a large number of Jews?

The fact is, there were numerous revolutionary groups in Russia during the lead-up to the revolution, all fighting among each other as much as with the Tsarist state. In that respect, Russia was very similar to other European countries that had experienced revolutions during the Revolutionary Year of 1848. Like 1917, right-wing extremists claimed that it was all the work of Jewish subversives. Yet when the Tsarist state collapsed in 1917, the Bolsheviks were as surprised as anyone. They just happened to be in the right place at the right time, and were able to take full advantage of the turmoil that ensued. There was no great master plan or conspiracy.

Inevitably, the *Protocols* became part of the Nazi propaganda arsenal, and was used to justify the persecution of the Jews. In 1934, Dr A. Zander, a Swiss Nazi, published a series of articles accepting the *Protocols* as fact, and the Nazi leadership began to quote from them to explain why Germany needed to eradicate the Jewish 'infection'. Nazi propagandists used the Jewish origins of some leading Bolsheviks—and their support for an international proletarian revolution—to present communism as a political idea created to benefit Jewish interests. This became known as the Jewish–Bolshevik conspiracy, and in support of it the Nazis pointed to Soviet legislation that made anti-Semitism a criminal offence.

This conveniently ignored Soviet hypocrisy. While Stalin claimed to be eliminating anti-Semitism, in reality he was an anti-Semite himself. In the late 1930s he purged the diplomatic services of most Jews in order to please Hitler, and later eliminated more Jews at higher levels in the party in the 1950s. Stalin distrusted Jews and regarded them as a threat to the multinational nature of the USSR. This distrust only increased when the state of Israel was created, an event that encouraged self-confidence among Soviet Jews. Stalin sought to eliminate any Jewish intellectuals from the party and accused his enemies of being Jews, among them Lavrenti Beria, head of the secret police. In the event, Beria seems to have moved too fast, since he later boasted of being responsible for Stalin's death, claiming to have poisoned him. There were some individual Soviet Jews, Trotsky for one, who did have plans for world domination and the obliteration of the Western way of life. But this idea arose from their communist ideals, not their Jewish origins, and is a far cry from constituting proof of a global Jewish conspiracy.

## Legacies

The ultimate legacy of the *Protocols* has been the immense damage done by its use in justifying Jewish persecution and repression, most infamously by the Nazis. After the defeat of Austria and Germany in World War I, many Germans yearned to create a unified Germany, especially after the loss of so many German-speaking territories in the Treaty of Versailles. However, Hitler and his followers were unwilling to blame

The front page illustration from Sergei Nilus' book that contained *The Protocols of the Elders of Zion*.

the German leaders whose political and ideological shortcomings had led the nation to defeat in the first place. Instead, blame was redirected to those suspected of having sabotaged the goal of national unification. And at the top of their list were Jews and communists, who became scapegoats for a people obsessed with German nationalist ideology, and deeply resentful of their current fallen state.

There is evidence to suggest that many Germans, including Hitler, believed that the Fatherland was forced to capitulate in 1918 as a result of a Jewish conspiracy in the ranks of the government that had taken over from Kaiser Wilhelm II in the final days of the war. Since Germany had signed an armistice before allied troops had actually invaded their homeland, these Germans would not believe that they had lost the war on the Western Front. In essence, they believed that Germany had been betrayed from within. It was this sense of betrayal that drove much of Hitler's own anti-Semitism, obsessed as he was with the glory of Germany. His hatred was reserved for those he saw as having robbed his adopted land of its rightful place as the leading nation in Europe, and the world.

## JEWS AND THE ENLIGHTENMENT

Given all of the accusations hurled at the Jews in the *Protocols*, it is surprising that the one major historical event in which they were heavily involved—the Enlightenment—is not mentioned anywhere in its pages.

When Jews of Spain were formally expelled from that country in 1492, after years of persecution, they wandered across Europe and many eventually found a home in the Netherlands. There they found an environment in which they could explore their political, religious and social identities in relative peace. It is not surprising, given the nature of the persecutions from which they fled, that they would be inclined to promote forms of expression and styles of government that were strongly secular, even specifically anti-Catholic. Such ideas played an important role in the Enlightenment of the eighteenth century, especially in its emphasis on individual conscience and personal choices unfettered by state-sanctioned religious authorities.

Of course, both Catholic and Protestant authorities saw such ideas as a threat against Christians everywhere. They believed that these developments were simply another manifestation of the conflict between Christians and Jews that had been going on for centuries. This was not the case, of course, since the thinkers involved no longer saw themselves as Jews in a religious sense, but as atheists who happened to be Jewish by descent. Such a distinction was not readily visible to mainstream Christian authorities, however, so distrust between the two groups remained.

With many individuals holding beliefs like this, *The Protocols of the Elders of Zion* found a willing audience eager to accept its lies and distortions. Hitler couldn't have made his belief in the *Protocols* any clearer than he did in the following passage from *Mein Kampf*:

> *To what extent the whole existence of this people is based on a continuous lie is shown incomparably by the* Protocols of the Wise Men of Zion, *so infinitely hated by the Jews. They are based on a forgery, the* Frankfurter Zeitung *moans and screams once every week: the best proof that they are authentic. [...] The important thing is that with positively terrifying certainty they reveal the nature and activity of the Jewish people and expose their inner contexts as well as their ultimate final aims.*

These claims made it much easier for the Nazis to round up Jews throughout Germany and deport them to concentration camps. Non-Jewish neighbours would not protest because removal of the Jews meant that they could not implement their plan for world domination, which the *Protocols* clearly stated was their objective. Anti-Jewish activities escalated throughout 1935–36 as Jews were forbidden government employment and subjected to the Nuremberg Racial Purity Laws and the Law for the Protection of German Blood and Honour. At the same time the Reich Citizenship Law was passed, which stripped all Jews, and anyone deemed to have Jewish blood, of their citizenship. By the time of Kristallnacht in 1938—when some 1500 synagogues, numerous Jewish cemeteries and more than 7000 Jewish shops and department stores were destroyed—the scene was set for the horrors to come. Some Jews were beaten to death while others were made to watch. More than 30,000 Jews were detained and removed to concentration camps, such as Dachau, yet this was only the beginning. Within seven years, six million would be dead, all of them victims of the lies propagated by the *Protocols*.

While most people today have rejected the *Protocols* as absurd and clumsy forgeries there are exceptions. Some fanatical groups and governments in the Middle East and elsewhere have attempted to use them as a tool in a propaganda war designed to whip up hostility against Israel. The Palestinian movement Hamas explicitly refers to the *Protocols* as being a factual account of the ultimate goals of the Jewish nation, claiming that: 'The Zionist plan is limitless. After Palestine, the Zionists aspire to expand from the Nile to the Euphrates. When they will have digested the region they overtook, they will aspire to further expansion, and so on. Their plan is embodied in *The Protocols of the Elders of Zion*, and their present conduct is the best proof of what we are saying.'

# PASSING THE BLAME FOR WORLD WAR I (1918)

*'Germany tried to bribe us with peace to desert our friends and duty.*
*But Great Britain has preferred the path of honour.'*
**Daily Mirror, 4 August 1914**

*'The search for someone to blame is always successful.'*
**Robert Half**

### LIE

Germany was responsible for starting World War I.

### TRUTH

All participants were equally responsible for the 'War to end all Wars'!

### CHIEF PARTICIPANTS

Kaiser Wilhelm II, Emperor of Germany and King of Prussia
Lloyd George, Prime Minister of Great Britain
Georges Clemenceau, Prime Minister of France

### THE STORY SO FAR

After existing for centuries as a loose federation of states and principalities, Germany became a unified nation in 1871 under the leadership of Kaiser Wilhelm I. With unification, Germany was finally able to exert an influence on European and world events that was appropriate for a nation with her population and industrial strength. As the twentieth century approached, the major European powers were entangled in a complex web of treaties. Britain and France were deeply suspicious of German intentions and so formed an alliance. Germany accordingly made an alliance with the Austro-Hungarian Empire to her south to counterbalance the perceived Anglo-French threat. Germany's support of the Austro-Hungarians alienated the Russians—since they were protectors of the Serbians, who were then subjects of the Austro-Hungarians—prompting them to join the British and French in a mutual alliance against aggression. Russia also had plans to move against the Ottoman Turks, but needed British approval to do so. The Turks knew this and duly aligned themselves with Germany to deter Russian aggression. In a

The assassination of Archduke Franz Ferdinand in Sarajevo in 1914 pushed the great powers into World War I.

situation so delicately balanced, any incident was liable to trigger a major conflict, and this duly occurred in June 1914 when Archduke Franz Ferdinand of Austria was assassinated in Sarajevo by a Bosnian Serb …

The case seems pretty cut and dried: Germany was driven by an egotistical and determined emperor who was bent on European domination. Britain was neutral and peace-loving, but would not stand idly by as Germany rode roughshod over nations that she had pledged to help. So when Germany declared war on France on 3 August 1914 and began its advance through Belgium, it triggered a European war that became a global war because colonies of the British Empire provided men and munitions in support of the Mother Country.

This, at least, was the story told by the Allies in the aftermath of their victory in World War I as they sought compensation for the costs of four years of conflict. Compensation required someone to be held accountable, and since Germany was the loser, she was the one declared to be responsible for starting the most bloody and destructive war the world had seen so far.

The problem with that story, however, is that it ignores the fact that World War I didn't occur in a vacuum, isolated from all previous history. Simply stating that the invasion of Belgium by Germany started the war by forcing Britain to honour its 1839 treaty guaranteeing Belgian independence, may appear to absolve other parties of any responsibility for the circumstances that made war inevitable. However, as is usually the case, the truth is far more complex, involving events that took place during a period of over 100 years, and involving stratagems and power plays in all parts of the world. Viewed from this longer perspective, Britain's imperial pretensions and her determination to maintain her place in the world—including conflict with Germany over her colonial ambitions—was far more important in laying the groundwork for the future war than was Germany's invasion of Belgium, which was merely the final act in a far more complex drama.

## The Official Story—Germany Started the War

In 1888, Kaiser Wilhelm II became Emperor of Germany, an empire that had been guided by the sure hand of its 'Iron Chancellor', Otto von Bismarck, since 1871. It was clear when Wilhelm took the throne that, although quick-witted, he was also emotionally unstable and had a violent temper. Impatient to have his own way in everything, no matter how trivial, he chafed at any restrictions. In his eagerness to extend Germany's power and influence throughout Europe and the rest of the world, he embarked on a program of rapid territorial conquest and military expansion that worried his European neighbours. When Bismarck tried to steer him towards a more cautious approach to foreign policy, the young emperor made it clear that he intended doing things his own way, and that he was not content to be merely a figurehead for an ambitious chancellor. Wilhelm's obsession with the armed forces meant that he came under the influence of the Prussian military elite, whose advice he sought with alarming regularity. Having been frustrated by his chancellor once too often, Wilhelm asked for, and obtained, Bismarck's dismissal from office.

With Bismarck's removal, Kaiser Wilhelm began to take Germany in a new and dangerous direction. The chancellors he appointed were weak and vacillating, reducing the government's effectiveness, which meant that Germany was now under his personal rule. Wilhelm's poor grasp of the political world of the late nineteenth century led him to make blunder after blunder. Believing his personal relationships with fellow monarchs were what counted, he allowed a defence treaty with Russia to lapse in 1890, enabling the Russians to forge a treaty with France instead. He maintained his alliance with the Austro-Hungarian Empire, even though it was on a collision course with Russia, an event that might lead to a war which would drag in France and Britain as well, because of treaties signed between the three nations.

The threatened conflict was finally triggered by the assassination of the Austrian Archduke Franz Ferdinand by a Bosnian Serb on 28 June 1914. Wilhelm offered his support to Austria-Hungary if it were to take action against the Serbians. As soon as Austria-Hungary declared war on Serbia, the Russians began to mobilise troops along both the Austrian and German borders. Seeing this, and recognising that since France had not declared itself neutral and would therefore come into the war on the side of Russia, military officials in Germany persuaded the Kaiser to sign the mobilisation order and initiate the Schlieffen Plan, by which Germany would attack France. Although Wilhelm was worried by the approaching conflict, he vacillated between asking for more time for negotiations and fully supporting his military commanders' approach. In the end, he gave approval for Germany to declare war on Russia on 1 August, and followed this with a declaration of war on Russia's main ally, France, on 3 August. When Belgium asserted its neutrality by denying Germany the right to cross its territory, the Germans invaded anyway on 4 August. Bound by treaties, Britain had no alternative but to declare war on Germany, which it did on 5 August.

In just five days, Europe had gone from a tense peace to a state of all-out war. Given Germany's declaration of war against several European powers, and its illegal occupation of Belgium, the British labelled the conflict as 'the Kaiser's War'. The Kaiser, like most of the other leaders involved, believed the fighting would be over by Christmas. He could not have been more wrong.

## The Truth—The Great Game

The Allied propaganda machine portrayed World War I as the fault of Germany alone. The German people were demonised, characterised as ruthless 'Huns', and depicted as bloodthirsty monsters who would willingly impale babies on their bayonets. Propaganda like this sought to turn the fight into a just one, a war against a nation that sought to dominate the world. But responsibility for World War I did not rest solely with Germany. Certainly, the immediate trigger and the official reason for Britain's intervention in the war was Germany's invasion of Belgium, but the real underlying causes of the war lie with Great Britain, and specifically with its foreign policy machinations.

To see British imperial policy in action, we need look only at the Crimean War of 1853–56. This war began with the Russian invasion of the Crimea, a peninsula thrust into the Black Sea, which at the time was part of the Ottoman Empire. The Russians were desperate to obtain an approach to the Mediterranean and also, if possible, to destroy the Ottoman Turks. This would give them Constantinople, the jewel of the Middle East, but to accomplish this they needed access to the Black Sea. The Ottoman Empire—known as 'The Sick Man of Europe' at the time due in part to its involvement in a series of calamitous wars resulting in lost territory—was by now on its last legs. Various central European powers, as well as the newly resurgent Balkan states, were circling, waiting for their chance to seize a piece of the corpse. When Russia invaded the Crimea, however, the British intervened on behalf of the Turks.

The reason Britain took this action was that it was fearful of losing the advantages of empire. Since the 1700s, Britain had slowly—and, allegedly, unwillingly—been building an empire. By 1850, it was the most powerful nation on earth, having beaten off the threat posed by Napoleon 35 years earlier. The British now saw Russian activities in the Bosphorus and the Black Sea as a potential threat, believing that Russian expansion southwards would eventually threaten their interests in India, then the jewel in the British crown. Russia had already expanded southward into Transcaucasia and was involved in Central Asia and Afghanistan, increasing British fears that the Russians would disrupt their lucrative trade with the subcontinent. This resulted in two Anglo-Afghan wars (1839–42, 1878–80) and the British invasion of Tibet (1903), among other incidents. The rivalry between Britain and Russia as they fought for supremacy in central Asia is still referred to as 'The Great Game', a name that disguises the deadliness of many of the moves made by both parties.

❧ ⌘ ☙

The Treaty of Versailles included an Anglo-American guarantee to prevent future German aggression against France, but this was later repudiated by the USA. Britain then followed suit by cancelling its obligations under the treaty as well.

❧ ⌘ ☙

## THE *DAILY TELEGRAPH* AFFAIR

'You English are mad, mad, mad as March hares. What has come over you that you are so completely given over to suspicions quite unworthy of a great nation?' With these words, Kaiser Wilhelm II tried to win over the hearts and minds of the British in what has to be one of the most inept attempts at international diplomacy ever seen. Seeking to allay British fears about Germany's naval build-up, the Kaiser had his views published in a popular British newspaper, the *Daily Telegraph*, in 1908. Rather than soothing and reassuring the British, however, his tactless emotional outburst managed to convey an image of a nation and a ruler completely out of touch with contemporary European concerns.

A grandson of Queen Victoria, the Kaiser believed he understood the British, and that all he needed to do was express his ideas on Anglo-German friendship in order to reassure them of his good will. He was singularly unsuccessful in achieving that aim, but worse was to come as he went on to outline his country's peaceful intentions towards the British by implying that France and Russia had tried to persuade Germany to enter the Boer War to fight with the Boers against Britain. This had the effect of alienating the French and the Russians; and when the Kaiser went on to declare that the German naval build-up was aimed more at Japan than Britain, he managed to alienate the Japanese as well. Having to endure the scorn and ridicule of fellow world leaders, it was many months before the Kaiser was able to summon the courage to step back into the limelight.

Events in Crimea and Central Asia in the second half of the nineteenth century are important for revealing how far Britain was prepared to go to preserve its empire; they also anticipate Britain's later foreign policy decisions that would play a major role in sending the world on its downward spiral to the Great War of 1914–18. For a start, British efforts to preserve the crumbling Ottoman Empire in the second half of the nineteenth century were to have disastrous consequences. In seeking to prevent its disintegration, they thwarted the ambitions of Balkan nations trying to wrest their freedom from the Turks. This led to almost continuous warfare for over 80 years, instead of a painful, but rapid dismemberment. The struggle also stoked the fires of Balkan nationalism, and the constant yearning for independence by various groups within the Balkans eventually began to destabilise the multi-ethnic Austro-Hungarian Empire. The passions that launched the bullet that ended Archduke Franz Ferdinand's life in Sarajevo in 1914 can be traced directly back to British policies of the nineteenth century. In fact, the British were so intent on keeping the 'Sick Man of Europe' alive, that they constantly turned a blind eye to the brutal repressions and atrocities committed by the Ottoman Turks, usually against Christian minorities. It is ironic that the Ottoman Turks eventually turned against their British allies in the Crimean War, and found a willing friend in Germany instead.

# HOW THE HUN HATES!

THE HUNS CAPTURED SOME OF OUR FISHERMEN
IN THE NORTH SEA AND TOOK THEM TO SENNELAGER.
THEY CHARGED THEM WITHOUT A SHRED OF EVIDENCE
WITH BEING "MINE LAYERS". THEY ORDERED THEM TO
BE PUNISHED WITHOUT A TRIAL.
THAT PUNISHMENT CONSISTED IN SHAVING ALL
THE HAIR OFF ONE SIDE OF THE HEAD AND FACE.
THE HUNS THEN MARCHED THEIR VICTIMS
THROUGH THE STREETS AND EXPOSED THEM TO
THE JEERS OF THE GERMAN POPULACE.

As for Imperial Russia, its humiliation at the hands of the British, meant that it turned its gaze to the Far East instead, leading to a disastrous confrontation with Japan in 1904–05. In eastern Europe, meanwhile, Russia channelled its ambitions into promoting the drive for Slavic independence, casting itself in the role of protector of the Balkan Slavs. This meant that Russia supported the Slavs in their struggle for independence from the Austrian Hapsburgs. As a consequence, Russia allied itself with France, which was also an enemy of the Hapsburgs. Paradoxically, this meant that Russia would eventually become an ally of its old enemy, Britain, when German expansionism began to play a major role in British deliberations.

## What Britain Would Have Done Anyway

Britain's fight to maintain its imperial dreams would have its greatest impact on Germany. The late nineteenth century was the last major era of imperialist expansion. All the great European powers were involved: Britain, Germany, France, even Belgium. It may have been fun and it may have been profitable, but in the end it was disastrous. Africa was rapidly carved up between the main European powers in the so-called 'Scramble for Africa', and harsh conditions were imposed on independent states that could not be conquered outright, such as China. However, this expansionist phase could not go on forever, and the time soon came when every available territory was claimed as a colony by one or other of the major European powers.

By the turn of the twentieth century, Germany was a rising force in the world, eager to acquire an empire comparable to that possessed by Britain. In 1871, the Germans had achieved their dream of unification, which their neighbour, France, had resisted for years in an attempt to keep them weak and divided. For centuries, Germany had been the place where power struggles between other European nations had been conducted, but that time was past. Since Germany was no longer directly involved in European wars or domestic disputes, it was determined to share in the scramble for territory abroad. As a result, it did achieve an overseas empire after 1884, but a small one compared to those administered by Britain and France.

> Owing to a difficult birth, Kaiser Wilhelm II was left with a withered left arm, which he always took pains to conceal when photographed.

In seeking to assert itself in the world, Germany became increasingly resentful of the power exercised by Britain. German imperialists argued that Britain's dominant position in the world gave it an unfair advantage on international markets, thus limiting Germany's economic growth and threatening its security. The scramble for

British World War I propaganda poster. Both sides tried to cast the other as brutes who eagerly committed barbaric acts.

colonies in Africa was driven by the idea that a nation's economic survival depended on its being able to offload surplus products onto overseas possessions. Britain, meanwhile, was determined to continue its expansionist plans because it foresaw a possible decline in its share of the world's export trade with the rise of competition from Germany, America and France.

During the period when Bismarck was Chancellor of Germany, he managed to gain what he wanted by subtle means, without overt confrontation. However, when the young and somewhat impatient Wilhelm II was made Kaiser, the situation started to spiral out of control. As Britain put pressure on Germany to limit the size of its naval fleet in the North Sea, the Germans were feeling hemmed in on land by the alliance between Britain, France and Russia. Germany also owned a piece of France—Alsace-Lorraine, acquired in the Franco-Prussian War of 1870—which the French wanted back. These were some of the factors that fed German resentment, which continued to fester until the moment came for it to explode.

Britain, meanwhile, was determined to maintain its dominant position in the world, and its actions in the lead-up to war speak volumes about where it saw its interests as lying. In 1902 Britain signed a new alliance with Japan, both to preserve its influence and to prevent German expansion in the area. And although Britain claimed that its alliances with France and Russia were about ending old disputes, rather than pledging to join those nations in the event of war, the Germans were worried. Despite British assurances to Germany, the fact remained that the country had allied itself with two nations that were convinced that Germany was their enemy.

The first Moroccan Crisis of 1905—over the colonial status of the North African country—saw Britain forced to choose between France and Germany, and it sided with France. Wilhelm II supported Moroccan independence—or at least its not being a protectorate of France—but the British supported French ambitions. Furthermore, Britain entered into military consultations with the French and delivered a blunt message to Germany, warning that it should not promote its ambitions too vigorously. In Britain itself, public opinion was turning against Germany as a result of that country's expanding naval program and the Kruger telegram—which had been sent by the Kaiser to the President of the Transvaal in what was seen as an attempt to interfere in a British sphere of influence. By the time of the second Moroccan crisis, Britain was firmly in the French camp, and Germany was convinced that Britain was seeking to encircle it with hostile alliances. In 1912, Britain signed a naval agreement with France pledging to defend the French coast along the Channel and the Atlantic, although once again Britain stressed to Germany that this agreement did not commit Britain to war if one were to break out

Among its punitive stipulations, the Treaty of Versailles required the German company Bayer to give up the trademark for aspirin.

between France and Germany. This was clearly not true, and Britain's real intentions were confirmed in 1913 when the British Expeditionary Force, comprising six divisions, was created to fight on the Continent.

The crux of the matter was that Britain could not afford for France to be defeated in another war with Germany. For that would make Germany the strongest nation in continental Europe, at a time when that country was attempting to gain control of the oceans and expand its sphere of influence into the Balkans and Turkey. Britain's leaders were aware that their nation would have to join France in standing against Germany sooner or later; all that was needed was the right pretext.

When war did come, it was inevitable that it would be an international conflict because of the web of alliances that came into play. Austria-Hungary declared war on Serbia; Russia declared war on Austria; Germany declared war on Russia; France declared war on Germany; and Germany invaded Belgium to get at the French, thus bringing Britain into the conflict. Britain was under no specific obligation to come to Belgium's aid, since the 1839 Treaty of London, which guaranteed Belgian independence, was a collective agreement among nations that did not include Germany. There was some legal wrangling over whether Britain was obliged to intervene, since the agreement was for a collective, not an individual response. But that didn't matter. It gave Britain the excuse it needed and had been looking for and the country's leadership took it.

## Legacies

The immediate legacy of the decision to lay the blame for World War I at Germany's door was the disastrous Treaty of Versailles (1918). Of the nations that participated in drawing up the treaty, only the United States sought some measure of leniency for Germany, seeing this as the path to a lasting peace in Europe. If only the other Allies had shared President Wilson's prophetic insight. As it was, while Britain was ambivalent, France under Georges Clemenceau, elder statesman of the Third Republic, wanted vengeance. The treaty explicitly stated that Germany accepted sole responsibility for the war and promised to pay reparations for all the damage done to the civilian populations of the Allies. Germany's military was to be permanently weakened, so it could never again threaten its neighbours. The army was limited to no more than 100,000 troops, the navy was severely cut back, an air force was forbidden, as was the manufacture and import of armaments. Finally, in an attempt to create a buffer zone with France, the Rhineland was to be turned into a demilitarised zone.

More devastatingly, Germany was forced to pay reparations, initially of 226 billion marks in gold (around £11.3 billion), although this was subsequently reduced to 132 billion marks. Even so, it was a ruinous amount, and meant that Germany could not effectively rebuild its own damaged economy. This, in turn, created a populous impoverished underclass that was ready to listen to and embrace radical revolutionary movements that promised to alleviate the country's plight and resurrect its fortunes. Perversely, at a time when the Allies were demanding this enormous sum, they stripped Germany of 13 per cent of its territory, including Alsace-Lorraine—a powerhouse of the German economy—which reverted to France. With the loss of this region, together with West Prussia, 16 per cent of its coalfields, half its iron and steel industry and all its overseas colonies, Germany faced a ruinous future.

---

After the German Revolution broke out in 1918, Kaiser Wilhelm abdicated and fled to the Netherlands, where he was granted asylum. Although the Treaty of Versailles called for Wilhelm to be extradited and prosecuted, Queen Wilhelmina of the Netherlands refused to comply. Wilhelm remained in the Netherlands until his death in 1941.

---

In the event, the Allies were either unwilling or unable to enforce the terms of the Treaty of Versailles, most importantly the prohibition on re-armament. Although they made some token effort to ensure compliance, Germany soon began to roll back the terms of the treaty. When a political party emerged in Germany in the late 1920s that promised to restore German freedom and pride—the Nazis—the Allies watched and did nothing. Even France, which had a clause inserted into the treaty that allowed for French occupation of the Rhineland should Germany ever attempt to remilitarise it, failed to act when the critical moment came in 1936. Vacillation simply encouraged extremists in Germany, who resented the treaty and interpreted a lack of action by the Allies as weakness.

The most important impact of the treaty was the effect it had on German political life. The Allies demanded the creation of a civil government, and so the Kaiser and his chancellor were replaced by a parliamentary democracy—the Weimar Republic—which was disliked by moderates and loathed by extremists on both the left and the right. Its inability to deal with the economic crises that occurred between 1919 and 1923 left its reputation in ruins among German workers, even after the economy began to pick up in the latter half of the 1920s. In practice, the parliament was so weak that any unscrupulous but determined groups willing to target dissatisfied workers had a good chance of securing power within the republic.

Of all of the legacies of Britain's ruthless imperial policy, the rise of Hitler was the most significant. In many respects, the horrors of the Holocaust and the misery caused by World War II are directly attributable to World War I and the subsequent ruin of Germany by the Treaty of Versailles. The Nazis were able to rise to power only because Germans were resentful and beset by economic and political crises. As Professor Richard J. Evans writes, the Nazis tapped into the 'incredulous horror [of] the majority of Germans [and] the sense of outrage and disbelief that swept through the German upper and middle classes like a shockwave'. These were some of the people who cheered as Hitler made clear his intention to discard the lingering military and territorial provisions of the Treaty of Versailles along with a promise to resurrect Germany's former glory.

Had it not been for Britain's imperial delusions, World War I may never have been fought in the first place. Even if Britain had not intervened, and Germany had defeated France in a European war, the circumstances that bred Hitler would probably never have eventuated. A German victory would have refashioned the face of Europe, with the next big war likely to have been a clash between Germany and the rising tide of communism in the east. World War II might also have been avoided. And with nothing to hasten the fall of the old imperial powers, the way would not have been so clear for the United States and the USSR to emerge as the two contending superpowers of the second half of the twentieth century.

# RUSSIAN PEASANTS AND STALIN'S PARANOIA (1930–1933)

*'Comrades! The revolt by the [...] kulak[s ...] must be suppressed without mercy. The interest of the entire revolution demands this, because we have now before us our final decisive battle with the kulaks. We need to set an example.'*
**Vladimir Ilyich Lenin**

*'The death of one man is a tragedy. The death of millions is a statistic.'*
**Joseph Stalin**

### LIE

Landowning peasants were the cause of all the Soviet Union's ills in the 1930s.

### TRUTH

Stalin's paranoia and his desire to create an internal enemy meant that millions of peasants were killed or sent to forced labour camps.

### CHIEF PARTICIPANTS

Joseph Stalin, General Secretary of the Communist Party of the Soviet Union (1922–35)
Vladimir Ilyich Lenin, revolutionary theorist and first leader of the Soviet Union

### THE STORY SO FAR

With the fall of the Tsars in 1917, the leadership of Russia fell to the Bolsheviks under Lenin. They immediately began creating a communist state, based on Lenin's interpretation of Marxist ideology. The control of the means of production by the state and the abolition of private property (even property owned by peasants) were the key components of this master plan. It failed, and Lenin was forced to reintroduce private ownership of property, all the while fighting a civil war between the communists and die-hard supporters of the Tsarist regime, which ended with a communist victory in 1923. With Lenin's death in 1924, the leadership of the party was contested by Stalin and Trotsky. Lenin did not want Stalin to become the next leader of the Bolsheviks, but Stalin won by out-manoeuvring Trotsky, who was eventually forced into exile, where he was assassinated. After consolidating

Russian farmers march to collective fields in 1931.

his grip on power, Stalin decided that the collectivisation of the peasants begun by Lenin back in 1918 should be resumed and ruthlessly pursued. The year was 1928 …

Life for the average Russian peasant was hard. It entailed hours of backbreaking toil from sun-up to sundown, 365 days a year to grow enough crops just to feed your family and yourself. Only in a very good year might there be a little something left over to sell at the market. Farm labourers in the West were little better off, but at least by the beginning of the twentieth century they no longer occupied the very lowest rungs on the social ladder. Illiterate, uneducated and backward, generations of Russian peasants squandered their lives in the fields, while the wealthy landowners grew fat on their suffering and toil.

Very occasionally, some would get lucky. A couple of particularly good years, some loosening of the ever-present restrictive laws, and it was possible to start making some progress. Extra labour could be hired, a field could be purchased from a neighbour who had fallen on hard times, and suddenly you were living a life of relative extravagance, far beyond anything previously dreamed of. But then, just when you thought the hard times were behind you, along came Stalin.

Stalin's policies towards the more wealthy peasants were based on a paranoid belief that they were conspiring to ruin the worker's paradise that was the Soviet Union. They were treacherous and greedy, and were the reason why the new socialist state was in danger of failing. This was a lie, of course, but it provided Stalin with an excuse to persecute and eliminate a section of society that he saw as a potential threat to his power. It also provided an example to the rest of the country of what could happen to anyone who fell foul of the communist system. As an example of the successful use of terror to silence a population, it has rarely been equalled. The legacy of this policy was to crush significant internal dissent, consolidate Stalin's power within the Soviet Union and in the process influence the course of world history for much of the twentieth century.

## The Official Story—The Enemy Within

Lenin and the Bolsheviks were confident that the future could be rosy and bright, were it not for the kulaks (rich peasants) who behaved like leeches, living off the toil and sacrifice of devoted factory workers and the poorer classes of agricultural labourers. Seeing their small wages disappear due to the rising cost of bread and other basic items—which the kulaks were obviously hoarding to inflate prices—the workers turned to the communist revolutionaries who were supposed to advance their interests. In the aftermath of the overthrow of the old Tsarist regime, the Bolsheviks accordingly abolished the whole notion of the private ownership of land and labour. The kulaks resisted, and the result was a disaster. Civil war followed, and in 1921 Lenin introduced the New Economic Plan (NEP), which restored private ownership to selected sections of the economy, farming in particular. The NEP allowed peasants to hire labour, and permitted them to retain any surpluses after paying a certain percentage to the government in taxes. Agricultural production increased greatly as a consequence, leading to a welcome economic recovery after many lean years of wars and crises.

Then came Stalin. Confident that the country was now ready to undergo long-planned changes, Stalin and the Bolshevik leadership began a process of collectivisation—the abolition of private agriculture. This policy change was triggered by the grain crisis of 1927. In order to get to the bottom of the problem, Stalin himself travelled to Siberia in January 1928 to investigate a drop in grain deliveries of some two million tonnes. He blamed the shortfall on those well-known enemies of the government—the kulaks—and arranged for the forcible collection of grain. The kulaks, he explained, had been hoarding grain in the hope of driving prices higher and thus increasing their profits at the expense of the poor, loyal factory workers.

Stalin and the political leadership decreed that drastic measures had to be taken to ensure that the precious grain got to where it was needed. Truculent peasants were accordingly herded onto collective farms, from which grain was forcibly seized and sold abroad. This, the officials explained, was necessary to allow the USSR to begin the rapid industrialisation program needed to produce the tanks, planes and heavy machinery that would help to transform the Soviet Union into a modern state. The private trade of food was suspended, and any kulak who did not deliver his grain was prosecuted as a speculator. Stalin's First Five Year Plan demanded an increase in production of 110 per cent, but it was the kulaks who offered the first resistance to this great leap forward.

Determined to succeed against its enemies, the government pushed forward with its plans, readying itself for the battle to come. The kulaks had to be destroyed once and for all, but they did not give up without a fight. They began their resistance by hiding their grain, and when this failed they resorted to destroying their own livestock, so the government countered by confiscating their land. Government officials were attacked as they carried out their work, but they pressed on regardless. Despite over 2000 rebellions during 1930–31, some 1.5 million kulaks were rounded up and deported to the most distant parts of the USSR, such as Siberia and Kazakhstan. Gradually, grain requisitions yielded lower and lower amounts, providing nowhere near the quotas demanded by Stalin. The government responded by pushing even harder. The Ukraine became a centre of kulak resistance, with the result that the government directed its energies there. The result was a famine in 1932–33, a disaster which was duly blamed on the kulaks who, it was said, were still resisting collectivisation.

Members of the Communist Youth League dig up bags of grain hidden by kulaks in a cemetery near Odessa.

By the time the kulaks were finally eliminated, millions had died of starvation, and millions more had been incarcerated in labour camps or sent into internal exile. Although grain could now be harvested and exchanged for the equipment that the Soviet Union so urgently needed, the price of victory had been very high indeed. Stalin later told Churchill that 'it was a terrible struggle', with the loss of 'ten million. It was fearful. Four years it lasted. It was absolutely necessary [...] it was no use arguing with [the kulaks]. A certain number of them had been resettled in the northern parts of the country [...] Others had been slaughtered by the peasants themselves—such had been their hatred for them.'

## The Truth—Who Were the Kulaks?

Stalin was a master at the 'big lie'. Almost everything about his life was a lie, even his name, which was actually Josef Vissarionovich Djugashvili. During his early attempts to dominate Soviet society he was often guilty of exaggerating the threat posed by enemies. He would even create imaginary enemies of the state—mostly those who stood in his way. In fact, Stalin's foes were from within the USSR itself, and in order to rid himself of them he would organise purges, despatching the unfortunate victims to forced labour camps. His first attempt at such a program—one that was to be the template for all those that followed—was the extermination of the kulaks.

A number of factors came together to cause the slaughter. First and foremost, there was Stalin's megalomania, paranoia and sadism. He believed there were conspiracies—both national and international—to overthrow him. He particularly feared war with the West, which he regarded as one of his most implacable enemies. The country had also experienced a large number of industrial and agricultural failures, brought about by Soviet incompetence. Collectivisation and the abolition of private ownership had created an extremely inefficient economy, one run by brainwashed and unhappy workers. In addition, the Bolsheviks were no strangers to the idea that mass murder could help achieve political ends, a lesson they had learned during the bloody civil war of 1917–23.

Mikhail Gorbachev, General Secretary of the Communist Party from 1985 until 1991, came from a family that had been classified as kulaks under Stalin. His grandfather was sent to a gulag for nine years for allegedly keeping grain for his own use.

So who were these kulaks who had to bear the brunt of Bolshevik paranoia and hostility? According to Soviet doctrine, the peasantry was divided into three classes: bednyaks, or poor peasants; seredniaks, or middle-income peasants; and kulaks, the more independent peasant farmers who owned their own land and were able to hire poorer peasants to work on it. However, it is questionable whether such clear distinctions really existed. Despite efforts to impose class-based ideology on every group within Soviet society, it would be more realistic to say that the peasants were just one large and homogeneous group, with individual families striving to better their situation.

Although kulaks were mentioned during the 1861 emancipation of the serfs, there is no evidence that they comprised a coherent group within Russian society. It was said that kulaks were more adventurous than other peasants, so they occasionally obtained more land by subdividing existing properties or absorbing common land into their farms. They also allegedly rented more land and grew non-traditional crops like flax. Yet their supposed wealth was a fiction, and payments for land they had acquired were often overdue. Their alleged oppression of their fellow peasants also seems to have been an exaggeration. There is little evidence that the kulaks were oppressed by bigger landowners, or that they oppressed peasants poorer than themselves. In fact, there seems to be no evidence to support the idea that there were any real social divisions within the peasantry at all. The peasant class as a whole was a fluid group, and the situation of individuals could either improve or worsen from year to year, or decade to decade.

If a peasant had a young family to care for, he would be quite hard pressed for a number of years. When his children were able to work on the farm, output would increase and he might be better off in the years before the children married and started farms of their own. A peasant could use that time to improve his farming methods, obtain new machinery and purchase new stock. He and his family would eat and dress better, which was normal for anyone trying to improve their lot. In the Soviet Union, however, such signs of prosperity were taken as an indication that you were guilty of exploitation and 'crimes against your class'.

## Ideology and Inefficiency

Given that there is little evidence that kulaks actually existed, it should come as no surprise that the Soviets, even Stalin himself, were unsure about what a kulak actually was. In 1930, Stalin's right-hand man, Vyacheslav Molotov, was given the task of overseeing the destruction of the kulaks. He proposed that they be divided into three categories—those to be eliminated, those to be imprisoned in labour settlement camps and those to be deported. This latter group comprised some 150,000 households, who were to be exiled to places such as Siberia. When Molotov began asking how kulaks were to be identified, no one knew. Stalin addressed the following angry question to himself during the planning phase: 'What does *kulak* mean?'

But the lack of an answer could not be allowed to hold things up when there were grain quotas to be met. Accordingly, when Stalin's trusted associates Lazar Kaganovich, Anastas Mikoyan and Molotov went out into the countryside with troops to obtain the grain and destroy the kulaks, they developed a pragmatic system of identification. Kulaks were those peasants who used hired labour; who owned a mill or had purchased complex equipment or machinery with a motor; had leased agricultural equipment or rented facilities; were involved in commerce; had sold their surplus, lent money or engaged in any other non-labour occupation.

In time, the forced requisition of enormous quantities of grain began to have an obvious effect: the peasants began to starve. In their despair, they attempted to force the government's hand by destroying livestock, but the powers back in Moscow were immune to this kind of tactic since they cared little for the fate of the peasants anyway. By the summer of 1931, it was evident that the food shortage was slipping into famine, but Stalin pressed on regardless. Over 180,000 party

Joseph Stalin, General Secretary of the Communist Party of the Soviet Union from 1922 to 1953.

workers were sent into the countryside to break up uncooperative villages. Over two million peasants were deported to Siberia and Kazakhstan, and a million ended up in forced labour camps. But still Stalin was not satisfied. Driven on by the need for more grain, he was convinced that the kulaks were responsible for causing the grain shortage. Historian Simon Sebag-Montefiore quotes one idealistic Soviet apparatchik describing how: 'I took part in this [...] searching for hidden grain [...] I emptied out the old folks' storage chests, stopping my ears to the children's crying and the women's wails [...] I was convinced I was accomplishing the great and necessary transformation of the countryside.'

## JOSEPH STALIN—THE 'MAN OF STEEL'

Joseph Stalin, known familiarly to the West as 'Uncle Joe' during World War II, was born in Georgia as Josef Vissarionovich Djugashvili. Like many other Bolsheviks at the time, he decided to signal his membership of the Communist Party by taking on a new name: one that would mark a break from family allegiances and a wholehearted commitment to the social revolution he wanted to bring about.

He was impressed when his fellow Bolshevik Vyacheslav Scriabin adopted the name Molotov—'the hammer'; it had the right industrial sound to it, and suggested someone to be feared. In his turn, Djugashvili decided that henceforth he would be known as Stalin—'Man of Steel'; the name would be an expression of his iron will and indomitable spirit.

Little could his friends and colleagues have known how true the name would turn out to be as Stalin degenerated into a despotic monster. Almost as soon as he came to power, Stalin began a series of brutal repressions of his own people that would see millions exiled to Siberia or Central Asia, executed, or dying of starvation as a result of his misconceived social and economic policies. Often driven by paranoid fears that he was surrounded by enemies, Stalin had no compunction in purging the military, the politburo, or even whole communities of ordinary workers. He ordered numerous ethnic groups to be forcibly resettled within the Soviet Union with no regard for the effect that this would have on families or societies.

The countryside was indeed transformed. By 1932–33, the USSR, and in particular the Ukraine, was in the grip of a great famine. 'The peasants ate dogs, horses, rotten potatoes, the bark of trees, anything they could find,' described one witness, quoted by Sebag-Montefiore. An American touring the Ukraine at that time came across a village near the Ukrainian capital Kiev where all of the people were dead, except for one woman, half-insane from hunger and suffering. Rats feasted upon the unburied corpses locked within their huts. There were countless other villages where the inhabitants had taken their own lives rather than succumb to the horrors of starvation and cannibalism. Still the leadership in Moscow refused to relent, now requiring the peasants themselves to identify the kulaks in their midst. Desperate for relief, the peasants turned on each other. The poor accused anyone better off than they themselves of being a kulak, only to be similarly accused by those who were even poorer. British journalist Malcolm Muggeridge reported: 'At a railway station early one morning, I saw a line of people with their hands tied behind them, being herded into cattle trucks at gunpoint—all so silent and mysterious and horrible in the half light, like some macabre ballet.'

It was ideology that drove Stalin and the Bolsheviks to create this situation. Inefficiencies inherent in the Five Year Plan and collectivisation were always going to result in circumstances where quotas could not be met. But in the Soviet Union at that time, failure was simply not acceptable. If quotas could not be met, enemies within the state must be responsible—in this case, the kulaks. That kulaks could not be found didn't matter. There were shortages and famine, so they must exist, otherwise how else could the shortages and famine be explained?

In creating this phantom threat, and deliberately engineering the famine in the Ukraine, Stalin bears responsibility for the deaths of over four million people. The peasants had always been the enemy of the Bolsheviks, whether they knew it or not. Fabricating the kulak threat allowed the Bolsheviks to break what little spirit the peasants possessed, thereby removing one potential source of opposition to Stalin and the Bolsheviks. The kulaks became Stalin's scapegoat in order to deflect criticism from his own failings when his promised utopia failed to materialise. As Nikita Khrushchev, Stalin's successor as First Secretary of the Communist Party, later wrote: 'Perhaps we'll never know how many people perished directly as a result of collectivisation, or indirectly as a result of Stalin's eagerness to blame his failure on others.'

## Legacies

The legacy of Stalin's assault on the Soviet Union's peasants was significant. In the first instance, it provided an opportunity to destroy peasant resistance to communist rule. The Bolsheviks had always recognised the peasants as a formidable force, especially if they made a serious attempt to loosen the young communist regime's tenuous grip on power. And the communist's hold on the country only became rock solid in the early 1930s. Even more importantly, the persecution of the kulaks demonstrated to everyone, at all levels of Soviet society, what treatment would be meted out to anyone who was considered an enemy of the state. Stalin's grip on power was assured in the wake of the catastrophe in the countryside. The enslavement of the entire Soviet Union and the subsequent oppression of Eastern Europe during the Cold War would not have been possible without techniques developed in the crusade against the imaginary kulaks. The basic principle of divide and conquer would be applied by all future communist states, destroying potential resistance before it had a chance to topple the regime.

The destruction of the peasants also came at a great cost to Stalin himself. The impossible production targets he had set were soon shown to be unattainable, a revelation he reacted to with characteristic violence. He blamed his subordinates for his own economic illiteracy, and any associations he had with party officials came close to disintegrating amid a welter of recriminations and betrayals. Some have speculated that Stalin suffered a nervous breakdown during this period, due to the pressure of the growing famine and the suicide of his wife in November 1932 after a violent row. Once he emerged from this crisis, Stalin saw conspiracies everywhere. Conflating the public with the personal, he became convinced that the destruction of his family was the result of a kulak conspiracy to overturn everything he had sought to build.

Despite the misery and destruction caused by collectivisation, it is nevertheless true to say that the requisitioning of enormous quantities of grain did help to fuel the expansion of Soviet heavy industry. The grain was used to raise money to build pig-iron smelters and tractors which would prove to be invaluable in attempting to drag the backward Soviet Union into the twentieth century. Although the country's factories were unable to meet the unrealistic production targets set by Stalin, and despite the fact that the tractors they produced often ended up in the hands of peasants who could not drive them, the push for modernisation was broadly successful.

The effort involved in transforming the Soviet Union from a basically agrarian society into a modern industrial power was huge. Collectivisation helped to provide the factories with the workers they needed, with up to 80 per cent of peasants moving from their farms to work in the cities. By the end of the First Five Year Plan, the Soviet Union had seen a 250 per cent increase in overall industrial development, with a mighty 330 per cent expansion in heavy industry. Similarly astonishing outcomes were achieved in electricity generation and the manufacture of steel. The scale of the expansion may have been impressive, but it came at great cost. American writer John Scott, who helped in the construction of the massive steelworks at Magnitogorsk in 1933, witnessed the suffering of:

> *A quarter of a million souls—Communists, Kulaks, foreigners, Tatars, convicted saboteurs and a mass of blue-eyed Russian peasants—building the biggest steel combinant in Europe in the middle of the barren Ural steppe [...] Men froze, hungered and suffered, but the construction work went on with a disregard for individuals and a mass heroism seldom paralleled in history.*

The story is not so positive for the agricultural economy of the USSR. Although industrialisation was a significant achievement for the Soviet state, the repression of the peasants did considerable damage to Soviet agriculture, which took years to recover. Apart from the disruption and pain caused by forced collectivisation, the entire process resulted in mutual distrust and hostility between rural workers and the Communist Party that lasted for years. In their inept attempts to create a rural proletariat, the communist authorities were more interested in the politics rather than the economics of primary industry. Farm workers were expected to be model citizens, while the practicalities of actually farming the land seemed to be of secondary importance. The government introduced a top-heavy bureaucracy to run state farms and ensure loyalty from the collectives. Any chairman of a collective who failed to meet the requirements of ideological purity was removed from his post. The bureaucracy cared little for the views of experienced farmers or farm managers who understood regional conditions. Such strategies reduced efficiency and squandered precious resources. The consequences continued to be felt to the very last days of the Soviet Union in the late 1980s, when Soviet farmers were on average about one-tenth as productive as their American counterparts.

# POINTING THE WAY TO
# PEARL HARBOR (1941)

*'Yesterday, December 7th, 1941, a date which will live in infamy, the United States of America was suddenly and deliberately attacked by naval and air forces of the Empire of Japan.'*
**Franklin Delano Roosevelt**

*'Naturally the common people don't want war [...] that is understood. But after all, it is the leaders of the country who determine policy, and it is always a simple matter to drag the people along, whether it is a democracy, or a fascist dictatorship, or a parliament, or a communist dictatorship. Voice or no voice, the people can always be brought to the bidding of the leaders. That is easy. All you have to do is to tell them they are being attacked, and denounce the pacifists for lack of patriotism and exposing the country to danger. It works the same in any country.'*
**Hermann Goering**

### LIE

The government of the USA had no idea that the Japanese were going to attack Pearl Harbor.

### TRUTH

President Roosevelt's administration had prior knowledge of a planned Japanese attack and used it as justification for entering the war!

### CHIEF PARTICIPANTS

Franklin Delano Roosevelt, 32nd President of the United States of America
Lieutenant Commander Arthur H. McCollum, US Office of Naval Intelligence

### THE STORY SO FAR

In the aftermath of World War I, the United States once again retreated into isolationism, refusing to ratify the Treaty of Versailles, and deciding against joining the League of Nations (the precursor to the United Nations). The majority of American citizens were keenly non-interventionist. Obsessed with the enormous industrial profits of the 1920s, the United States was unprepared for the 1929 stock market crash and the Great Depression that followed. These events occupied the country's attention for the next decade. As Europe moved

The battleship USS *Arizona* sinks into Pearl Harbor after being bombed by Japanese planes.

closer to war, the Roosevelt administration, pressured by groups such as the America First Committee, introduced a series of Neutrality Acts between 1935 and 1939 to ensure that they would not get involved in foreign conflicts, as had happened in World War I. It was only with the Lend-Lease Program of 1941, in which material resources were shipped to the Allies, that Roosevelt began to steer America carefully towards involvement in World War II. Then came 7 December 1941 …

Visitors step off the boat and approach the solitary white building at Pearl Harbor, Honolulu, Hawaii. They enter—the young, the old, men, women and children. Quietly they make their way through the building until they stand in the assembly room. Around them are seven large open windows on both the walls and the ceiling, and before them, on the floor, an opening to the waters below. The visitors look on as a number of young children gather around the opening and drop flower leis into the water, in honour of the dead. Moving through the building the visitors come to the shrine room, where everyone stops talking and a profound silence descends upon all, aware that they stand over a tomb of the fallen. Before them is a marble wall with names engraved upon it, commemorating those who died for their country. This marks the final resting place of the 1102 crewmen of the USS *Arizona* who lost their lives on 7 December 1941, their bodies forever entombed within the sunken wreck below.

Everyone who gathers there is deeply aware of the significance of that site and of the date: the day when the United States was dragged into a world war that it wanted no part of. The people had made it clear that the war raging in Europe and the Pacific was none of their concern, and President Roosevelt had promised not to get them involved. It would take an attack on American soil to change the mood of the country.

Yet, despite appearances to the contrary, the US administration was desperate to enter the war against Germany, and all it needed was the right sort of excuse. It therefore set about the task of manipulating Japan into launching an attack on the United States; an attack, moreover, that would appear to be unprovoked. In fact, the attack on Pearl Harbor was not unprovoked, although it has gone down in history as one of the most successful surprise attacks ever carried out.

## The Official Story—A Surprise and Unprovoked Attack

The negotiations were going nowhere, that much was certain. Annoyed Japanese diplomats waved their arms in frustration, exasperated at the apparently indecisive approach of the United States administration. The Japanese had been having lengthy discussions with the US since May 1941, and they were becoming more annoyed with each passing month. The war in China and Southeast Asia was going well, but the US had imposed an oil embargo on Japan, which threatened its ability to pursue its military ambitions in the area. Consequently, in early November, the Japanese leadership decided to continue their diplomatic efforts to secure US cooperation for a further three weeks only. If an agreement could not be reached by then, they would launch an attack against the US on 7 December 1941.

In preparation for this contingency, a Japanese flotilla had been despatched in mid-November from the Kurile Islands, some 4800 km (3000 miles) away. They were maintaining complete radio silence as they stealthily approached Hawaii from the north, avoiding the sea lanes generally used by merchant shipping. As the days counted down, parts of the US Pacific Fleet were despatched from Pearl Harbor. On 28 November, USS *Enterprise* was directed to leave, together with 11 of the United States' most modern warships, to deliver aircraft to Wake Island. Then on 5 December, the USS *Lexington* was despatched with eight other warships to Midway Island. Those remaining on Hawaii, including Admiral Kimmel, Commander-in-chief of the Pacific Fleet, and Lieutenant General Walter Short, commander of US military installations, were blissfully unaware of the approaching threat.

---

One of the most vocal opponents to America's entry in World War II was the America First Committee, and one of its strongest spokesmen was the aviator Charles Lindbergh, famous for being the first man to fly non-stop across the Atlantic. During the war he continued to oppose further American involvement, but still flew many combat missions as a civilian consultant.

American participation in the war with Germany was guaranteed by the Axis Tripartite Pact between Germany, Italy and Japan, signed on 27 September 1940. By declaring war on Japan, America was automatically at war with Germany and Italy as well.

---

Japanese officials on the mainland received a communiqué on 6 December, advising them to break off all negotiations the following day. They had concluded from America's response that it was obvious there was going to be no diplomatic settlement. Accordingly, as the sun rose over Hawaii on the quiet Sunday morning of 7 December, the first planes from the Japanese attack group approached the island of Oahu. Reaching it at 7.48 am, they set about their assigned task of incapacitating all US military air bases on Hawaii, and as many of the ships anchored in Pearl Harbor as possible. Sleepy-eyed US servicemen aboard the ships were woken by a cacophony of sirens, explosions and gunfire as they scrambled to get into position. But they were already far too late.

Almost all fighter aircraft on the ground were destroyed, with only a small number making it into the air. The aircraft, parked nose to tail, wingtip to wingtip for protection against Japanese insurgents were sitting ducks. A total of 2117 Navy and Marine Corps personnel lost their lives; 18 ships were either sent to the bottom of the harbour or severely damaged; 161 aircraft were destroyed and 102 damaged. The battleship USS *Arizona* exploded and sank taking with her over 1100 servicemen, whose bodies remain entombed within the wreck to this day, accounting for over half the American dead. The Japanese also attacked using midget submarines.

The Japanese armada consisted of five aircraft carriers and a total of 441 aircraft, including fighters, torpedo-bombers, dive-bombers and fighter-bombers. Of these, 55 were lost during the battle. The planes attacked in two waves, with Admiral Nagumo abandoning a third attack in favour of pulling back to avoid the risk of further losses, believing that he had crippled the US Fleet. The Japanese congratulated themselves on a job well done, while the Americans greeted news of the death and devastation with bewilderment and anger as their president moved the United States closer to being a country at war.

## The Truth—Reasons for War

The attack on Pearl Harbor brought America into World War II, but it was not the surprise it was claimed to be. To understand why, we need to take a look at just what was happening in the world in the years leading up to the conflict.

Although the United States was a rising power, it had not yet achieved the dominance enjoyed by the traditional powers—Britain, France and Germany. The situation was gradually changing, however, as the major powers struggled to recover from the devastation caused by World War I. This process was helped by America's reluctance to enter the war against Germany and Japan. For the first two years the United States were quite content to look on as the fading colonial powers exhausted themselves. All that was to change in June 1941, when Hitler took the insane decision to invade Russia—a campaign codenamed Operation Barbarossa—a move he had been planning for many months. The warning signs were obvious by late 1940 to those who were paying attention. Stalin certainly knew about it by September 1940, having been informed by his spies that Hitler had signed 'Directive 21' ordering preparation for Operation Barbarossa. It is certain that the Western powers knew about it as well.

Military strategists in the United States thought that if Russia entered the war it would defeat Germany, and eventually come to dominate Europe. Although American leaders routinely condemned Hitler, they had no doubt that the real enemy was going to be the Soviet Union, with its antipathy towards the American way of life. In the 1920s, America had sent troops into Russia in an effort to halt the Bolshevik revolution, so they had made their minds up about who the real enemy was as far back as then. Although the German invasion of Russia increased the US administration's unease about the outcome of the war, these concerns could not be shared with the public. Over three-quarters of the American people were opposed to any intervention in the war, so it would take something drastic to make them change their minds—something like an attack on Americans living on American soil.

With the US government committed to provoking one of the Axis powers into attacking, the next question was: which one? It was Secretary of the Interior Harold Ickes who provided the answer, writing in his diary on 18 October 1941: 'For a long time I have believed that our best entrance into the war would be by way of Japan.' But what would be needed to provoke Japan into attacking a far larger neutral power, inviting retaliation and almost certain defeat? There was also the problem of how to get America involved in the European war, even if Japan could be provoked into an attack.

## Skilful Manipulation

To get America involved, the Roosevelt administration was counting on the Axis Tripartite Pact, signed by Germany, Italy and Japan in September 1940. If Japan could be manipulated into starting a war with the United States, that would activate the mutual assistance clauses of the Tripartite Pact, bringing America into the European war against Germany; once in Europe, the United States would be in position to counter the eventual Soviet threat. Lieutenant Commander Arthur McCollum of the Office of Naval Intelligence duly detailed eight acts designed to aggravate and provoke the Japanese into aggressive action. One of these was to base a large part of the US Fleet in Hawaii, and tempt the Japanese to attack it.

On 8 October 1940, President Roosevelt summoned the Commander-in-chief of the US Fleet, Admiral James O. Richardson, to the White House. The admiral was instructed to place the fleet in an exposed position at Pearl Harbor. He objected, not unnaturally, saying that this would put his sailors and ships in danger. Since Richardson was clearly going to cause problems, he was removed and replaced by Rear Admiral Husband E. Kimmel, who was given command of the fleet in Hawaii. Kimmel was promoted to four-star admiral to give him greater prestige, and given charge of the fleet in early February 1941. To complete the clandestine preparations, Major General Walter Short was promoted to three-star Lieutenant General, and installed as commander of army operations and bases in Hawaii.

Gradually throughout 1941, Roosevelt, as Commander-in-chief, ordered the other seven key McCollum recommendations to be carried out. These included an embargo on key resources—particularly oil and steel—being traded with Japan. With very limited oil production and virtually no refined fuel reserves, Japan's military exploits against China and Indochina were in danger of collapsing. The embargo increased Japan's determination to conquer and exploit areas in Asia containing the vital resources they needed. They believed the United States wouldn't remain inactive when the invasions began, so their chief military commander, Admiral Yamamoto, began to explore ways of eliminating American power in the Pacific. It was then that Japanese attention turned to the exposed US Fleet in Pearl Harbor.

Further evidence that the attack on Pearl Harbor was deliberately provoked can be found in a memo written by Secretary of the Interior, Harold Ickes, to President Roosevelt on 23 June 1941, the day after Germany invaded the Soviet Union. In it, Ickes wrote that: 'There might develop from the embargoing of oil to Japan such a situation as would make it not only possible but easy to get into this war in an effective way. And if we should thus indirectly be brought in, we would avoid the criticism that we had gone in as an ally of communistic Russia.'

On 22 July, Roosevelt received a report from Admiral Richmond Turner, stating: 'It is generally believed that shutting off the American supply of petroleum will lead promptly to the [Japanese] invasion of Netherlands East Indies […] it seems certain she would also include military action against the Philippine Islands, which would immediately involve us in a Pacific war.' Within a few days of receiving that report, Roosevelt froze all Japanese assets in the United States, setting in motion the inevitable march to war. It was also from this date that vital pieces of intelligence information were withheld from the commanders in Hawaii.

It is certain that Roosevelt was constantly briefed about Japanese responses to American actions through intercepted and decoded diplomatic and military communications, although the intelligence wasn't shared with the commanders in Hawaii. In fact, the United States obtained plans for the attack on Pearl Harbor well before the event. According to author Robert B. Stinnett, on 24 November 1941, Admiral Yamamoto sent a radio message containing instructions to Admiral Chuichi Nagumo, Commander of the Pacific Striking Fleet: 'The task force, keeping its movement strictly secret and maintaining close guard against submarines and aircraft, shall advance into Hawaiian waters, and upon the very opening of hostilities shall attack the main force of the United States fleet in Hawaii and deal it a mortal blow.'

The Japanese had no idea that at least 1000 military and diplomatic radio messages were being intercepted every day by monitoring stations across the world.

OWI-38539-ZC

Battleship row, Pearl Harbor, in the aftermath of the Japanese air assault.

The contents were summarised for the Roosevelt administration, and the message they contained was crystal clear: Japan was planning an attack somewhere in the Pacific. The Roosevelt administration hoped that the target would be Pearl Harbor. A week before the attack, Admiral Kimmel and Lieutenant General Short were ordered by President Roosevelt himself not to go on an alert footing, because 'the United States desires that Japan commit the first overt act'.

The major counter-argument against American foreknowledge of an attack asks why Roosevelt was willing to sacrifice most of the Pacific fleet, and possibly one of the most important American naval bases in the Pacific. This would cripple US operations against Japan for the next two years, by which time the Japanese were very likely to have taken over the Pacific and begun operations against the west coast of America.

The answer is that, first, Japan could not move against the United States until China was subdued, and it was looking increasingly unlikely that China would fall; second, Roosevelt had already saved all the important elements of the fleet from destruction.

In the northern spring of 1941, Roosevelt sent a significant portion of America's naval strength into the Atlantic, in response to attacks by Germany. He ensured that the aircraft carrier USS *Saratoga* was kept on the west coast of America and, most importantly, that two aircraft carrier groups were sent out of Pearl Harbor in the weeks prior to the anticipated attack, which meant that not only they, but also their fast escort ships, would be saved. In essence, all of the newer ships stationed at Pearl Harbor were removed from harm's way. Only obsolete World War I vessels remained anchored at the base. As Admiral Bloch, commander of the local Naval District at Pearl Harbor, testified to Congress later: […] the Japanese only destroyed a lot of old hardware. In a sense they did us a favour.' It is abundantly clear that Roosevelt knew very well which ships remained at Pearl Harbor. Within minutes of hearing of the attack, and before any confirmed reports had been received, he reportedly told Lord Halifax at the British Embassy that: 'most of the fleet was at sea […] none of the newer ships were in harbour.

## Legacies

With the United States finally in the war, an Allied victory looked more certain. If the United States had remained on the sidelines, the war in the Pacific would have been won by Japan. Their conquests might not have extended to Australia, but they would certainly have consolidated the areas they already occupied. The Japanese Empire would have become a reality, and they would have been the only great power in the Pacific. With Britain exhausted as a result of fighting a war in two theatres, Japan would have concentrated all her efforts on overcoming China, although there is no guarantee that it would have emerged victorious from that struggle.

In Europe, while Hitler would almost certainly have been defeated by Soviet forces, the lack of an American presence would have allowed Soviet troops to sweep across the Continent, resulting in the creation of Soviet-style satellite states as a buffer against the West. In fact, it is hard to see that anything could have prevented the Soviet Union from dominating all of Europe—certainly not a tiny and exhausted Britain. Had the United States not intervened, therefore, Europe would have been dominated by a communist superpower, and Asia by a militaristic and expansionist Japan. It seems certain that at least one of those powers would then have turned their eyes towards an isolated and friendless United States. It is fortunate that events did not turn out that way, both for the United States and the rest of the free world. What happened instead was that the United States became a superpower.

Until the late 1930s, the United States was suffering the effects of the Great Depression, which had lasted for nearly ten years. The country was finally dragged out of its sustained slump by the vast amount of money spent by the federal government to support the war effort. Between 1939 and 1944, America's production capacity increased twofold. Unemployment tumbled from 14 per cent in 1940 to less than 2 per cent in 1943, as the labour force was expanded by ten million. This effort was sustained after World War II, as the United States managed to turn its formidable war economy into a booming consumer culture in a relatively short time. It was this that provided the launching pad for America's post-war prosperity, making it an economic powerhouse and turning it into the pre-eminent superpower at the beginning of the twenty-first century.

## THE THIRD WAVE—WHAT MIGHT HAVE BEEN

The Japanese attack on Pearl Harbor consisted of two waves of aircraft. When the second wave had returned to their aircraft carriers, discussions took place on whether a third wave should be launched or not. A number of Japanese officers, including the one who planned the assault, were keen to despatch a third wave. Its objective was to have been Pearl Harbor's fuel storage depot, as well as maintenance and dry dock repair facilities. Their destruction would have crippled the base, preventing it from being used in the immediate future by an American fleet seeking to engage the Japanese.

The decision rested with Admiral Chuichi Nagumo, who decided not to proceed. His reasons were all very sensible. The Japanese had sustained large casualties during the second wave, since the element of surprise had gone. This could only get worse if there was a third attack. There was also a possibility that the ships would run out of fuel on the return journey, and Nagumo wasn't sure of the location of the American aircraft carriers, and whether they would be able to attack the retreating Japanese fleet. Taking all of these factors into consideration, he gave the order to withdraw.

With the benefit of hindsight, it seems obvious that a third strike would have been a good idea. Even though the two previous attacks had destroyed several battleships and other naval craft, together with a large number of aircraft, the fact that the aircraft carriers were not at Pearl Harbor meant that an important part of the Pacific Fleet remained a threat. With fuel and repair facilities intact, this meant that the base could still be used to counter Japanese activities in the Pacific. The future course of the war may well have been determined by Admiral Nagumo's decision that December morning.

America's entry into the war after the attack on Pearl Harbor also contributed to its greatness in other, unexpected ways. As American armies overran Nazi facilities, they acquired German scientists who were at the forefront of numerous military research projects, including rocket research. America's victory in the space race would not have been possible without the know-how of those German scientists, among them Wernher von Braun, who played a key role in designing the V2 rocket, Germany's last-ditch attempt to bomb Britain into submission. After the war, von Braun went on to help design the first intercontinental ballistic missiles that helped keep the United States in the forefront of the arms race; and, later, he led the NASA team that developed the enormous Saturn V rockets that propelled American astronauts to the moon. The development of the atomic bomb and the hydrogen bomb were also made possible only with help supplied by captured German scientists and technicians. As historian Norman Naimark points out, the physicist Werner Heisenberg, 'was worth more to us than ten divisions of Germans. Had he fallen into Russian hands, he would have proven invaluable to them.'

Perhaps most significant of all, America owes its position as the world's pre-eminent superpower to World War II and its aftermath. While America came out of the conflict immeasurably stronger, the same could not be said of Britain and France. By the close of the war, millions were homeless, many European economies had collapsed, and most of Europe's industrial infrastructure was in ruins. Britain found it could no longer afford to retain its colonial possessions, with the result that they slipped away one by one. Into Britain's shoes, as the world's impartial policeman, stepped the United States, determined to halt the spread of communism and not afraid to put its former allies firmly in their place if they went against American interests. The protection of America's interests demanded not only an aggressive foreign policy, but also the economic and military means to defend them should that have become necessary. Victory in World War II had guaranteed that.

Sailors on leave read about the attacks on Hawaii and the Philippines.

# OFFICIAL DECEPTIONS & COVER-UPS

*'The Press was protected so that it could bare the secrets of the government and inform the people. Only a free and unrestrained press can effectively expose deception in government. And paramount among the responsibilities of a free press is the duty to prevent any part of the government from deceiving the people.'*

## JUSTICE HUGO L. BLACK

A fourteenth-century illustration of a council meeting to discuss the conflict between Philip IV and Pope Boniface VIII over the taxing of the clergy.

# THE PHARAOH ERASED FROM HISTORY

## (1336 BC)

*'But when you rise again, everything is made to flourish for the king; since you did create the earth and raise it up for your son, who came forth from your body: the King of Upper and Lower Egypt, [...] Akhenaten.'*
**Akhenaten**

*'May you never forget what is worth remembering, nor ever remember what is best forgotten.'*
**Anonymous**

### LIE

Pharaoh Akhenaten never existed.

### TRUTH

The Egyptian priests erased all mention of the reign of Akhenaten and his son Tutankhamun!

### CHIEF PARTICIPANTS

Pharaoh Akhenaten, ruler during the 18th dynasty of Ancient Egypt
Pharaoh Tutankhamun, Akhenaten's son
Horemheb, commander of the Egyptian army, who became pharaoh after
    Tutankhamun's death

### THE STORY SO FAR

For over 100 years, from about 1648 BC, the Nile delta and Middle Egypt were under the sway of foreign invaders whom the Egyptians called the Hyksos ('foreign rulers'). The south of the country (Upper Egypt) was ruled by an Egyptian royal family whose centre of power was the city of Thebes. From here, a succession of Theban pharaohs launched attacks against the foreign kings of the north until, finally, in around 1540 BC, Pharaoh Ahmose I expelled the Hyksos from Egypt and reunited the country. This event marked the start of the New Kingdom and the Eighteenth Dynasty, whose warrior-kings spread Egyptian power and prestige across Africa and the Middle East, from Sudan in the south to the borders of modern Turkey. By the time Pharaoh Amenhotep IV ascended the throne in 1352 BC, Egypt's power seemed assured …

The king list of Abydos depicting Pharaoh Seti I, his son Rameses II and their ancestors.

'Feverishly we cleared away the remaining last scraps of rubbish on the floor of the passage before the doorway, until we had only the clean sealed doorway before us.' Thus Howard Carter recalled the momentous day in November 1922 when he was about to open the sealed entrance to the tomb of Tutankhamun. Amid all the wonder and excitement of the discovery of the tomb and its riches, there would have been one thing that all Egyptologists were eager to discover—the name of the pharaoh. When the hieroglyphs were translated, and the name Tutankhamun was deciphered, this presented a puzzle. According to the list of kings found at Abydos in Upper Egypt, no such pharaoh from the Eighteenth Dynasty ever existed. In fact, none of the available king lists mentioned the name of the now famous boy pharaoh.

The solution to this mystery was to be found in the reign of Tutankhamun's father, Akhenaten, a man who turned Egypt upside down for a period of 15 years; a man who so alienated the rich and powerful that every attempt was made to erase any mention of his existence. The same was done to his son, and anyone else involved in Akhenaten's attempt to completely change the Egyptian world view. Statues were torn down, names erased and a vast city abandoned to the swirling desert sands as the people of ancient Egypt tried to forget the very name of the heretic king.

Akhenaten was to be the victim of the world's first and most successful example of historical revisionism. Nowhere else has the very existence of a ruler been so thoroughly and deliberately erased from the historical record.

## The Official Story—The Kings of the Eighteenth Dynasty

The illustrious Pharaoh Seti I, ruler of Upper and Lower Egypt from 1294 to 1279 BC, decided to construct the greatest temple that his country had ever seen at the great religious centre of Abydos. The temple was so ambitious that it was not completed during Seti's lifetime, but was finished by his son, Rameses II, and was considered the most beautiful ever constructed. Over 170 m (558 ft) long and clad in white limestone, it was dedicated to all the gods and former kings of Egypt.

Within the temple, Seti sought to legitimise his occupation of the throne by divine right by having a list of the names of all the kings of Egypt who had preceded him carved on the walls of a narrow corridor: the so-called king list of Abydos. His father Rameses I was no longer merely a commoner who had been raised to high office by the Pharaoh Horemheb. Instead, he was listed among the 75 names of all the known pharaohs of Egypt from the dawn of time to Rameses I's reign. Seti's son, Rameses II, would later order that Seti's own name be added to the list of royalty gracing the walls of this greatest of Egyptian temples.

The king list of Abydos included not only Seti's own dynasty—the nineteenth— but also the dynasty from which Seti himself claimed to have sprung—the eighteenth. These were the great and powerful rulers who had rescued the sacred land from foreign domination and set it back on the path to greatness. Here was Ahmose I, who had founded the dynasty and completed the conquest and expulsion of the hated Hyksos. He was succeeded by Amenhotep I, who consolidated his father's successes in the north and the south. Then there was Tuthmose I, the Hammer of the Nubians, who fought and killed the Nubian king and hung his body from the prow of his ship. He was followed by his son Tuthmose II, who had subjugated the Kush. Next was Tuthmose III, the ruler who had forged the greatest empire Egypt had ever seen, extending from the fourth cataract of the Nile in Nubia, to the scorching deserts of Syria. His son, Amenhotep II, had killed seven rebel princes at Kadesh in single-handed combat, and returned to Egypt with 745 kg (1643 lb) of gold and 54,800 kg (120,833 lb) of copper, as well as 550 Mariannu captives, 210 horses and 300 chariots. Next came Tuthmose IV, the conqueror of Syria, and the pharaoh who restored the Sphinx to its former glory. The penultimate eighteenth-dynasty name on the wall belonged to Amenhotep III, who saw peace and tranquillity established throughout the empire. Finally, there was Horemheb, the great reformer who had restored order throughout the land and curbed the power and abuses of state officials. These were the great kings of the ancient land of Egypt, whose names would live forever in the halls of the Great Temple of Seti at Abydos.

## The Truth—The Reign of Akhenaten

Tall, spindly and potbellied, Akhenaten did not cut an attractive figure. The son of Amenhotep III, he had originally been given the name Amenhotep IV. A poet, philosopher and religious revolutionary, Akhenaten ruled Egypt from 1353 to 1334 BC, establishing the world's first monotheistic religion, Atenism. This elevated what had originally been an obscure minor god—the Aten, the life-giving disc of the sun—to the position of supreme deity, and eventually to the status of the only god.

At the beginning of his reign, Akhenaten attempted to place his radical movement in a recognisable Egyptian religious context by describing the Aten as a reinvention of the familiar supreme deity, Amun. However, by the ninth year of his reign, Akhenaten decided that the Aten was not just the supreme god among many other Egyptian gods, but was, in fact, the only god. To reinforce his own position in the newly established faith, Akhenaten declared himself to be the only link between the Aten and his people. To the consternation of many, the pharaoh ordered the desecration of Amun's temples throughout Egypt, removing any mention of the god's name. He also demonstrated a desire to crush the independent authority of the traditional Amun priesthood, who controlled Egypt's wealth and produce. These actions offended large sections of the Egyptian population.

Akhenaten also banned all idols and declared that no physical representation of the sun god, the Aten, was to be allowed. The only exception was the depiction of the rayed solar disc, with the sun's rays shown as having hands at their ends, representing the hidden spirit of the Aten. Unlike idols, however, these images were clearly identified as being representations, not real manifestations, of the god. A revolution was underway in the ancient land of Egypt, a land where innovations were regarded with suspicion as dangerous and un-Egyptian.

Modern scholars believe that the principal reason the city of Akhetaten was abandoned was due to a plague that ravaged Egypt around the time of the death of Akhenaten.

The new religion needed a new religious centre, so Akhenaten started work on a new capital in the fifth year of his reign. Named Akhetaten ('Horizon of Aten'), and located at a site beside the Nile now known as Amarna, it was built to centralise Egyptian religious practices, avoiding any sacrilegious taint that might come from worship associated with other cities in the past. As work started on the new capital, the pharaoh changed his name from Amenhotep IV to Akhenaten ('He Who Works for Aten'), to show that the old order and the old ways were now to be cast aside. Akhenaten also supervised the assembly of some of the largest temple complexes in ancient Egypt, including one at Karnak, close to the old temple of Amun.

After Akhenaten's death in 1334 BC, worship of the Aten fell out of favour almost immediately. Akhenaten's son Tutankhaten was forced to change his name to Tutankhamun within the first two years of his reign, and he deserted the city of Akhetaten. With the pharaoh gone, the new city lost its reason for being, with the result that all the people who had moved there during Akhenaten's reign were now obliged to move yet again. The once mighty city of Akhetaten, with its temples and statues, fell into ruin and was eventually covered by the desert sands. When Tutankhamun died nine years later, his successors Ay and Horemheb tore down the remaining temples built by Akhenaten, including the magnificent temple at Thebes, and used the rubble to construct temples of their own.

A bust of Akhenaten, also known as Amenhotep IV, depicting his unusually elongated face.

## Historical Revisionism

In the wake of Akhenaten's death, all his political, religious and artistic reforms were abolished as the old power elites restored Egyptian life to the way it had been for hundreds of years before. Almost all of the art and buildings created during Akhenaten's reign were defaced or destroyed in the years immediately following his death, although some were incorporated into the temples and tombs of subsequent pharaohs. To ensure the eradication of all trace of Atenism, and anyone associated with this unfortunate period, all mention of Akhenaten, Tutankhamun and Ay (Tutankhamun' successor) were removed from official lists of pharaohs. Akhenaten's reforms had annoyed a great many people, who were determined to ensure that all memory of the man and his achievements were forgotten. King lists from that time on insisted that Akhenaten's father Amenhotep III was immediately followed by Horemheb. Akhenaten's name was banished forever.

For 3000 years, Akhenaten remained unknown and forgotten. It was not until the second half of the 1800s that archaeologists discovered information about him as they unearthed the few monuments that remained from his reign. The site of the lost city of Akhetaten at Amarna was found and partly recorded, first by scientists accompanying Napoleon's Egyptian expedition of 1798–1801, and later by a Prussian expedition in 1843. However, it wasn't until 1887 that the importance of the site became clear, when a cache of nearly 400 clay tablets inscribed in cuneiform was uncovered. Now known as the Amarna Letters, they are an archive of mostly diplomatic correspondence between the Egyptian administration and its representatives in what is modern-day Palestine. The name of Amenhotep IV occurs repeatedly in the correspondence, a name that had previously not been seen anywhere in Egypt. This sparked considerable interest in Amarna, leading to expeditions by Alessandro Barsanti and Sir Flinders Petrie in the early 1890s, and by Ludwig Borchardt in 1907–14. Borchardt excavated the northern and southern suburbs of the city, and uncovered the workshop of the sculptor Thutmose, where he found the now famous bust of Akhenaten's wife, Nefertiti.

All this archaeological work revealed the reign and radical innovations of Egypt's most idiosyncratic of pharaohs, finally restoring him to the pages of history. Our knowledge of the pharaohs of the Eighteenth Dynasty was finally completed in the 1920s, when Tutankhamun's tomb was discovered by the British archaeologist Howard Carter. Father and son had both been consigned to the dustbin of history

Due to the occasional collapse of Egyptian authority over the centuries, even the Egyptians of the Nineteenth Dynasty did not have complete records of the pharaohs who preceded them. Thus, although the Abydos King List implies that Rameses II was the 77th pharaoh since the dawn of time, he was in fact the 188th pharaoh since the reign of the first king, Menes.

because of their involvement in one of the world's most radical and momentous revolutions—the introduction of monotheism. However, the revolution was so hated by the traditional religious caste in ancient Egypt that they set out to destroy all memory of the heretic pharaoh and his blasphemy. It is ironic that while few people today would recognise the name of Menes, who unified Egypt, or Khufu, who built the great pyramid, or Rameses II, who expanded the boundaries of Egypt to their greatest extent, they do know the name of Tutankhamun, the son of the heretic pharaoh whose name was almost erased from history.

## Legacies

Akhenaten's impact was limited in Egypt itself, since his reforms lasted for only a short time, to be forgotten as rapidly as the pharaoh himself. It is, however, quite possible that his impact was felt elsewhere, as a small tribe of Semites in the land of Canaan started to speak about their god. Like Akhenaten's god, theirs also was the only god; a god of which no idol or graven image was permitted to be made; and one that could be worshipped in only one place, through the intercession of a divinely chosen individual. Perhaps Akhenaten's most important legacy exists as an echo in the next faith to declare its belief in a single god—Judaism.

Akhenaten's removal from the historical record also provides us with the world's first and most successful example of historical revisionism. There have been many attempts to rewrite history to suit the victor in some conflict, with varying degrees of success. Some have denigrated individuals or groups in order to 'prove' that they were in the wrong and that those who triumphed over them were in the right—the demonising of King Richard III being a case in point. On other occasions, such as the French Revolution, the past has been considered so obnoxious that it had to be completely eradicated, in order that a new historical era could begin. And, in the case of Mao Zedong's China, the nation's history was deliberately rewritten to conform with Mao's vision of it.

Similarly, during Stalin's tyrannical rule of the Soviet Union, a concerted effort was made to expunge the memory of Leon Trotsky, one of the leaders of the revolution with Lenin. After Trotsky tried unsuccessfully to oppose Stalin's rise to power in the 1920s, his days as a member of the leadership were numbered. He was first expelled from the Communist Party, then deported from the country, and finally murdered in exile on Stalin's orders. Thereafter, every mention of Trotsky as a leading figure in the Russian Revolution was revised over a period of two decades. He was 'edited' out of photographs that showed him with Lenin and other Bolsheviks. Official histories of the time refer to him only as an 'enemy of the people'. They make no mention

# THE ORIGINS OF MONOTHEISM

The worship of Aten, introduced into Egypt by Akhenaten, is the first verifiable example of monotheism in the world. Not surprisingly, there has been considerable discussion about a possible link between it and Judaism, the next great monotheistic faith to come out of the Middle East.

One of the first people to advance this theory was Sigmund Freud. He argued that Moses could have been a priest in the worship of Aten, and that he had been forced to leave Egypt with his followers during the counter-revolution that followed Akhenaten's death. This would mean that the Exodus story records the overthrow of monotheism in Egypt, and its transfer to Canaan by the exiled members of the cult. Scholars have debated this ever since. Most have strong objections, pointing out that the texts of the Torah do not have any similarities to Aten worship, except for the focus on a single god. They also point out that Atenism used visual imagery of the solar disc, whereas such imagery is not found in early Judaism. And they argue that the three most important Judaic expressions for God, 'Yahweh', 'Elohim' and 'Adonai' are not linguistically related to the name 'Aten'.

Arguments in favour of the theory point out that the Exodus story signifies that something important happened in Egypt, and that it involved a large number of people fleeing from that country. According to this view, any new religion is bound to generate a number of true believers who will remain converts for the rest of their lives. Since we now know that there was a purging of Atenism after the death of Akhenaten, it is possible that those who had been converted to the worship of Aten would have fled the country. And where would they have fled, but east, in the direction of the rising solar disc, the Aten itself? They then wandered the Sinai Desert for many years before entering the land of Canaan and introducing their worship of one god to the locals. As they intermingled with the native Semites, their religion merged with local religious customs to form a new religion—Judaism. It is widely accepted that there are clear resemblances between Akhenaten's 'Great Hymn to the Aten' and the Biblical Psalm 104.

The historical observation that Akhenaten's reign occurred some one hundred years before the time of Moses might seem to present a problem for this theory. However, a period of 300 years between the Aten worshippers' flight from Egypt and the emergence of Judaism would account for changes in the worship of the one god, and the emergence of the new religion.

of his work in bringing down Tsarist Russia and stabilising the rule of the Soviets, particularly his leadership of the Red Army during the civil war. Yet his reputation and legacy survived Stalin's best efforts at eradication.

Only in the case of Akhenaten has the ruler of an entire nation been so thoroughly eradicated from the historical record for such a long time. Yet for all the efforts of the state and religious authorities to remove all vestiges of the Amarna experiment, some consequences still reverberated in the years that followed Akhenaten's death. Post-Akhenaten Egyptian theology, though supposedly a restoration of the traditional worship of the old gods, had been subtly modified by the intrusion of monotheism. Where prior to Akhenaten's rule the chief Egyptian god Amun was merely the most important in the pantheon of deities, by the time of Rameses II, Amun had been fused with the concept of an animating spirit that was behind the existence of all the other gods, indeed of all of creation. This innovation of Ramessid theology was in reality a merging of the Amarna concept of a single, all-powerful god—the Aten—responsible for maintaining all of creation with the pre-eminent god of the New Kingdom pharaohs—Amun. Though the old gods were once again worshipped, their place in Egyptian world-view was forever diminished. According to German Egyptologist Professor Jan Assmann, this reorientation of Egyptian theology would be transmitted from the Age of Rameses right through to the Graeco-Roman era, and in fact is the genesis of the notion of a god who *is* all and is *in* all.

By the third century BC, when the Egyptian historian Manetho compiled a king list, knowledge of events during the Eighteenth Dynasty was obviously faulty. Although some names on Manetho's list can be linked to known historical rulers, others remain obscure. In Manetho's list, for example, the pharaoh who should correspond to Akhenaten is named Orus, while the one who should correspond to Tutankhamun is named Rathotis. We cannot assume that these are alternative names for the kings who actually reigned, so it would seem that attempts by the priests to eradicate all mention of Akhenaten had been successful.

# THE FORGERY THAT GAVE WORLDLY POWER TO THE POPES (C. 750 AD)

*'In imitation of our own power, in order that for that cause the supreme pontificate may not deteriorate, but may rather be adorned with power and glory even more than is the dignity of an earthly rule: behold we—giving over to the oft-mentioned most blessed pontiff, our father Sylvester the universal pope, as well our palace [...] as also the city of Rome and all the provinces, districts and cities of Italy or of the western regions; and relinquishing them, by our inviolable gift, to the power and sway of himself or the pontiffs his successors—do decree [...] and do concede that they shall lawfully remain with the holy Roman church.'*

**Donation of Constantine**

*'It is true that you may fool all of the people some of the time; you can even fool some of the people all of the time; but you can't fool all of the people all of the time.'*

**Abraham Lincoln**

### LIE

The Emperor Constantine ceded power over most of the Roman Empire to the popes, as shown by the document known as the *Donation of Constantine*.

### TRUTH

An unknown forger created this document to help the pope to assert his authority at a time when Rome was under threat from foreign invasion!

### CHIEF PARTICIPANTS

Constantine I ('The Great'), Roman Emperor, 306–337 AD
Pope Sylvester I, leader of the Catholic Church, 314–335 AD
Pepin the Short, King of the Franks, 751–768 AD
Pope Stephen II, leader of the Catholic Church, 752–757 AD

### THE STORY SO FAR

After the fall of the Western Roman Empire in 476 AD, Italy was ruled by a succession of foreign kings, while 'Roman' power was exercised by a Byzantine emperor based in Constantinople. In 540 AD, the emperor Justinian briefly achieved the impossible by winning back control of North Africa and Italy, but in 568 AD the Byzantines

A fresco showing Constantine I visited by Saints Paul and Peter in a dream.

179

were driven back by a Germanic people, the Lombards, who invaded from the north. By 600 AD, the Byzantines retained only a fraction of the Italian peninsula, including the city of Rome, which they administered through an exarch (governor) located at Ravenna. The city of Rome itself was managed by the pope, the Catholic Church being the only hierarchy that survived the collapse of the empire intact. But relations between the pope and the exarch were rarely easy, and easily boiled over into open opposition. Then the Lombards captured Ravenna, killing the exarch, and Pope Stephen II feared for his own safety and the future of Rome. Turning to the Frankish King Pepin the Short for help, he set in motion a chain of events that would bring undreamed of secular power to the papacy for the next 1000 years …

O n 21 February 1513, Pope Julius II died after a reign of ten years. Less than a year later, an anonymous satire, *Julius Excluded from Heaven*, was published. Believed to have been written by the Dutch humanist Desiderius Erasmus, it satirised Julius' worldly power and obsession with preserving territory he had inherited as pope—the Papal States. In one famous scene, Julius defends the pomp and ceremony of the papacy before the Gates of Heaven:

PETER: But tell me who first of all befouled and burdened with these ornaments of yours the Church that Christ wanted to be supremely pure and unencumbered?
JULIUS: What does that matter? The main thing is that I've got them, I possess them, I enjoy them. Some people do say that a certain Constantine transferred all the riches of his empire to pope Sylvester, armour, horses, chariots, helmets, belts, cloaks, guardsmen, swords, gold crowns (of the very finest gold), armies, machines of war, cities, entire kingdoms.
PETER: Are there any proper records of this magnificent donation?
JULIUS: None, except one codicil mixed in with some old decrees.
PETER: Maybe it's a fable.
JULIUS: I've often suspected as much. What sane man, after all, would bestow such a magnificent gift even on his own father? But when anyone has tried to question it, I've been able to silence him with a threat or two.

This scene satirises the incongruity of the popes possessing riches and territories in central Italy that they had acquired as the result of a lie. The lie, created in about 750 AD, was that the Emperor Constantine had bestowed his authority, together with most of the territories belonging to the Roman Empire, on the popes in Rome. This lie was used to legitimise the acquisition of lands, power, money and property for a thousand years.

## The Official Story—Constantine Bequeaths the Roman Empire to the Popes

Constantine had been emperor since his troops proclaimed him thus at the Roman garrison town of York in England in 306 AD. He was a man who knew how to reward his friends, and so it was that on 30 March 315 AD, he issued a letter to Pope Sylvester I in gratitude for his intercession in a frightening situation. The emperor was afflicted with leprosy, one of the most feared of diseases. His physicians had been unable to cure him, so he consulted the pagan priests in Rome, who advised him to soak in a bath filled with the blood of innocent babies. He issued the order, but the cries of the mothers made him change his mind. That night he was visited by the spirits of Saint Peter and Saint Paul, who told him to go in search of Pope Sylvester, who would cure him of his affliction. Sylvester had the emperor wear a hair garment in penance, then, after adopting the faith of the Catholic Church, he was immersed in water and the leprosy instantly vanished.

In gratitude for this miraculous cure, Constantine fell to his knees and granted the Vicar of St Peter—both the current occupant of the post and his successors—a series of generous gifts, which became known as the *Donation of Constantine*. First, the pope would be pre-eminent over the patriarchal sees of Antioch, Alexandria, Constantinople and Jerusalem, as well as over all other churches throughout the entire world. Second, the signs of supreme power—the diadem and sceptres, the imperial raiment and the Lateran Palace—would be transferred to the popes in perpetuity. Finally, Constantine decreed:'we have granted them our gift of land in the East as well as in the West; and even on the northern and southern coast [...] Judea, Greece, Asia, Thrace, Africa and Italy and the various islands [...] that all shall be administered by the hand of our most blessed father the pontiff Sylvester and his successors.'

After taking control of the empire, a succession of powerful popes ruled successfully over it; men such as Leo I, who saved Rome from the armies of Attila the Hun in 452 AD. The empire fell, however, and the power of the papacy declined. The *Donation* was all but forgotten, remaining hidden in the archives of the Lateran Palace until it was rediscovered during the pontificate of Leo IX in the mid-1050s. Leo was at that time in the process of restoring the power of the papacy, and he used the *Donation* to bolster his claim for universal jurisdiction over the Church, particularly the Church in the East. He failed, and the Roman Catholic and Eastern Orthodox churches split in what became known as the Great Schism. However, the *Donation* continued to be used by medieval popes to prove their ownership of the Papal States—a broad area of central Italy—and to assert their right to a position of pre-eminence in the Christian world.

## The Truth—The Papacy under Threat

Ever since the Lombards first entered Italy in 568 AD, the safety of Rome had been threatened. Driving back the Byzantine armies, the Lombards conquered more and more of Italy, until they had control of most of the peninsula. By 700 AD, only a few areas remained securely in Byzantine hands: the duchies of Rome and Naples, the Duchy of Calabria in the south, and a strip containing Ravenna and Venice in the northeast, while a narrow ribbon of heavily contested territory linked Ravenna and Rome.

In spite of the threat posed to them by the Lombards, relations between the pope in Rome and the Byzantine exarch in Ravenna were never easy. Over time, the papacy became increasingly resentful of having to take orders from the emperor's secular representative, and matters were not helped by a growing sense of frustration over a lack of military aid from Constantinople. The emperor had problems of his own in the form of Bulgars to the north and Arabs to the east, so was unable to help the Italians militarily. As a result, the papacy needed to take an ever-increasing role in defending Rome, usually through diplomacy, threats and bribery, but also by raising a Roman militia. Realising that if they didn't look after their own interests properly, no one else would, the popes of the early 700s became as much concerned with politics and state affairs as with theology and the spiritual welfare of their congregations.

Matters came to a head in 751 AD, when the Lombards stormed Ravenna and killed the Byzantine exarch. Realising that Rome could be next, Pope Stephen II travelled to Paris to plead for help from Pepin the Short, a duke of the powerful Frankish Empire. To encourage Pepin's compliance, Pope Stephen arranged for an elaborate ceremony at the Basilica of St Denis, where he anointed Pepin as King of the Franks, and conferred on him the title 'Patrician of the Romans'. In response, Pepin brought his armies into Italy, drove the Lombards out of Ravenna, and helped secure for Stephen a swathe of territory that would become the foundation of the future Papal States.

In 781 AD, Charlemagne (the son of Pepin the Short) stipulated the regions over which the pope would rule. These included the Duchy of Rome, Ravenna, the Pentapolis—on the Adriatic coast of the Italian peninsula—and parts of the Duchy of Benevento, Tuscany, Corsica, Lombardy and a number of Italian cities. The pope's authority was to be guaranteed by the Frankish Empire, which assumed the role of papal protector. Pepin the Short and then Charlemagne both acted as they did in large part because of the *Donation of Constantine*.

> The *Donation* forms part of an even larger series of forgeries referred to as the Pseudo-Isidorian Decretals, supposedly written by Isidore Mercator. Among the many rulings it documented, it decreed that eternal damnation awaited anyone who attempted to prosecute a bishop.

For it was at about that time that the *Donation* first came to light, and it seems likely that the document was produced by a cleric, either in Rome or at the Frankish court, with the aim of strengthening papal power in Italy. If it was devised in Rome, the *Donation* could be seen as an attempt to convince the Franks that the land the pope sought to control was originally church land, and that the Byzantines were usurpers. Alternatively, if the Franks themselves cooperated in creating the document, it could be seen as allowing Pepin to declare that he was returning papal lands to their rightful owner, the Church, rather than bestowing them by his own authority.

It has also been suggested that there may have been an older oral tradition about Constantine's donation, which the eighth-century forger felt he was simply helping to confirm. According to this view, the *Donation* would not have been seen as a cynical fabrication, but as an attempt to safeguard a truth that had been handed down from generation to generation. Since the original document was lost, it became necessary to re-create it in order to preserve a prerogative already possessed by the Church. But whatever the reason for its creation, the *Donation* provided a legal basis for the convenient political alliance between the Catholic Church and the Franks.

## Evidence of Fraud

The contents of the *Donation of Constantine* were widely accepted by Western Christendom without question for close on 500 years, which was understandable, given the trust and authority vested in the papacy. Over centuries, as the popes began to resemble secular princes, the Church made regular use of the *Donation* to ward off the territorial ambitions of France, Spain and Germany. Naturally, there were those who objected to the document on principle, believing that such power would not have been handed to the successors of St Peter, to whom Christ had given 'the keys to the Kingdom of Heaven'. And some had their own reasons, such as the Holy Roman Emperor Otto III (996–1002), who expressed doubts over the authenticity of the document. In his case, however, he was seeking to bolster his own power against that of the current pope, and needed to remove one of the pope's principal pillars of support.

It was not until the Renaissance—as classical learning was revived after almost a millennium in retreat—that it was possible to compare the *Donation* with authentic ancient Roman texts. Gradually, people started to realise that events portrayed in the *Donation* were at odds with the facts as described in many ancient documents. Finally, in 1440, a Catholic priest named Lorenzo Valla, a man who was also a humanist and a rhetorician, wrote an essay entitled 'Discourse on the Forgery of the Alleged Donation of Constantine' demonstrating that the *Donation* could not be genuine.

A fresco from the Vatican depicting the *Donation of Constantine*.

Valla based his arguments on a number of issues. First, he argued against the validity of the *Donation* from a lawyer's perspective, focusing on legal arguments. Second, he analysed its language, showing that the Latin in the document could not have been written in the year 324 AD. Although Valla was not able to fix the period in which it was written, the current consensus is that it was probably written around the time of the fall of the exarchate in Ravenna in 751 AD. Third, and most importantly, he identified a number of historical irregularities and anachronisms within the body of the text. Some of the major inconsistencies are detailed below.

*Historical anomalies:* First, the *Donation* claimed that Constantine passed jurisdiction of the empire to the papacy in 315 AD. Yet there are documents proving that Constantine continued ruling after the date mentioned in the *Donation*. There is also no evidence that Sylvester began administering the empire from 315. Second, there were numerous Roman emperors crowned after the reign of Constantine, such as Theodosius the Great. They should not have ruled if the claims of the *Donation* were correct.

*Historical anachronisms:* The *Donation* refers to Constantinople as one of the patriarchal sees, alongside Rome and Jerusalem. Valla correctly pointed out that, at the time of the supposed *Donation*, not only was Constantinople not a patriarchate, but it hadn't even been built (the city was consecrated in 330 AD). There was also confusion over the nature of the diadem given to Sylvester in token of his new role. The *Donation* describes it as made of gold, but the Romans in the West only ever used diadems made of cloth, expressing contempt for kings of the East who wore such trinkets. A golden diadem would also have been too like a crown, which the Romans would never have tolerated.

> Although Constantine halted the persecutions of the Christians, and later claimed that he owed his victory to the God of the Christians, he did not formally accept the Christian God during his reign. He continued the traditional worship of pagan gods and was only baptised on his deathbed.

*Incorrect terminology:* Parts of the *Donation* refer to members of Constantine's retinue of courtiers as 'satraps'. This is anachronistic, as Roman officials of the time were never referred to in that way. There were praetors, aediles and others, but the higher officials known as satraps appear only in the middle of the eighth century—at the time when the *Donation* is thought to have been forged. Then there was the reference to the people of Rome as a 'subject people'. They should properly have been referred to as the Senate and the People of Rome. Finally, the clergy were referred to as 'patricians and consuls', but in imperial Rome there was never a position known as a 'patrician' and there were only ever two consuls.

Another error that Valla did not identify is confusion over dates. The Romans dated years by naming the consuls who were in office at the time, and the *Donation* refers to the year 315 AD as falling in the fourth consulship of Constantine and a certain Galligano. However, Galligano is not a Roman name from the time of the empire. What the forger probably meant was Gallicanus, but he was not consul until 317 AD. The only year in which Constantine (for the seventh time) and Gallicanus were consuls together was 329 AD, but even so the mismatch of names and dates remains.

Not surprisingly Valla's groundbreaking work was not well received by the Vatican. Instead, the papacy simply stopped appealing to the *Donation* in power and territorial disputes, and even placed Valla's book on its list of banned publications. It was not until the early seventeenth century that the Catholic Church officially accepted that the *Donation* was a forgery of the eighth century, and not an authentic document from the fourth.

## Legacies

The immediate legacy of the *Donation of Constantine* was the creation of the Papal States, a large area of Italy that became the focus of wars and disputes for the next 1000 years (see page 188). It can also be said to have set the Catholic Church on a quest for power and money that would lead to its corruption and the eventual collapse of the unity of Western Christendom during the Reformation.

Responsibility for the Papal States involved the popes in the politics of the Italian peninsula, which had two effects. First, it meant that leaders of the Church began to be more interested in the temporal world rather than in the spiritual; and, second, that since they were the rulers of a state, unscrupulous and ambitious individuals would seek to become head of the Church in order to rule over its lands. This meant that just when the popes had freed themselves from the Byzantine emperors, they became mired in the murky world of local Italian politics. Efforts by the popes to reinforce their authority and their territorial claims led to a never-ending series of wars, both local and international. One of these was a dispute with the Holy Roman Empire, which brought political turmoil to northern and central Italy for over three centuries. It was only in the sixteenth century that the papacy could claim genuine control over all its territories. By then the papal territory had expanded greatly and the pope was one of Italy's most important secular rulers as well as head of the Church.

Perhaps the most important consequence of the *Donation* flowed from its assertion that the pope was the ruler of the territories of the Roman Empire, since many medieval states considered that they descended from the glorious achievement that was Rome. This welded a diverse group of people into a shared partnership, that even the dissolution of the Western Empire in 476 AD could do little to shake. Successor states in Europe during the Middle Ages, such as Spain, France and Germany were still welded together by the ghost of the Roman Empire. And many empires that followed all claimed to be the heirs of Rome, even down to the twentieth century: The Holy Roman Empire, Napoleon's empire and even Mussolini's fascist Italian state. In the Middle Ages, however, because Europeans saw themselves principally as Christians, regardless of where they lived, their sense of a shared heritage acted as a glue to keep

Constantine, on the right, handing over his crown and imperial power to Pope Sylvester I.

them united. This accounts for the term given to that united entity—Christendom—and thus the belief that the popes had supreme authority within Christendom.

This sense of a shared Roman heritage meant that people in the West always looked respectfully on papal authority, while the popes themselves, when challenged, would produce the *Donation of Constantine* to show that they were successors not just of St Peter, but of the Roman emperors themselves. And they were helped by the fact that people in Western Europe for a long time did not think of themselves as belonging to a nation state, such as England, France, Germany or Spain. The principal reason for this was the feudal system, which encouraged people to see themselves as subjects of a higher local authority and not members of a state as such. Thus the peasant was in the service of a knight, who was in the service of a duke, who was in the service of the king, who fought wars of conquest for his own personal fiefdom or dominion, not for a state or nation. This is why the popes could wield such power in

# FALL OF THE PAPAL STATES

At their height, during the eighteenth century, the Papal States included most of central Italy—Latium, Umbria, Marche, and the Legations of Ravenna, Ferrara and Bologna, extending north into the Romagna. Also included were the small enclaves of Benevento and Pontecorvo in southern Italy, and the larger Comtat Venaissin around Avignon in southern France. It took only a few decades for the popes to lose almost all this territory in the social and political upheavals of the first half of the nineteenth century. By 1870, Italy was completely unified, thanks to the armies of Giuseppe Garibaldi, leaving only Rome and parts of Latium in the hands of the pope.

In 1870, the new Italian government declared war on the last of the Papal States, and Rome was captured with minimal fuss. The invasion was denounced by Pope Pius IX, but to no avail. The government presented the pope with the option of being left in charge of the old Leonine City, on the west bank of the Tiber, but Pius dismissed the proposal. Deciding to show how impotent the pope actually was, in 1871 the government moved the capital of Italy from Florence to Rome. The pope retreated into the Vatican, all the while protesting against the illegal seizure of his territory. He declared that he was now a prisoner, and that he would never again venture forth or set foot in St Peter's Square until he was liberated. Pius also forbade all Italian Catholics from taking part in elections in the new Italian state, on pain of excommunication.

To the pope's surprise, the Italian state did not fail, nor did other Catholic nations come to his aid. It took 50 years for the popes to recognise the futility of their position. In 1929, Pius XI abandoned claims to the Papal States and signed the concordat with Mussolini that created the State of the Vatican City, forming the sovereign territory of the Holy See. This is now the only existing remnant of the Papal States that were created 1200 years earlier under the privileges granted through Pepin's acceptance of the *Donation of Constantine*.

medieval Europe, since they were at the top of a chain of authority that unified the peoples of Europe spiritually. It was only with the dissolution of the feudal system in the fifteenth century that the growing merchant and middle classes needed to identify themselves as something other than Christians or servants of a lord. This led to the new concept of a geographical region that provided a common bond linking each individual to others sharing a similar economic and cultural heritage.

Over time, this concept of common unity gave way to the concept of a nation, with people seeing themselves as members of a state. This change was at odds with the idea of a unified Western Christendom, with the pope as its head. The Church demanded unity and obedience to the spiritual head, while the state demanded obedience to the temporal head—a king, queen or governing body.

With the rise of the nation-state and the Reformation came the final fragmentation of what was left of the Roman Empire in the West. The existence of the *Donation of Constantine* aided this process of fragmentation. Wealthy bishops ruled their dioceses, and many high-ranking churchmen saw the Church as a means of achieving authority, not only over the humble faithful, but over princes, kings and emperors as well. The nobility saw the Church as a means of consolidating more power in their hands, and were thus the principal source of recruits for posts as archbishops and cardinals. There was also an extraordinary amount of wealth invested in the Church, leading many in authority to spend too much time and effort tending these worldly treasures.

Those who would reform the Church were contemptuous of its laxity and softness, demanding harsher rules for the clergy and the congregations, as well as a stricter interpretation of the Bible. While the would-be reformers had some legitimate grievances, the papacy was never going to change a system that was working so well for those in power. Given the papacy's history of centralising power, and its views on its own role in setting Church doctrine and policy, the confrontational approach of Protestant reformers was only ever going to end in conflict and division.

# THE BETRAYAL OF THE KNIGHTS TEMPLAR (1312 AD)

*'If some among them [the Templars] are innocent, it is expedient that they should be assayed like gold in the furnace and purged by proper judicial examination.'*
**King Philip IV of France**

*'The dictum that truth always triumphs over persecution is one of the pleasant falsehoods which men repeat after one another till they pass into commonplaces, but which all experience refutes.'*
**John Stuart Mill**

### LIE

The Knights Templar were heretics who worshipped false idols.

### TRUTH

The Knights Templar were destroyed because they were a rich order of military monks who owed allegiance to the pope and thus stood outside the authority of the nation-state!

### CHIEF PARTICIPANTS

Philip IV ('The Fair'), King of France
Pope Clement V, leader of the Catholic Church
Jacques de Molay, Grand Master of the Order of the Knights Templar

### THE STORY SO FAR

In the victorious aftermath of the First Crusade, many young aristocrats were inspired to take up the cross in order to protect pilgrims travelling to Jerusalem and the Holy Land. One particularly dedicated group decided to become a religious military order—a band of knights who would take monastic vows in the service of the Church. They were constituted by the pope in 1119 with the title, Poor Knights of Christ and of the Temple of Solomon; hence, the abbreviated English name, Knights Templar. Owing obedience only to the popes, they were originally very poor, but were soon granted considerable powers, enabling them to travel between countries without the consent of the kings whose territories they crossed, and to set up chapter houses across the length

King Edward I of England paying homage to Philip IV, King of France.

and breadth of Europe. Drawn mainly from the ranks of the nobility, the order became extremely wealthy, investing its profits in land. As long as the Templars were dedicated to fighting Muslims, all was well. Problems arose, however, when the crusader kingdoms in the East fell one by one, with the final outpost in Acre surrendering in 1291. The Templars then became a military order without a purpose, but with some vague dream of reclaiming the Holy Land. It was then that the monarchs of Europe turned their worried gaze upon them, in particular King Philip IV of France …

Aprominent critic of the government is seized outside his place of work in broad daylight by government security forces under orders from the head of state. He is taken to an interrogation cell, tortured for a week and made to sign a false confession detailing his crimes against society. He is then forced to make accusations against other members of his organisation, which are used by the government as an excuse to round up further supposed enemies of the state. He is then kept in prison for two years until a show trial can be arranged, at which he does not attempt to answer the charges brought against him. After a trial lasting a year, he is imprisoned for another four years until he is finally sentenced and executed in a public ceremony.

Such events might not have been unusual in Hitler's Germany, Stalin's Soviet Union or Mao Zedong's communist China. However, this travesty of justice occurred 700 years ago in medieval France, when a monstrous lie was concocted that led to the destruction of a great and noble military fraternity. In the name of greed, and because of the pride of a malevolent monarch, the order of Knights Templar was accused of villainy and heresy, and its leaders executed by being burned at the stake.

## The Official Story—The Crimes of the Templars

Rumours began to circulate in 1305. There was talk of blasphemy, devil worship and other bizarre practices performed by members of one of the pillars of the Church—the militant order of monks, the Knights Templar. To head off accusations being made by disgruntled outcasts of the order, the Templar Grand Master, Jacques de Molay approached Pope Clement V in 1307 to discuss the matter. The French pope agreed that the accusations were false, but Clement felt obliged to write to King Philip IV of France, seeking his help in an investigation. The king, as the paramount Christian sovereign in Europe, was deeply troubled by what he heard.

The Grand Master then spent the summer of 1307 in Paris, where he spoke to the king. Although Philip did have some concerns, Jacques de Molay left reassured that there were going to be no problems with the investigation. Returning to Poitiers, where the pope was in residence, he requested that Clement establish an inquest to swiftly exonerate the order and end the malicious gossip. Clement, being his friend, did as he was asked, declaring that the inquest would meet on 24 August 1307. Philip was disturbed by this development, suspecting that it might lead to a sham investigation in order to cover up the truth about the Templars. Consequently, on 14 September, with utmost secrecy, he issued orders to arrest all Templars in the kingdom, including the Grand Master, and to confiscate their property.

During subsequent lengthy interrogations, the Templars confessed to a number of crimes, including forcing new recruits to deny Christ, followed by spitting upon, trampling or urinating on the image of Christ crucified. Each recruit was then made to kiss the Templar who received him on the mouth, the navel, the buttocks, the lower back and the penis. They declared that they worshipped a demon called Baphomet, who was conjured in the shape of a cat, a skull or a head with three faces. Cords that had been exposed to the demon's head were then tied around the waists of the Templar knights in an act venerating the demon. Finally, they were accused of betraying the Holy Land to the Muslims. These crimes shocked Christians everywhere, calling into question all deeds performed by the Templars in Europe and in the Holy Land.

Taken before royal interrogators, the Grand Master confessed only to 'denying Christ and trampling on the Cross' as part of the ritual of initiation. He was then ordered to dictate a letter commanding all Templars to confess to these acts. In light of these revelations, publicised by the French king, Pope Clement V ordered the arrest of all Templars throughout Christendom. Still disinclined to believe the stories, the pope sent two cardinals to Paris in December 1307 to put further questions to Jacques de Molay, who retracted the confessions he had made to the agents of the French King.

As commissions of inquiry were set up throughout Europe, the Grand Master was once again questioned, this time before representatives of both Clement and Philip, and once again he confessed to his crimes. Another two years were to pass before he and the other Templar knights were summoned to appear, by which time Jacques de Molay was silent regarding the charges made against him and his order.

The commissions of inquiry found the same stories repeated throughout other kingdoms of Europe where Templars were based. Having confessed, the Templar knights were unable to offer any defence against the charges brought against them, and by the time the Archbishop of Sens sentenced fifty-four Templars to be burned at the stake on 10–12 May 1310, the reputation of the order was in tatters. At the Council of Vienne in France, on 22 March 1312, the pope dissolved the military order and directed that its possessions be handed to another military order, the Knights Hospitaller.

Sergent del.

M.me De Cernel sculp.

1789

# PHILIPPE IV, SURNOMMÉ LE BEL,

## ROI DE FRANCE ET DE NAVARRE;

né à Fontainebleau en 1268; sacré à Rein

le 6 Janvier 1286; mort à Fontainebleau le 29 9.bre 1314.

The final act took place in 1314, when Jacques de Molay and Geoffrey of Charney, preceptor of the knights in Normandy, both recanted their confessions, declaring the order innocent of all charges. King Philip declared them relapsed heretics and ordered that they be burned at the stake. On the evening of 18 March 1314, Jacques de Molay and Geoffrey of Charney were taken to the Ile-des-Javiaux in the River Seine where they were burned. That night, after the fires were extinguished and the French nobles had returned to their many pleasures, a large number of Parisian locals, including some nearby monks, searched through the embers for the charred bones of the dead Templars. These would be kept for the day when the men's honour would be redeemed and their relics venerated.

## The Truth—Envy and Greed

If anyone needed a public relations officer it was surely the Templars. Administered by men who were clever, ruthless and rich, the organisation had received a lot of bad publicity over the years. Regardless of the rumour and innuendo, however, the truth was that the Templars were simply a religious order, nothing more and nothing less. They were established after the fall of Jerusalem during the First Crusade by Hugh of Payns, a knight who envisioned a community of his fellows that would follow the rules of a monastic order. Their principal purpose was to protect pilgrims in the Holy Land. In 1119, Hugh and eight other knights took vows of poverty, chastity and obedience before the Latin Patriarch of Jerusalem. Thus was born 'The Poor Fellow-Soldiers of Christ and of the Temple of Solomon', who in time became known as the Templars. By 1129, they had received approval from the Church to be recognised as a new monastic order and had convinced the Cistercian abbot St Bernard of Clairvaux to draw up the 73 clauses of the Templar Rule of Life. This meant that the Templars effectively became an offshoot of the Cistercian order, following many Cistercian rules, but with extensions covering military matters.

The focus from the start was on recruiting men from the nobility, regardless of whether they had wives or not. Whatever their marital status, all knights had to observe strict monastic rules. They were compelled to sleep dressed in a shirt, breeches, belt and shoes, with the lights on. They had to eat in silence, with meat restricted to three meals a week. Friday was a fast day, and for the six months between the feast of All Saints and Easter, knights had to eat a minimal amount of food. In common with all monastic orders, they also had to celebrate the regular daily round of prayer and worship.

There were three main causes for the downfall of the Templars. First, creating a military unit with monastic discipline resulted in a standing army of the sort not seen in Europe since the fall of the Roman Empire in the West. This was a force that

Portrait of Philip the Fair, at the time the most powerful monarch in Europe.

owed no loyalty to a liege lord, and was thus outside the feudal system. The order was exempted from complying with local or national laws, as instructed by Pope Innocent II in his bull, *Omne Datum Optimum*, of 1139, which allowed the Templars to move without restraint through all the countries of Christendom. The order didn't have to pay any taxes, and since they were under the direct control of the popes, they didn't have to answer to anyone else, not even the kings in whose lands they had established their headquarters. This was a potentially dangerous situation, and one that concerned many rulers.

The second reason for the order's downfall was their wealth. After they had been formally recognised by the pope, they became one of the most favoured charities in Christendom. As with other monastic orders, the Templars all took vows of individual poverty, but, in common with most monastic orders, they received enormous sums of money from donations and investments. Adroit management of assets was to make the Templars one of the richest organisations in Europe.

While the order's principal duty was to serve in a military capacity, only a tiny proportion of its members was deployed to fight in the Holy Land. The remainder acted in supporting roles, helping the fighting knights individually or administering finances. These non-combatants outnumbered the fighting knights seven to one. The costs of running the order, including maintaining a presence in the crusader states, was astronomical. It has been estimated that a fully armed knight with his attendant squires and sergeants cost as much to maintain as a heavy tank in a modern army. To generate the funds needed to manage such a large operation, the Templars bought large estates in Europe and the East, and also invested the wealth of individual members. It was not uncommon for noblemen who participated in the crusades to place all their assets under Templar management while they were abroad. These would be invested, yielding significant financial returns.

With this combination of bequests and investments, the Templars created extensive financial networks across Europe and the Holy Land, their wealth and activities making them conspicuous in medieval society. The wealth also generated envy, with the result that it was not uncommon for people to accuse them of avarice, and for greedy kings to cast envious eyes on their grand castles and large cash reserves, conscious always of their own lack of funds.

---

It is believed that the only Templar admission that was true was that they denied Christ and trampled on the Cross. The Templars did this in order to desensitise themselves should they ever be captured by Muslims and forced to desecrate the Cross and deny their faith. For many years, the date of the arrest of the Templars—Friday 13 October 1307—was thought to be the origin of the unlucky Friday 13th superstition. This is not the case.

---

The final reason for the fall of the Templars was the collapse of the crusader kingdoms, which left them without any real role. Without pilgrims to protect or assets to defend, they no longer had any reason to exist. After Jerusalem was lost to Saladin, Sultan of Egypt and Syria, in 1187, the Templars were forced to move their headquarters to the seaport of Acre (located in modern-day northern Israel), which they held until 1291. When the crusaders were finally forced out of the Holy Land altogether, European monarchs began to withdraw their support for the order. While the Templars were defending the Holy Land, Christian sovereigns were prepared to accept that the order was outside their control. They were, however, distinctly uneasy about a powerful army that had lost its main purpose, that owed them no allegiance, was able to move freely through their lands, and was answerable only to the pope.

Times had changed, and by the end of the thirteenth century the popes were making strenuous claims for authority over all the kings of Christendom. They were hampered only by the lack of a standing army to enforce the papal will. Now, with the Templars stationed throughout Europe under the command of the pope, all it needed was for one pope to issue a fateful command to overthrow all royal authority and replace it with the rule of the papacy. The popes had already destroyed the Hohenstaufen dynasty in Germany during the thirteenth century, without help from the Templars, who were busy at the time defending the last of the crusader kingdoms. Now that the Templars were free, what more could the papacy achieve with such a force at its disposal? This was a possibility that alarmed many European monarchs, particularly Philip IV of France.

## The Final Act

Philip IV was a tall and attractive man with pale features. He was also cold, stern, humourless, stubborn and vindictive, and determined to strengthen the French monarchy at any cost. One contemporary critic, Bernard Saisset, Bishop of Pamiers, said of Philip: 'He is neither man nor beast. This is a statue.' In a troubling sign of what was to come, the bishop was arrested in 1301 for his insolence and charged with heresy, simony, sorcery, treason, fornication and blasphemy.

Tension between Philip and the Templars erupted suddenly as a result of a simple request. Philip was desperately short of funds for his war against the English, and he asked the Templars for a loan. They refused, claiming that the primary purpose of their wealth was to recover the Holy Land. Philip was therefore forced to issue a decree allowing him to tax the French clergy, and tried to get Pope Boniface VIII to excommunicate the Templars. Boniface refused, excommunicating Philip instead and issuing a papal bull in 1302 asserting that he had supreme authority over everyone on earth. Philip then hatched a plot to kidnap Boniface on the usual false charges of sodomy, blasphemy and heresy, and sent French troops to invade the papal palace at Anagni. The plot failed, but Boniface's health deteriorated and he died within a month, to be replaced by a weak and vacillating Frenchman, Clement V, in 1305. Events at once began to move more rapidly. Philip used the accusations of former disgruntled Templars to begin an investigation into the order. Before Clement could get the formal investigation underway, Philip had arrested the Grand Master and all Templars throughout France and seized all the order's property.

Under instruction from Philip, the Templars were tortured to extract confessions of their various 'crimes'. Members of the order were placed on the rack, where their limbs were stretched to a point where joints were dislocated. Others were suspended from their wrists, which were tied behind their backs. Many had fat rubbed into the soles of their feet which were placed before a fire. All were kept in chains, given only bread and water, and denied sleep. It was little wonder that the men confessed to any crime they were accused of. When Philip declared the Templars guilty of heresy, simony, sorcery, treason, fornication and blasphemy, Pope Clement refused to believe the charges, since Philip had used the very same ones against other opponents in the past.

## THE CURSE OF THE GRAND MASTER

After being imprisoned for several years, Jacques de Molay, Grand Master of the Knights Templar, stood up and recanted his forced confession. In fury, King Philip IV ordered that he be burned at the stake as a relapsed heretic. On 18 March 1314, Jacques was duly brought to the Ile-des-Javiaux in Paris to face his terrible fate. He asked to be tied facing Notre Dame cathedral, with his hands bound together in prayer. Showing great courage, he died singing hymns, even as the flames rose around him. As the flames reached their peak, his voice thundered from the inferno with an awful prophecy—Pope Clement and King Philip would soon meet him before God. This last despairing cry was probably given little thought by the two men the Grand Master had both served and trusted. However, as fate would have it, Clement was dead within a month, and Philip would die before the end of the year in a hunting accident.

Philip increased the pressure, whipping the Parisian mob into a frenzy as it demanded action against the blasphemers. Clement finally gave in, issuing the bull *Pastoralis Praeeminentiae,* which directed all Christian kings to detain the Templars and seize their assets. Dozens of Templars were burned at the stake during the show trials that followed. Finally, with Philip threatening to use force unless Clement agreed to obey his requests, the pope acquiesced. At the Council of Vienne in 1312, he issued the papal bull *Vox in Excelso*, which officially dissolved the order. It was a spineless act that betrayed the principles that his predecessors had so carefully built up since the 1050s, and exposed the papacy as a potential puppet of any ruler ruthless enough to impose his will on it.

Although Clement, in a small act of rebellion, decreed that Templar assets were to be turned over to the Knights Hospitaller, Philip seized the considerable Templar treasury located in Paris for himself. Two years later, the Grand Master met his fate at the stake, and the history of the grandest and most successful military order of the Middle Ages ended in ignominy and shame. It would take 700 years before the Vatican finally laid the ghosts of the Templars to rest. When transcripts of the trials were finally published in 2007, they confirmed what many had already known—that Clement had initially absolved the Templars of the crime of heresy, only to reverse his decision under pressure from Philip.

## Legacies

The Knights Templar were one of the medieval papacy's principal supports, and their destruction helped to cripple the power of the papacy, leading to the rise of the nation-state. The power of the popes was built on the militarisation of the Catholic Church, principally as a result of the crusades. Previously, papal claims were merely empty phrases, with no real weight behind them. Any powers the popes exercised involved the spiritual manipulation of kings, with threats of excommunication. The creation of military orders, such as the Templars, provided the papacy with a force that was not beholden to any temporal power. The popes used the military orders to bolster their claims to power, and the orders supported the expanded role of the papacy. The fact that these military orders could boast a presence in every European state meant that the pope had a body of soldiers willing and able to carry out his instructions.

With the loss of the Holy Land and the crusading spirit fading, the popes were under pressure to abandon their power to the emerging European nations. The destruction of the Templars sent a clear signal that the militant Christianity proposed by the medieval popes—and so warmly endorsed by St Bernard—was on the wane. Philip IV's reign began the decline of papal power, and the removal of an organisation that was the embodiment of a universal Christendom created a vacuum in the power structures of Europe that was filled by the emerging nation-states. As author Piers Paul Read points out, the popes 'failed to see, until it was too late, the threat posed by the predatory nation-state. Who could have envisaged that the grandson of Saint Louis [King Louis IX of France] would be the instrument for the downfall of the Roman pontiffs?'

These nation-states and their rulers no longer had the welfare of Christendom as their primary concern. They were now mostly worried about events within their own realms, and with their subjects, who were beginning to regard themselves as citizens of the realm, rather than primarily as Christians within Christendom. This crucial change robbed the popes of their most potent weapon in the fight against the rise of the nation-state. It was only a matter of time before the nation-states turned against the inheritors of the Roman Empire—the popes—to assert their long-suppressed desire for independence. When this happened it tore Europe apart. Longing to overthrow—or at least curtail—the reach of Rome in their courts, they eagerly grasped at the opportunity afforded by the Reformation to sever their ties with Rome.

The presumed guilt of the Templars was used by Protestants and sceptics during the Reformation as a stick with which to beat the Catholic Church. The Anglican divine, Thomas Fuller, wrote that it was 'partly their viciousness, and partly their wealth' that caused the Templars' 'final extirpation'. Even the great eighteenth-century English historian Edward Gibbon referred to 'the pride, avarice and corruption of these Christian Soldiers.' It was this perception of the Templars, based on the lies told about them in their final years, that formed the basis of the description of the Templars in Sir Walter Scott's novel *Ivanhoe*. Scott describes the Templar Brian of Bois-Guilbert as being 'stained with their usual vices; pride, arrogance, cruelty, and voluptuousness'.

Legends that built up around the Templars have been used in modern times to construct elaborate fantasies about secrets the order was supposed to possess, secrets that would cast doubt over the basic tenets of Christianity. Many of these stories rely on the fact that the Templars' first headquarters was on Jerusalem's Temple Mount, which they occupied for 75 years. This is where the ruins of the Temple of Solomon are situated and where the Ark of the Covenant was supposed to have been kept. Modern conspiracy theorists claim that the Templars discovered documents hidden on the Temple Mount which 'proved' that Jesus either survived the crucifixion—or was never crucified in the first place—and that he married Mary Magdalene and had children with her. The purpose of the fantasy is to convince people that the core belief of Christianity is a lie. Since the resurrection of Jesus lies at the heart of Christian faith, without it everything else collapses like a house of cards. The fantasists seek to turn St Paul's words into reality: 'If Christ has not been raised, your faith is vain.' Unsurprisingly, since Jerusalem had been in Christian hands for 300 years until its capture by the Muslim Arabs, there is no evidence to support the belief that the Templars discovered something on Temple Mount. Nor is there any evidence to suggest that the order was destroyed because they discovered such a secret. Other legends woven around the Templars link them to freemasonry, or claim that the Holy Grail, used by Christ at the Last Supper, was found by the order and taken to Scotland or Northern Spain during the suppression of the Templars in 1307.

Strange as it may seem, the final chapter in the history of the Templars is still to be written. In 2008, members of the Association of the Sovereign Order of the Temple of Christ, a group claiming to be the heirs of the Knights Templar, launched a lawsuit in Spain against the Catholic Church. They were seeking compensation for the estimated 100 billion euros worth of property confiscated when the order was dissolved. Where money is concerned, it would seem that nothing is ever truly forgotten.

# THE FICTION THAT JUSTIFIED D-DAY (1944)

*'You will bring about the destruction of the German war machine, the elimination of Nazi tyranny over the oppressed peoples of Europe, and security for ourselves in a free world.'*
**General Dwight D. Eisenhower**

*'In wartime, truth is so precious that she should always be attended by a bodyguard of lies.'*
**Winston Churchill**

## LIE

The Allies needed to open a second front to help the Soviet Union defeat the Nazis.

## TRUTH

The Allies needed to invade France to ensure that they were able to reach Germany before Soviet troops got there!

## CHIEF PARTICIPANTS

Franklin D. Roosevelt, 32nd President of the United States of America
Winston Churchill, Prime Minister of Great Britain
Joseph Stalin, leader of the Soviet Union

## THE STORY SO FAR

In September 1939, after forging a pact with the Soviet Union, German forces invaded Poland, starting the European phase of World War II. By 1940, Germany had subdued Belgium, the Netherlands and France, and had intervened in Greece to help its Italian ally. The Blitzkrieg had overcome all resistance, leaving Great Britain alone to take on the German military machine. Believing its western flank secure, in June 1941 Germany invaded the Soviet Union, launching the Eastern Front. Stalin, who only three years previously had drastically thinned the ranks of the Soviet military during the Great Purge, found his army ill prepared to fight the Nazis. He pleaded with the Allies to launch a second, Western Front as soon as possible. Britain was keen on a second front, but wanted to launch it from North Africa, penetrating 'Fortress Europe' via the exposed Italian peninsula. With America's entry into the war in December 1941, the Soviet Union tried to get them to agree to launch a second front in France. Nothing happened until the 1943 Tehran Conference, when Great Britain, the United States and the Soviet Union agreed to the creation of a second front in France. The planning of Operation Overlord had begun …

D-Day, 6 June 1944. A landing craft vacated by invasion troops points towards a fortified beach on the Normandy coast as American soldiers wade to shore under heavy German machine-gun fire.

———— ❧ ✦❀✦ ❧ ————

Monday 2 June 2004 was the sixtieth anniversary of the Normandy landings—the first phase of the Allied invasion of northwest Europe. Gathered together on a cliff top at the French coastal town of Arromanches-les-Bains were world leaders, including those from the United States, France, Germany and Great Britain, all present to commemorate events that took place on that spot so many years before. Veterans who could, marched in their blue blazers and berets, pushing their frailer companions in wheelchairs. There were speeches, glasses raised in toasts, and promises made to remember always the great Allied counter-offensive against Germany; the beginning of the end for Hitler's tyrannical regime. The same platitudes are repeated almost every year and, like all good myths, they are uplifting and inspirational. That is not to denigrate the sacrifices and the lives lost during the Normandy landings, but history tells a different tale, one that questions the need for the Normandy landings and asks why so many brave young men had to lose their lives on those beaches so long ago.

The stated goal of the Normandy landings was to breach Hitler's 'Fortress Europe', and to bring an end to the war. While this was certainly a goal, it was not the main point of the operation. Its principal purpose was really to prevent the entry into Europe of an enemy America and Britain feared even more than Hitler—the Soviet Union. The second front was opened in order to stop Soviet troops from overrunning Germany and gaining access to its scientists and the advanced technology they had been busy developing. The real success of the Normandy landings, and the operations that followed, was in preventing the Soviet Union—and the 'scourge' of communism—from dominating Europe.

## The Official Story—A Second Front

Stalin was desperate, paranoid and deeply afraid. His desperation stemmed from the fact that his armies had been driven back with horrendous casualties, leaving the Soviet Union's extensive oilfields exposed to the German onslaught. His paranoia focused on his belief that the Allies had abandoned him to face Hitler's war machine alone while they regrouped. His fear stemmed from his rash decision in the mid-1930s to purge his army chiefs, leaving him with a fighting force that was short of experienced officers. As December 1941 approached, what Stalin really wanted for Christmas was a second front opened against Germany somewhere in Europe. He had to wait until 1942, however, for Allied leaders to feel that the time was right to commit to such a move, in principle at least.

By that stage, a second front was considered vital. France had fallen in 1940, Greece was under occupation, Britain and its Commonwealth allies were fighting the Nazis in North Africa, and the Soviet Union was bearing the full brunt of invading

German forces. Accordingly, Roosevelt, Churchill and Stalin issued a joint statement announcing that a second front was urgently needed. But, at the same time, Churchill informed Soviet Foreign Minister Molotov that the Allies lacked the resources to undertake an invasion. This was partly due to the weakness of the British, and partly to the recent entry into the war of the United States, which needed time to build up troop numbers and armaments production.

While the British preferred to attack Germany from the south via Italy—seen as Europe's weak underbelly—the Americans were strongly in favour of an attack via the shortest route, using Britain as a base. The preliminary proposal for a full-scale invasion was named Operation Roundup, which foresaw an invasion in 1943. It was this proposal that formed the basis of the plan that eventually became Operation Overlord, which was delayed until June 1944.

The formal process for organising the invasion did not really get underway until after the Tehran Conference, held in late 1943 between Stalin, Churchill and Roosevelt. It was there that Roosevelt offered Stalin the guarantee he had been waiting for since June 1941. This was that the Americans and the British would open a second front in France in May 1944, designed to coincide with an escalation of Soviet attacks on Germany's eastern border. Responsibility for the operation was handed to the Supreme Headquarters Allied Expeditionary Force, commanded by General Dwight D. Eisenhower. General Sir Bernard Montgomery was named as commander of the invasion's ground forces, and he was asked to come up with the invasion plan.

Owing to limitations in the range of British air support, the Normandy coast was selected as the preferred landing site, although it presented a number of problems. The principal one was that it had only one usable port, Cherbourg, which was well protected by German fortifications, artillery and troops. A proposal to attack the port directly was rejected, partly because of difficulties the Allies had experienced in a raid on the Port of Dieppe in August 1942. Despite those problems, however, it was argued that landing on a broad front in Normandy would see the Allies ideally positioned for a thrust towards Paris and onwards to the German border. The Normandy coast was also poorly defended, since the Germans did not believe that an invasion would come at that point.

However, Field Marshall Rommel, who was in charge of German Atlantic coast defences, had recognised that existing defensive fortifications protected only the ports. He had accordingly initiated a program to improve defences along the beaches, although crucially, work on the Normandy sector was nowhere near complete by the time of the invasion.

To ensure that Operation Overlord would have the greatest possible chance of success, a series of phoney invasion plans were leaked to the Germans in the weeks leading up to the campaign. They included proposed attacks on the Pas de Calais, the Balkans, the south of France and, most brazen of all, 'Operation Fortitude

North', which purported to be an invasion plan of Norway. With preparations complete, a force of 156,000 British, Canadian and American troops crossed the English Channel on 6 June 1944 to land on the Normandy beaches and fight their way into history.

## The Truth—What about Italy?

The official reason given for launching the landings in Normandy was that this would open a second front in Europe to take the pressure off Soviet troops fighting on the Eastern Front. It was vital for the Western Allies to break into Hitler's 'Fortress Europe' in order to bring about a rapid end to the war. This explanation looks superficially plausible, but it ignores the fact that by June 1944 the Allies already had a second front—in Italy.

The Allies considered Italy a soft target for many reasons. Italian troops had not proved to be particularly effective in the war so far, the Italian government's commitment to the war was suspect, and there was a significant internal problem with anti-Fascist groups, keen to overthrow Italy's vainglorious leader, Benito Mussolini.

Churchill in particular was enthusiastic about prosecuting the war through Europe's 'soft underbelly'. According to Churchill, the British government believed the Anglo-American forces in North Africa, which had first hand experience fighting and defeating the Germans, should not be allowed to remain idle. Keen to pursue the enemy as continuously and intensively as possible, he pushed for the invasion and capture of Sicily as an important first step, with the full-scale invasion of Italy and the critical occupation of Rome as the way forward. This was one of the principal reasons why British and Commonwealth troops were so heavily involved in fighting the Germans in North Africa during 1942: the area was seen as an ideal launch pad for an invasion of Italy. Regardless of US President Franklin Roosevelt's supposed reservations about Churchill's plan, and his view that the Allied invasion should be launched in France, the Americans nevertheless provided significant troops and resources for the invasion of Italy.

The second front was accordingly opened in July 1943, when Allied troops landed in Sicily. They spent the next 12 months crossing to the Italian mainland and fighting their way northwards in what proved to be a gruelling campaign. When the Italians surrendered in September 1943, the Allies were confident that they could push through Italy very rapidly. But the Germans would have no talk of surrender. Hitler decided to regard Italy's capitulation as an act of disloyalty and accordingly treated the country as an occupied territory. Using Italy's mountainous terrain to their advantage, German troops put up stiff resistance, slowing the Allied advance significantly. Although Rome didn't fall to the Allies until June 1944, they were nevertheless making steady headway and seemed certain to be able to fight their way into Austria, France and Germany. In essence, therefore, the Allies were already in Europe. The Western Front had been created and vital German resources were being drained from the Eastern Front. Why, then, should the Allies invade Normandy? The answer was the West's bogeyman—the Soviet Union.

## THE CROSSWORD PANIC OF MAY 1944

During the planning for the Normandy landings, certain key activities and locations were given codenames. Thus the codename for the overall invasion was 'Operation Overlord'. As might be expected, all aspects of the operation, particularly the date and place of the landings were protected with the tightest possible security.

Preparations were reaching fever pitch in May 1944, when members of the British secret service noticed that crossword puzzles printed in the *Daily Telegraph* newspaper contained a surprisingly large number of words that were codenames relating to the coming invasion. The answers to two clues were 'Utah' and 'Omaha'—names that had been given to beaches in Normandy where American troops were to disembark. Shortly afterwards, crosswords were published containing the answers 'Mulberry', the codename for the floating harbour, and 'Neptune', a codename for naval support.

At first, security agents were tempted to dismiss the whole matter as a coincidence, but when a clue was given referring to a 'Big-Wig', with the answer 'Overlord', they began to worry that the crossword was somehow being used to warn the Germans. Two officers were duly despatched to interview the crossword compiler—a 54-year-old teacher named Leonard Dawe. After some close questioning, the agents became convinced that Dawe had no knowledge of the impending landings, and that his clues and their answers had indeed been a series of strange coincidences.

The Germans were losing the war. It was obvious to everyone by the end of 1943 that the Russians were going to overrun the overstretched German troops on the Eastern Front. Even without the Normandy landings, Germany would therefore have been defeated in late 1945, or possibly early 1946. However, the thought of the Soviets reaching Germany and seizing all its scientists filled Western leaders with horror. Suspecting—rightly as it turned out—that the Soviet Union would turn into an enemy after the fall of the Nazis, Western leaders decided that their troops

needed to get to Germany first. But what could they do, with the Italian campaign proceeding so slowly? The answer was an invasion designed to land a sufficient force in northern Europe so that they could get to Germany before Soviet troops had a chance to seize it all for themselves—the Normandy invasion.

The real objective of the Normandy landings could not be disclosed, since that would have alienated Stalin. The operation was therefore described as the great Western offensive to topple Hitler. While this was certainly a secondary reason for the invasion, the primary reason was always to halt the Soviet advance, which had the potential to go far beyond Germany. There was the possibility that Belgium, France, Greece and Italy might all be brought under Soviet control if communist troops were allowed to proceed unchecked. Such an outcome was unthinkable, and so it was that the Cold War began on those northern beaches in the early summer of 1944.

By early 1945, with the German military machine all but defeated, the need for secrecy was over and plans were drawn up to prevent Soviet troops from penetrating any further into Europe. 'Operation Unthinkable' was delivered to Churchill on 22 May by his Chief of Staff, Lieutenant General Sir Hastings Ismay. As the plan makes clear: 'The overall political object is to impose upon Russia the will of the United States and British Empire.'

## Fooling Stalin

Fear of the Soviet Union had been around since the Bolshevik Revolution of 1917. The West had been eager to support the White Russians during the Civil War of 1918–22, and hostility towards the Bolsheviks had not diminished during the intervening years. It was certainly important in Churchill's thinking, being one of the reasons why he advocated the invasion of Italy in 1943, believing that such an operation would create an obstacle for a Soviet advance into Europe. Churchill was a vehement anti-Bolshevik, and nothing had changed his view of Stalin as an enemy to be feared and watched, however useful he might be in the fight against Hitler.

In spite of his wariness of the Soviet Union, Churchill discussed the possibility of opening a second front against the Germans with Stalin as early as 1941. Both men knew that a second front was urgently needed to confront the victorious German military machine and to put pressure on Hitler. However, Churchill was always opposed to a second front in France, preferring to persevere with his plan to attack Italy. He secretly hoped that Germany and the Soviet Union would exhaust each other on the Eastern Front, leaving the Western powers free to deal with both of them easily when the time came. At the Tehran Conference in November 1943, Churchill, Stalin and Roosevelt discussed Operation Overlord in detail, and agreed

The legacy of D-Day: Checkpoint Charlie, with Russian and US tanks facing one another, 28 October 1961. After a 17-hour standoff, Russian tanks retreated from the border.

that an invasion of France should be launched in May 1944, even though it was already apparent that the war was no longer going smoothly for the Germans. In fact, within a few months it was evident that the Germans had over-reached themselves. While the Allies were making slow progress through Italy, the Russians had not only halted the German advance, but were pushing them back. Defeat for Germany seemed only a matter of time.

As it was, the struggle on the Eastern Front was to play a major role in the eventual defeat of Germany. In the months following the Normandy landings, the war in western Europe was fought between fifteen Allied and fifteen German divisions, whereas on the Eastern Front, more than 400 Soviet and German divisions battered each other for four years. Nearly 90 per cent of German military losses in World War II occurred on the Eastern Front in fighting that ranged from major tank battles to desperate house-to-house skirmishing that the Germans came to call Rattenkrieg—the Rats' War.

Yet it would seem that Stalin, at Tehran, could not yet see that the Germans were beginning to falter, and was accordingly desperate for another front to be opened in Europe. He did not predict—as the other Allies did—that the Germans would rapidly become overstretched and that Soviet forces would either hold them indefinitely or eventually overrun them. It was therefore in Stalin's interest to have another front opened in France. The Western Allies, particularly Roosevelt, were also eager for a new front in France, but for different reasons, and they did not want to appear to be too eager in case they aroused Stalin's suspicions about the true objective of Operation Overlord—which was to get to Germany before the Russians did.

Having seen how easily Hitler had fooled Stalin prior to the invasion of Poland in 1939, Roosevelt and Churchill manipulated Stalin at the Tehran conference. Roosevelt appeared to support Stalin, engaging his trust by expressing a desire to see the British Empire brought to heel in the aftermath of war. As American historian Robert Dallek writes: 'Roosevelt's candour was calculated to encourage Stalin to see the President as a trustworthy ally. He "ostentatiously" took Stalin's side in some of his disputes with Churchill.' Churchill, meanwhile, expressed his doubts about an attack through France, wishing to concentrate Western intervention in Italy. This appearance of disunity worked brilliantly, fitting perfectly with Stalin's view that the British were a major enemy and the principal force to be reckoned with. He failed to see the real objective of the Normandy invasion and failed to anticipate that America would become the dominant Western power after the war. The apparent disunity between Roosevelt and Churchill convinced him instead that there was no great Western conspiracy to oppose the Soviet Union. Instead, he believed that the Western nations were suspicious of each other, and therefore divided. Roosevelt and Churchill manipulated Stalin into believing that it was he who convinced them to launch the Western offensive, and that it was his 'alliance' with Roosevelt against Churchill that would ensure the outcome he wanted.

Roosevelt maintained this charade for the remainder of his presidency, always ensuring that any correspondence he drafted was positive towards Stalin and the Soviet Union, although he did occasionally express some personal doubts. During all his personal encounters with Stalin, he took great pains to develop a friendly camaraderie with the dictator. Since he had chosen to adopt a pro-Soviet role, he left it to others to become the anti-Bolshevik standard bearers. One of these was Churchill; another was Roosevelt's running mate for the 1944 election, the noted anti-communist Senator Harry Truman, who became president when Roosevelt died in April 1945.

Stalin eventually realised his mistake when the race for Berlin began between the Red Army and US troops. But by then it was too late. The Normandy landings had served their purpose, giving the West an opportunity to halt communism before it had a chance to overrun the whole of Europe.

## Legacies

The main legacy of the Normandy deception was that it achieved exactly what it set out to do: it prevented communism from gaining more of a foothold in Europe than it eventually did. But it was a close run thing. Hitler's major miscalculation was that the Soviet economy was fragile and that its obsolete and inferior military forces would break down under stress. He didn't believe that Stalin would sacrifice millions of his people to ensure victory, with the result that the German military was swamped by sheer weight of numbers. Soviet and American troops eventually met at the River Elbe on 25 April 1945, cutting Germany in two. Berlin and eastern Germany were taken under Soviet control, with northwest Germany, Denmark and Holland entering the American and British spheres of influence. It was this outcome that determined the front line in the coming ideological battles of the Cold War. Had it not been for the successful Normandy landings, the situation could have been much worse, with the Red Army overrunning all of Germany, and possibly occupying France and Italy as well.

In the aftermath of the war, the Soviet Union had to be satisfied with control over the eastern half of Europe. Stalin eagerly installed puppet regimes in East Germany, Poland, Romania, Hungary, Czechoslovakia, Bulgaria, Albania and Yugoslavia. The aim was to create a series of buffer states in order to prevent hostile nations from attacking the Soviet Union directly, something that would not have been necessary had Soviet troops overrun the whole of the continent. The Normandy landings allowed the Allies to halt the Soviet advance, sparing the people of western Europe the torture chambers, gulags and brutality of the 'perfect worker's paradise'.

Thanks to the Allied victory, democratic governments and capitalist market systems were able to flourish in West Germany, France, Italy, Greece, Austria, Belgium, the Netherlands and Scandinavia, bringing prosperity and economic reconstruction to a war-ravaged continent. Leaders in the United States assumed that if American-style governments and markets were established as widely as possible, countries could resolve their differences peacefully through international organisations such as the United Nations and NATO. This was in stark contrast to the economic vandalism of the communist state-planned economies.

The liberation of Europe following the Normandy landings also brought about a deep-seated change in Europe's political identity. Europe had been a fragmented society before the end of World War II, one constantly plagued by wars since the fall of the Western Roman Empire some 1600 years earlier. Now, for the first time, it was possible for Europe to become a symbol of hope. In today's Europe, the legacy of all those sacrifices made in defeating fascism and communism is plain for all to see as countries in the European Union offer one another mutual support and understanding.

It was long believed that the Germans had received details about Operation Overlord via the Cicero Affair. Cicero was the codename given to a spy who obtained classified information from the British ambassador to Turkey.
It is now known that the only concrete detail the Germans obtained from Cicero was Overlord's codename.

It was NATO, and particularly the United States, that helped bring about the downfall of communism in Europe, and eventually in the Soviet Union as well. The inefficient communist economies proved incapable of paying the enormous costs needed to maintain totalitarian military states. Had the Soviet Union been able to establish satellite states throughout Europe, the Americans would never have been able to bring pressure to bear upon them in the way that they did. It was the presence of American troops in western Europe, together with the bases and the missiles aimed at the heart of their empire that forced the Soviets to spend a large proportion of their gross domestic product on the military, forcing them into an arms race that they could never hope to win.

US President Ronald Reagan understood the true legacy of D-Day. In his memorable 1984 speech, he noted that not all that followed the war's end was planned, as some liberated countries were lost. In Warsaw, Prague and East Berlin, the Soviet troops who came in 1945 did not leave when peace came to Europe.

They were still there forty years later, unwanted and uninvited. And it was because of *them* that the Allied forces were still encamped in Western Europe, with one key purpose: to guard and preserve democracy. Then, as forty years before, the American armies were prepared to defend freedom from the Communist aggressors; the only European territories the Americans held were the memorials and the graves of their dead. Having learned the truth after two world wars, in which America initially did not wish to participate, they now understood it was better to protect the peace instead of waiting to respond when freedom had been lost.

The Cold War was necessary to hold back communist expansion, while simultaneously helping to build American power in the world. That it was successful is something for which the west should always be grateful.

# POLITICS AND THE PARTITION OF INDIA (1947)

*'The Hindus and the Muslims belong to two different religions, philosophies, social customs and literature [...] To yoke together two such nations under a single state, one as a numerical minority and the other as a majority, must lead to growing discontent and final destruction of any fabric that may be so built up for the government of such a state.'*
**Muhammad Ali Jinnah**

*'Distrust, therefore, all those who decry human reason, and who require you to abandon it, wherever religion is concerned. Once they have gained this point, they can lead you where they please and impose on you every absurdity which they wish you to embrace.'*
**Joseph Priestly**

### LIE
The Muslims in India had always been separate, so they needed a separate state.

### TRUTH
Hindus and Muslims had lived side by side for centuries in India, and it was the Muslim leadership that was fearful of losing its power and influence!

### CHIEF PARTICIPANTS
Muhammad Ali Jinnah, first President of Pakistan
Jawaharlal Nehru, first Prime Minister of India
Lord Louis Mountbatten, final Viceroy of the British Indian Empire

### THE STORY SO FAR
In 1858, after the chaos caused by the Indian Mutiny had subsided, the British government decided that administering India through a private organisation, the Honourable East India Company, was inefficient and problematic. It therefore brought the greater part of the Indian subcontinent under the direct rule of the India Office, and left several hundred 'princely states' to govern themselves more or less autonomously. Eighteen years later, in 1876, Queen Victoria was declared Empress of India. Until that time, India was a patchwork of states with both Hindu and Muslim populations living side by side in peace. As the decades passed, there were increasing demands for home rule, and by the

Hindus and Sikhs, crowding this train on 17 October 1947, flee the newly created Muslim state of Pakistan.

1930s many leading Indians were advocating a single unified and independent state, although all attempts to force the British to abandon the county were unsuccessful. Given that the majority of the people were Hindu, they were bound to dominate any new state, and this worried the Muslim minority, headed by Muhammad Ali Jinnah …

The world of the British Raj in the early years of the twentieth century—a world so vividly described by Rudyard Kipling and E.M. Forster—was relatively tranquil and stable. It was a world of tiffin, pukka sahibs, memsahibs, spacious bungalows, polo, cricket and tea. From the dark jungles of the interior to the colourful markets of villages, towns and cities, their narrow streets teeming with life, thousands of Indians went about their daily business, Hindu and Muslim living side by side. Now fast-forward to the very same country 50 years later and you would be greeted with scenes of devastation, of streets littered with corpses, gutters clogged with blood and rivers dotted with the bloated bodies of men, women and children. Hindu, Sikh and Muslim had turned on one another as rage and paranoia mounted in the dying days of the British Empire. The competing claims of the Indian National Congress and the All India Muslim League tore the subcontinent apart in an orgy of sectarian violence. As the last British troops departed through the grand Gateway to India in Mumbai (Bombay) in February 1948, they were witnessing the birth pangs of not one, but two countries.

It has become fashionable to blame Great Britain for the horrors of partition—the division of India into two separate nation states—but that is to an extent unfair. Britain at that time was a power in decline, one that lacked the strength or the will to impose a solution on increasingly outspoken political rivals. It was also unwilling to have a showdown with the All India Muslim League, which argued ever more stridently that the Hindu majority was distinct from the Muslim minority, that they had always been separate and thus needed separate states. Yet the truth was that Hindus and Muslims had lived side by side for centuries in India, and it was simply that the Muslim leadership feared losing power and influence when India became independent. Their paranoia resulted in the slaughter of around one million people, and the largest mass migration in modern history as between 12 and 14 million people left their homes to take up residence in one or other of the two new countries. Echoes of the conflict can still be heard to this day, in the arguments and occasional fighting over Kashmir, the continuing tensions—now with the added threat of nuclear weapons—between India and Pakistan, and the movement of Hindus from Bangladesh to India.

## The Official Story—Separate People, Separate States

Muhammad Ali Jinnah was a worried man. For years he had been involved with the Indian National Congress, an organisation dedicated to promoting some form of home rule for all native-born Indians. However, Jinnah was increasingly troubled by the domination of Hindus in the Congress, and began to see future problems unless certain safeguards were in place to protect the Muslim minority. He had been aware of the existence of the All India Muslim League for some time, but had been hesitant about joining. A reserved and dignified man, Jinnah always dressed immaculately in English suits, but he was not strict in his observance of Islamic custom and law. He ate pork, attended prayers at the mosque only rarely and addressed meetings in English rather than Urdu, the language spoken by most Indian Muslims. Despite his reservations, Jinnah did eventually join the League and became its leader, although he remained a member of the Congress for some years after.

What drove Jinnah away from Congress was the arrival of Mahatma Gandhi, whose style of leadership, refusal to wear Western-style clothes and preference for an Indian language instead of English all seemed to be expressions of an Indian identity that was not Muslim. Jinnah was also opposed to Gandhi's policy of non-violent civil disobedience, preferring instead to conduct his struggle via constitutional means.

Jinnah left India in 1927 when the Muslim League fractured, but he was drawn back in 1934 to take charge of the League once again. By this stage his beliefs had changed considerably. He had originally been against the partition of India into two separate states, but the increasing power exercised by Hindus in Congress had changed his mind. When the British passed the 1935 *Government of India Act*, allowing Indians to vote for their own local governments (overseen by the Governor-General), the Congress was able to form governments in a majority of provinces. However, in creating their Cabinets, they refused to appoint any Muslim ministers who had not renounced membership of the Muslim League. It was at this point that Jinnah began to approach the British directly, arguing the need for a separate state for Indian Muslims.

Jinnah advanced two arguments. First, he claimed that unless safeguards were in place to ensure freedom and a political voice for the minority Muslims, a united India would lead to the marginalisation of Muslims and eventual civil war. Jinnah's second argument sought to persuade the British that a two-state solution was the correct and just one. He declared:

> It is extremely difficult to appreciate why our Hindu friends fail to understand the real nature of Islam and Hinduism. They are not religions in the strict sense of the word, but are, in fact, different and distinct social orders, and it is a dream that the Hindus and Muslims can ever evolve a common nationality, and this misconception of one Indian nation has troubles and will lead India to destruction if we fail to revise our notions in time. The Hindus and Muslims belong to two different religious philosophies, social customs,

*literatures. They neither intermarry nor inter-dine together and, indeed, they belong to two different civilizations which are based mainly on conflicting ideas and conceptions. Their aspect on life and of life are different. It is quite clear that Hindus and Mussalmans [sic] derive their inspiration from different sources of history. They have different epics, different heroes, and different episodes. Very often the hero of one is a foe of the other and, likewise, their victories and defeats overlap. To yoke together two such nations under a single state, one as a numerical minority and the other as a majority, must lead to growing discontent and final destruction of any fabric that may be so built for the government of such a state.*

Jinnah's argument in essence was that the Muslims on the subcontinent formed a distinct and separate nation from the Hindus. He cited evidence from the eleventh century, when the Persian scholar Al-Biruni had observed that Hindus and Muslims differed in all matters and habits. The states that had arisen in the subcontinent were each based upon one or other culture—Muslim, Hindu or Sikh—and there had never been a state or a government that was a mixture of any of these. As a result, regardless of the fact that they had shared the subcontinent for 1000 years, relations between Hindus and Muslims could never be truly equable.

Jinnah's views seemed to have been confirmed as India spiralled towards sectarian violence in 1946 as partition approached. As he noted ominously: 'We shall have India divided, or we shall have India destroyed.' The British accepted Jinnah's arguments for a separate state, making disaster inevitable.

## The Truth—Unity Through Diversity

Before partition and with a population of some 370 million people, the followers of different faiths lived side by side in every province of India, as they had done for centuries. The Hindus were the largest group making up over half the population, with Muslims forming a significant minority (over 50 million people), most of them descended from the soldiers of conquering armies who had arrived 700 years earlier from central Asia. There were also a large number of Sikhs—a reformed Hindu sect—with most of the balance of the population made up of Parsees, Jains, Christians, Buddhists and Jews.

The subcontinent had witnessed the rise and fall of many empires since at least 500 BC, the majority ruled by Hindus. The Gupta Empire, for example, ruled northern India until 550 AD, during what became known as India's 'Golden Age', when Hindu culture and science flourished.

A major change occurred with the rise to power of the Islamic empires, starting with the Delhi Sultanate in the thirteenth century. This sparked an Indian cultural renaissance, the resulting blend of Hindu and Muslim cultures producing enduring

Gandhi led a campaign of non-violent resistance against British rule in India, alienating the Muslim minority.

works in architecture, music and literature. Islamic influence reached its peak at the time of the Mughal Empire, which was established by Babur, a descendant of Genghis Khan. The Mughal Empire, which had extended its power over almost the entire Indian subcontinent by 1600, began to decay slowly after 1707, and finally came to an end after the Indian Mutiny of 1857. During the period of the Mughal Empire's slow decline, new empires sprang up, such as the Hindu Maratha Empire, the Muslim princes of Hyderabad, and the Sikh Empire. All were swept away in the wars that brought about the creation of British India.

The one constant that most of these states shared was a pluralistic and tolerant approach to the various religious groups among their subjects. The people were united in their diversity, seeing in the policies of the ruling classes an openness and a spirit of understanding that was not interested in pitting one group against another. All subjects were members of the Mughal or the Maratha empires, regardless of religious affiliation. There were exceptions, of course. In the early stages of the Mughal Empire, the emperors married local royalty, allying themselves with regional Maharajas and trying to merge their Turko-Persian culture with ancient Indian styles, producing a unique Indo-Saracenic architecture. Emperor Akbar even went so far as to propose a merging of the two religions into a new faith. However, during the decline of their empire they discarded these principles and reintroduced Shari'a Law, demanding strict adherence to Islam, abandoning the religious openness of their predecessors. This alienated the Hindu majority and hastened the end of the Mughals.

> When the Maharaja Hari Singh asked for Nehru's help to ward off the tribal invasion from Pakistan, Nehru convinced him to sign accession to India as the price of military support.

While those in power in India's successive empires may have been Muslim, Hindu or Sikh, the people they ruled over were a mixture of many religions; the concerns of the empire builders were not their concerns, which were focused more on local or regional issues. Looking back at Indian history, there is no evidence to support Jinnah's contention that Muslims and Hindus could not live in harmony in one state.

## British Stratagems

The notion of an India united under one government was a British creation, one that they claimed had given the Indians peace, unity and equal religious rights. In seeking to create one administrative entity where there used to be many, British colonial policy was one of divide and rule—always to favour one minority group over the majority. As author Shirin Keen writes:

*The British had followed a divide-and-rule policy in India. Even in the census they categorised people according to religion and viewed and treated them as separate from each other. They had based their knowledge of the peoples of India on the basic religious texts and the intrinsic differences they found in them instead of on the way they coexisted in the present. The British were also still fearful of the potential threat from the Muslims, who were the former rulers of the subcontinent, ruling India for over 300 years under the Mughal Empire. In order to win them over to their side, the British [...] supported the All-India Muslim Conference [...] As soon as the League was formed, they were placed on a separate electorate. Thus the idea of the separateness of Muslims in India was built into the electoral process of India.*

It was therefore British policy that promoted a belief in the separateness of the peoples of the subcontinent. So it is hardly surprising that when the Indians began their quest for independence, the social and religious differences identified by the British were reflected in demands for freedom, self-government and, most especially, measures to safeguard the Muslim minority in the new, single state of India. Even so, the very thought of being a minority and under the yoke of a people their ancestors had ruled over for centuries proved too much for many in the Muslim leadership. Disempowered and discontented, fearful of being swamped by the Hindu majority, and with thoughts of past glories firmly in mind, Jinnah and his colleagues began to demand a separate state for Muslims. Their rhetoric inflamed a people who, until then, had never thought of themselves as separate from their Hindu neighbours.

The British saw in the Muslim League a way of thwarting the ambitions of the Indian National Congress and their plans for independence. Gandhi's leadership and political acumen forced the British to the negotiating table, but once there they used Jinnah and the League to try to hinder Gandhi's plans. The League's leadership knew that this was their tactic and told the British: 'It is the old maxim of divide and rule. But there is a division of labour here. We divide and you rule.' Gandhi's demand for complete independence was hindered by the Muslim leadership who wanted assurances that they would be treated as a separate community with separate representation, which Gandhi rejected. When World War II broke out, the Congress refused to support Britain, while Jinnah and the League earned Britain's gratitude by giving it their unqualified support.

Jinnah then began to push hard to ensure that his would be the only Muslim voice heard by the British, especially as the Congress had the support of many Muslims in the Punjab and Bengal. He continued to agitate for division, while the Congress held out for unification. In the aftermath of the war, Britain no longer had the will or the economic power to hold on to India, a fact recognised by both Hindus and Muslims. Consequently, both sides started to promote violence as a way of forcing a solution, unconcerned by the rising death toll.

The British government finally acquiesced, appointing Lord Louis Mountbatten as Viceroy after the end of World War II to oversee the withdrawal of British troops and the transfer of authority to the Indians. Mountbatten formally suggested partition and managed to convince Jawaharlal Nehru, President of the Indian National Congress, that unless India was divided, there would be no end to the violence. He and the rest of the Congress—except for Gandhi—agreed.

In the final analysis, Jinnah's fears were largely unfounded. While it is true that there was a faction within the Congress that was keen for a 'Hindu only' nation, the principal players—Gandhi and Nehru—were determined to preserve Indian unity for all Indians, Muslims as well as Hindus. They had gone to great lengths to ensure that the Congress contained a significant number of prominent Muslims. There has always been a question about how real Jinnah's concerns actually were, and whether they were a cover to mask his real ambitions. Whatever the case, it was Jinnah's intransigence that prevented a compromise solution, and it was his manipulation of the British that allowed him to achieve his aims. His defenders have argued that Jinnah genuinely believed that Pakistan would be a smaller version of secular India and that even as late as 1946 he was prepared to consider a federated state solution, as proposed by the British Labour Government. But that was never a serious suggestion. Jinnah's demands for an undivided Punjab and Bengal, plus Sind, Baluchistan and the North-West Frontier, to be part of a Muslim state was always going to cause sectarian bloodshed. When Mountbatten met Jinnah and warned him that partition would mean the division of Bengal and the Punjab, he replied: 'I do not care how little you give me, as long as you give it to me completely.' This was the response of a man whose pride and fierce ambition refused to let him compromise his belief in a separate state. The price of that pride was to be a catastrophe.

## Legacies

The consequences of partition were felt almost immediately. Mountbatten declared that Britain would hand over power to two countries, India and Pakistan, on 15 August 1947. Acting in great haste, his officials drew up the partition boundaries. It is doubtful that anyone, even with unlimited time, could have mapped out a frontier that ensured that all Hindus were on one side and all Muslims on the other. It is also safe to assume that it didn't help that the man in charge of drawing up the partition boundaries had never been to India before.

India and Pakistan duly came into being on 15 August, and on that same day a group of Muslim women in a town in East Punjab were raped by a Sikh mob and paraded naked through the streets before being killed and burned. Also on 15 August, across the border in the newly created Pakistan, a Sikh temple was burned to the ground by Muslims, who cheered as the worshippers trapped inside perished in the flames.

There followed the largest mass migration seen in modern history as between 12 and 14 million people crossed the newly declared borders of East and West Pakistan. Neighbours and friends found themselves divided by nationality as well as religion, and in the heat of the moment turned on each other, spurred on by howling mobs and tales of atrocities committed against co-religionists. Trains filled with desperate and frightened Muslims were attacked by Hindus and Sikhs, with all on board being slaughtered. Meanwhile, Hindus travelling in the opposite direction were butchered by Muslims. Those who delayed their departure too long were tortured and killed. There were stories of men on both sides shooting or stabbing their wives and daughters to save them from the fate that awaited them.

The British looked on in helpless horror as the sectarian violence reached a crescendo in September 1947. But there was nothing they could do, since there were almost no British troops left in India by this time. The Boundary Force, which had

# THE ASSASSINATION OF MAHATMA GANDHI

Anxious, as always, to seek the non-violent path, Gandhi urged the Hindu citizens of Delhi to allow Muslims to return to their homes in the city in the aftermath of partition. Always the champion of the oppressed, he was becoming an irritant to intolerant Hindus keen to purge India of those they hated. Accordingly, on the afternoon of 30 January 1948, as Gandhi was making his way through a crowd towards his daily prayer meeting, a young man stepped up to him, bowed low and shot him three times in the chest at point-blank range. Gandhi's last words were 'Hi Ram'—'Oh God'.

Hearing the news, both Nehru and Mountbatten forced their way through the crowd to see if it was true. When Mountbatten heard someone in the crowd shout that the assassin was a Muslim he responded instantly. 'You fool,' he snapped, 'don't you know it was a Hindu?' Very quietly, his press secretary asked him how he could possibly know that. 'I don't,' was his reply, 'but if it really were a Muslim, India is going to have one of the most ghastly massacres the world has ever seen.' As it turned out, the assassin was indeed a Hindu, the editor of an extremist newspaper who believed that by preaching non-violence and toleration of Muslims, Gandhi was undermining both Hinduism and the newly formed Indian nation.

Partition had claimed one more victim, the life of the one man who had fought more tenaciously than any other to prevent the division of India from ever taking place. Many would say that, with the loss of such a man, the cost of partition had been too high. But Gandhi himself would have been horrified by that thought, believing that the life of any one of the millions who perished was equally as valuable as his own.

been established to oversee the hoped-for peaceful transfer, was overwhelmed by the ferocity of the fighting. Eventually, as the numbers of refugees began to decline, there were fewer and fewer atrocities and retaliations as the rage began to burn itself out. Pakistan and India finally emerged from the horrors of partition but, observing the relationship of the two nations since partition, it is unlikely they will ever be able to fully trust one another again.

Jinnah got his wish. He was made Governor-General of the newly created Pakistan by Mountbatten, but would not survive to enjoy his victory long. Already suffering from tuberculosis and lung cancer, he died within a year of partition. His legacy was a state that has never been quite comfortable with democracy. There have been a succession of military coups, and the nation's hardline Islamic extremists have never forgiven the Hindus for atrocities committed in 1947. It was a military coup that toppled the elected government of Zulfikar Ali Bhutto in 1977, and it was an Islamic extremist who assassinated his daughter, opposition leader Benazir Bhutto, on 27 December 2007 as she was campaigning for the return of democracy to Pakistan. Both of these groups distrust the Western democratic tradition: the military for its perceived tendency to descend into disorder, and the Islamists because they feel it undermines Islamic traditions.

India, on the other hand, has managed to establish a flourishing democratic system that manages a multi-ethnic state, although not without occasional accusations of corruption. However, India shares with Pakistan the problem of political assassinations. Mahatma Gandhi was murdered by a Hindu extremist in 1948, Prime Minister Indira Gandhi was shot dead in 1984, and her son Congress President Rajiv Gandhi was killed by a suicide bomber in 1991.

Relations between India and Pakistan have generally improved since the troubled days of partition, but the countries have fought three major wars, in 1947–48, 1965 and 1971. There is also still one issue that is a source of continuing tension, the region of Kashmir on the border with China. At the time of partition, those regions that were controlled by hereditary princes were given the right to decide whether they wanted to be part of Pakistan or India. Kashmir had been ruled since 1925 by the Maharaja Hari Singh, a Hindu. Even though the majority of Kashmir's population was Muslim, the Maharaja joined the secular Union of India after local tribes from Pakistan invaded his land. This decision was met with fury from Pakistan, which despatched troops to force the issue. India, which had a document of accession signed by the Maharaja on 26 October 1947, also responded by sending troops, thus triggering the first Indo-Pakistan War. Pakistan doubted the legality of the accession, but the British accepted it as legitimate, although they did insist on a plebiscite to determine the wishes of the Kashmiri people. The United Nations also requested a plebiscite, but a vote has never taken place. India insists that until Pakistan removes its troops from the northwestern sector of the state, no election can be held. To complicate matters further, part of northern Kashmir was ceded to China by Pakistan in 1963, though this has never been accepted by India.

The Kashmir question has occupied the minds of generations of Indian and Pakistani politicians, and it has triggered numerous clashes. The first, in 1947, created roughly the boundary that exists today, with Pakistan possessing about one-third of Kashmir, and India two-thirds. The line established at the ceasefire—known as the Line of Control since 1972—became the de facto border between India and Pakistan in most of the region. Further conflicts erupted in 1965 and 1999, each one failing to resolve the deadlock. Yet tensions remain high, and have escalated even further as first India and then Pakistan developed nuclear weapons, and then tested missiles with which to deliver them.

None of this would have happened if the multi-faith and multi-ethnic country that was India had not been needlessly partitioned. The lie that Pakistan had to be an independent state ultimately led to the deaths of millions of innocent people and a conflict that continues to this day. Unity was sacrificed for the sake of political ambition. National leaders who continue to stoke the fires of racial and religious hatreds are condemning generations yet unborn to what is essentially a fruitless struggle.

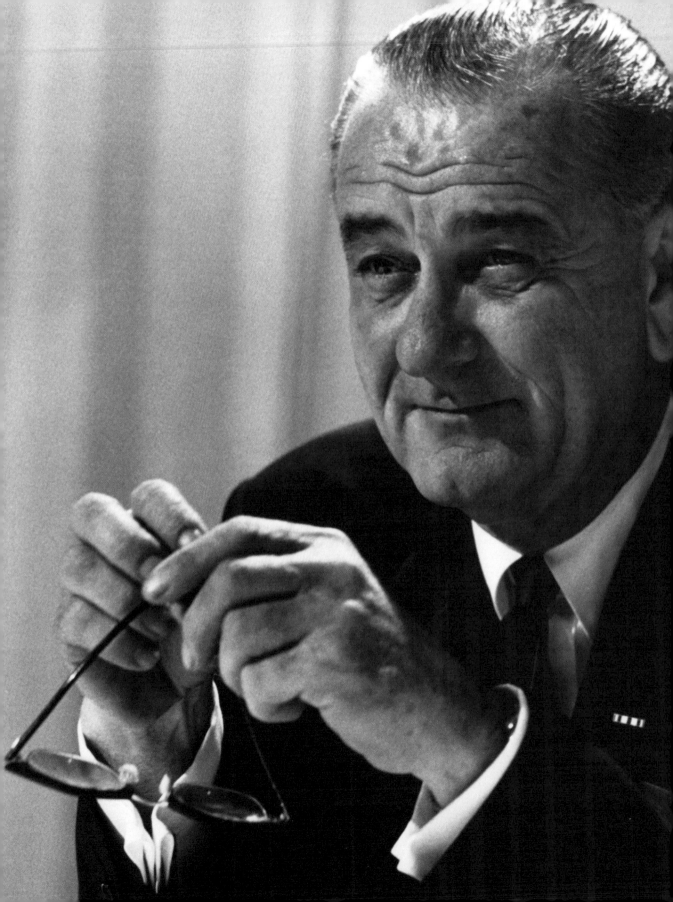

# SEND TROOPS—THE NORTH VIETNAMESE ARE ATTACKING! (1964)

*'If in order to avoid further communist expansion in Asia and particularly in Indo-China, if in order to avoid it we must take the risk by putting American boys in, I believe that the executive branch of the government has to take the politically unpopular position of facing up to it and doing it, and I personally would support such a decision.'*
**Richard M. Nixon**

*'Assumption is the mother of the screw-up.'*
**Angelo Donghia**

## LIE

The North Vietnamese began the Vietnam war by attacking US forces in South Vietnam.

## TRUTH

An over-eager sonar man was a bit too jumpy!

## CHIEF PARTICIPANTS

Lyndon B. Johnson, 36th President of the United States of America
Robert McNamara, US Secretary of Defense
John Herrick, Captain of the USS *Maddox*

## THE STORY SO FAR

In the late nineteenth century, the French claimed the region now occupied by Vietnam, Laos and Cambodia as a French colony, which was named French Indo-China. The French ruled this region until the Japanese invaded in 1941 during World War II. In Vietnam, a resistance movement under the leadership of Ho Chi Minh was created with the aim of driving the Japanese out and establishing an independent state. With the defeat of the Japanese in 1945, Ho Chi Minh occupied Hanoi, the capital of Vietnam, and declared independence. The French, unwilling to relinquish their colonial possessions, despatched armed forces to restore French rule. This resulted in the First Indo-China War, which ended in defeat for the French in 1954. Because Ho Chi Minh was a communist, and had established a communist state, the United States, guardian

President Lyndon B. Johnson, who gave the go-ahead to US military escalation in Vietnam.

of freedom and democracy in the world, insisted that the treaty that had ended the First Indo-China War would divide Vietnam between a communist north and a supposedly democratic state in the south. Even though the people of Vietnam wanted unification and independence, the Cold War was raging and the United States would not tolerate a unified state where the communists were in control …

'The Vietnam War was', in Professor Donald Goldstein's sober assessment, 'arguably the most traumatic experience for the United States in the twentieth century. That is indeed a grim distinction in a span that included two world wars, the assassinations of two presidents and the resignation of another, the Great Depression, the Cold War, racial unrest, and the drug and crime waves.' Given the amount of money and resources, and the number of military personnel, that America poured into Vietnam for almost a decade, one might imagine that only an event as serious as the attack on the World Trade Center would compel the nation to commit itself to such a conflict. The French had wasted years in Indo-China and limped away empty-handed, but now circumstances had changed. America was increasingly concerned about the spread of communism in Southeast Asia, and was convinced that it had to do everything within its power to shield those countries that had not yet succumbed.

Yet far from being as momentous as the 2001 attack on the World Trade Center, the event that triggered US intervention was a supposed attack on American destroyers patrolling waters around North Vietnam on 4 August 1964. Declaring that they would not stand for such blatant provocation, the US administration, led by President Lyndon B. Johnson, took the decision to increase American involvement in Vietnam.

In fact, no such attack ever took place. Although US forces believed they had come under fire from the North Vietnamese, it became obvious very shortly afterwards that there had been no engagement with the enemy. The confusion was the result of false alarms and mistaken reports. This didn't prevent the Johnson administration from using sketchy details of the incident to declare that US forces were under attack, even though the President and his Secretary of Defense, Robert McNamara, didn't believe that to be the case. The result was that the United States was committed to intervene in a civil war between North and South Vietnam. The short-term consequence was defeat and humiliation for the United States, while the long-term consequences were a perception that the American war machine was not invincible, and that there were serious internal divisions within US society. In the aftermath of the Vietnam debacle, the United States backed away from major foreign policy initiatives and focused much more on domestic issues. It was not until the First Gulf War in 1990 that the ghosts of Vietnam were laid briefly to rest.

## The Official Story—US Forces under Attack

On the night of 4 August 1964, US destroyers were patrolling just outside North Vietnamese waters in the Gulf of Tonkin, under orders to gather electronic intelligence. The seamen on board were jumpy. Two nights previously they had been attacked by North Vietnamese torpedo boats, and were therefore keeping a sharp lookout for enemy vessels. Their worst fears seemed to come true when a radar operator on board USS *Maddox* spotted what he thought were five torpedo boats about 58 km (36 miles) to the northeast at about 7.40 pm. The US vessels also received radio signals that they believed indicated that another attack by the North Vietnamese navy was imminent.

The USS *Maddox* and the USS *Turner Joy* prepared for action. When the approaching vessels were about 8 km (5 miles) away, the *Maddox* fired star shells to light up the sky, which was pitch black, with no moon and heavy cloud cover. When sonar indicated that the contacts were about 5 km (3 miles) away, the *Turner Joy* began firing her guns, using radar for aiming. The *Maddox* also began firing, even though her radar showed no attacking vessels. However, four sailors on the *Turner Joy* and one crewman aboard *Maddox* did report seeing the silhouette of an enemy ship, and a seaman claimed that he saw a searchlight briefly pierce the darkness. There were also sonar reports of as many as 22 torpedoes being fired at the *Turner Joy*.

The engagement lasted for a total of about two hours, and when it was over Captain John Herrick of the USS *Maddox* wired Washington with sketchy details of the attack. His first communication stated only that they appeared to have been attacked. Admiral Ulysses S. Grant Sharp, Commander in Chief of the Pacific Fleet in Honolulu responded with an urgent cable asking: 'Can you confirm absolutely that you were attacked?'

At 1.27 pm Washington time, Herrick sent a response indicating that the 'review of action makes many reported contacts and torpedoes fired appear doubtful. Freak weather effects on radar and overeager sonarmen may have accounted for many reports.' He qualified this an hour later, cabling that: 'Entire action leaves many doubts except for apparent ambush at beginning. Suggest thorough reconnaissance in daylight by aircraft.' Three hours later, Herrick confirmed that he was 'certain that the original ambush was bona fide'.

In his final report that night, Herrick stated that: 'The first boat to close in on the *Maddox* probably fired a torpedo at her which was heard but not seen. All subsequent *Maddox* torpedo reports are doubtful in that it is suspected that sonarman was hearing the ship's own propeller beat.' In spite of these uncertainties, President Johnson met with his top advisers and the National Security Council, and began considering the possibility of an air strike against the enemy vessels and their bases. Secretary of Defense Robert McNamara claimed later that he had 'unimpeachable' intelligence— widely believed to have been intercepted North Vietnamese radio messages—showing not only that Hanoi had planned an attack on the US destroyers, but also that it was informed of the attack's progress.

USS *Maddox*. Its coming under fire started a chain of events that led to the United States declaring war against North Vietnam.

President Johnson ordered a retaliatory attack against North Vietnam, and announced shortly after 11.30 pm (Washington time) on 4 August that the US was sending its armed forces into battle for the first time since the Korean War. A few minutes later, 64 fighter jets from USS *Ticonderoga* and USS *Constitution* were sent to attack North Vietnamese torpedo boat bases and fuel facilities. The next day, headlines in the *Washington Post* announced: 'American Planes Hit North Vietnam After Second Attack on Our Destroyers; Move Taken to Halt New Aggression'.

## The Truth—It's All a Big Mistake

Amid all the claims and counter-claims made about events in the Gulf of Tonkin in August 1964, a few things are certain. The North Vietnamese admitted that three of their torpedo boats did attack the USS *Maddox* on 2 August. American aircraft were launched from USS *Ticonderoga*, which attacked the retiring torpedo boats.

The USS *Maddox* suffered minor damage as she withdrew to South Vietnamese waters, where she was joined by the destroyer USS *Turner Joy*. The US administration subsequently claimed that this had been an unprovoked attack, which was the first lie of the Gulf of Tonkin incident.

Rather than being on a routine patrol on 2 August, as had been claimed, the USS *Maddox* was actually carrying out an intelligence-gathering exercise, in coordination with attacks on North Vietnam by the South Vietnamese navy and the Laotian air force. John Prados' essay on the 40th Anniversary of the Gulf of Tonkin incident described the encounter between the USS *Maddox* and the North Vietnamese on 2 August 1964 as being sparked by a series of covert US-led 34-A maritime raids on North Vietnamese coastal targets. Senior Johnson administration officials were well aware that such covert naval commando raids were being undertaken, and that there was a relationship between the raids and the *Maddox*'s intelligence cruise, referred to as 'DeSoto Patrols'. Secretary McNamara at one point did mention the 34-A raids, but maintained that they were operated by the South Vietnamese, with no American input. Yet documents show he was well aware that the 34-A missions were run and paid for by the United States, using boats obtained and repaired by the US navy and attacking targets identified by the CIA. South Vietnamese input was limited to providing the men who were recruited as commandos, and who were then led by American Special Forces, as well as administrative responsibility should anything go wrong.

The reports of Captain John Herrick make it clear that there was confusion about what actually happened the night of 4 August, but it is hard to avoid concluding that a jumpy sonar operator made an error of judgment and that there was no attack on US forces. This appears to be confirmed by the North Vietnamese, who were happy to take credit for the attack on 2 August, but who denied firing at the US ships on August 4. Other evidence comes from squadron commander James Stockdale, a navy pilot on duty that night. 'I had the best seat in the house to watch that event,' recalled Stockdale, 'and our destroyers were just shooting at phantom targets—there were no PT [torpedo] boats there [...] There was nothing there but black water and American fire power.' Lieutenant Raymond Connell, in charge of the guns on the USS *Maddox* recalled: 'We were hopping around up there, trying to figure out what [the USS *Turner Joy*] were shooting at. We fired a lot of rounds, but it was strictly a defensive tactic.'

There was certainly no physical evidence whatsoever to confirm the alleged attack on 4 August. This is despite claims made by the captain and four servicemen aboard the USS *Turner Joy*. A searchlight was reported, as well as boat cockpit lights, smoke at the spot where they believed their guns had hit a North Vietnamese ship and at least one torpedo wake. However, there were no dead bodies and no debris, despite navy claims that their ships had destroyed two attacking torpedo boats.

McNamara's 'unimpeachable' evidence—the intercepted North Vietnamese transcripts—were declassified in 2003. According to a National Security Archive essay by John Prados discussing the Gulf of Tonkin incident, the documents clearly show that the cables were not intercepts of North Vietnamese radio broadcasts as claimed, but reports by US forces summarising the content of the radio broadcasts. It was therefore not possible that the Hawaii headquarters of the Commander-in-Chief of the Pacific or Washington could have had the raw intercepts simultaneously passed to them.

President Johnson and the National Security Council could not, therefore, have had the transcripts when they decided to launch a counterattack on North Vietnam. Their decision was based on older transcripts that mentioned preparations

## THE KENT STATE MASSACRE

Antagonism towards the Vietnam War, and the force used to crush dissent, were nowhere more clearly demonstrated than at Kent State University in Ohio on Monday 4 May 1970.

Richard Nixon was elected president in 1968, promising to end the Vietnam War. Instead, he replaced the military draft with a lottery and expanded the war, announcing on 30 April 1970 that US forces had invaded Cambodia. Students at Kent State University began to protest the invasion of Cambodia on 1 May, and for the next two days there were large demonstrations that began to spiral out of control. Ohio's Governor Rhodes called out the National Guard, and on 3 May held a press conference and called the protestors un-American. 'They're worse than the brownshirts and the communist element and also the nightriders and the vigilantes,' Rhodes said. 'They're the worst type of people that we harbor in America. I think that we're up against the strongest, well-trained, militant, revolutionary group that has ever assembled in America.'

The following day, an estimated 2000 students gathered on the university commons for a planned protest. The National Guard were called out and ordered the crowd to move on, using tear gas to reinforce their demands. The protestors retaliated by throwing stones. Realising they were not going to disperse, a troop of guards began to advance on the students with fixed bayonets. They were initially successful in dispersing the protestors, but many students soon returned, still throwing stones. Shortly after noon, a number of National Guardsmen fired their semi-automatic rifles into a group of students gathered near some campus buildings. Four students were killed and nine wounded. Two of those killed had taken part in the protests, while the other two were merely walking to class.

Protests and demonstrations erupted across the country in the days that followed the shootings. In Washington DC, 100,000 people demonstrated against the war and the killing of student protesters. To many Americans, this act represented the ultimate betrayal of the people by their elected officials. One Nixon administration official declared in disbelief: 'This can't be the United States of America. This is not the greatest free democracy in the world. This is a nation at war with itself.'

for launching some patrol boats on that night, along with the conflicting details from the events of 4 August. This information was clearly relayed to the White House, along with Hanoi's denials of the attack. Even the president had his doubts, declaring that: 'For all I know, our Navy was shooting at whales out there'. The fact is that the Johnson administration had already decided to order a strike against North Vietnam; the Gulf of Tonkin incident merely provided them with the excuse they needed.

## Faulty Dominoes

The Johnson Administration was eager to enter into the Vietnam conflict because of the prevailing theory about the spread of communism—the so-called domino principle. This was originally put forward by President Eisenhower, who declared that: 'the "falling domino" principle [is where] you have a row of dominoes set up, you knock over the first one, and what will happen to the last one is the certainty that it will go over very quickly [leading to] a disintegration that would have the most profound influences'. By 1960, American foreign policy experts believed that the Soviet Union, and especially China were seeking to promote the growth of communism in Southeast Asia. Both countries were believed to be actively subverting democratic states, with the hope that the collapse of one would lead to the collapse of others in turn, like a row of dominoes. The Americans believed that they had to take a stand against the communists, and a line in the sand was to be drawn with Vietnam.

However, the entire premise was based on two incorrect assumptions: the first was that the situation in Vietnam was principally a communist takeover; the second that the communist world was a unified foe. In fact, the conflict in Vietnam was essentially a war of independence, firstly against the French and then against the Americans, although it also had some features of a civil war. Vietnam was a poor country with very little industrial development. It did, however, have a highly organised and efficient army, led from the north by the communists. When the supposedly democratic Republic of Vietnam was established in the south in 1955, it had no support from the majority of the people, who wanted a single unified state. The Republic's main supporters were Catholics who had fled the communists in the north. America supplied vast quantities of aid to support the South Vietnamese leadership, but the puppet government was unable to gain the loyalty of the people. The Vietcong became the preferred party to govern Vietnam, principally because they were fighting a war of independence, not because they were communist. Within Vietnam itself, the conflict with America was referred to as the 'American War', emphasising its origins in a struggle to end Western colonialism in Southeast Asia.

The principal flaw in the domino theory was the way in which its supporters understood the relationships between the various communist nations in the region. The monolithic foe, seen by the Americans as united in a struggle against the West, was a figment of fevered imaginations in Washington. The relationship between China and the Soviet Union had broken down to such an extent in the 1960s that there were numerous border skirmishes between them. And, after the Vietnam War was over, tensions arose between Vietnam and China over Vietnam's overthrow of the Khmer Rouge in Cambodia, which was also a communist regime and a close ally of the Chinese. This led to more wars, this time between Vietnam and China. Clearly, the communist world had its own internal disputes, just as the West did. There was certainly no grand communist plot to take over the countries of Southeast Asia one by one. The fact that communism failed to gain a foothold in Thailand, Indonesia and other large Southeast Asian countries after the end of the Vietnam War demonstrated that the domino effect had no basis in reality. In Vietnam, and elsewhere, the Americans had simply confused communism with nationalism. When the United States backed a regime in an effort to halt the spread of communism, the group they supported almost always ended up being loathed by the locals. They were inevitably corrupt and generally guilty of human rights abuses, which triggered civil and military opposition to their rule. Popular support was given instead to the principal party opposed to the Americans—the communists. In reality, the supposed leaders of a global communist conspiracy were merely seeking to expel unwelcome foreigners from their countries, which they wanted to govern for themselves.

## Legacies

The Gulf of Tonkin incident led directly to the Vietnam War, perhaps America's biggest foreign policy blunder. The costs associated with the war were astronomical. In Vietnam, three million people on both sides of the north–south divide were killed. At least one million Laotians and Cambodians also died. The Southeast Asian countryside was ravaged, with the Americans dropping around 6.7 million tonnes of bombs, compared with 2.7 million tonnes dropped on Germany during the entirety of World War II. The war continues to exact a price today, with land mines and unexploded ordnance having injured or killed 100,000 Vietnamese since the fall of Saigon in 1975, and with many people in the countryside still suffering genetic defects as a result of 'Agent Orange', the notorious defoliant used by America to clear jungles used by the Vietcong as cover for their operations.

US Secretary of Defense Robert McNamara, architect of the Vietnam War.

The war was also disastrous for America, although in different ways. The United States may have delayed a communist victory in Vietnam by perhaps 15 years, but the communists took over in the end anyway, and the delay came at immense cost. Nearly 2.59 million American servicemen fought in Vietnam, 58,169 being killed and some 304,000 wounded. Between 1965 and 1973, the United States spent almost $120 billion on the war, causing inflation that damaged even the gargantuan American economy. American prestige also suffered a near mortal blow. The extent and ferocity of the conflict damaged America's moral leadership in the world, and began weakening the bonds that had bound Europe and the United States tightly together since the end of World War II.

The moral ambiguity of the war plagued America's conscience, and the defeat badly damaged the country's self-confidence, with disturbing effects on the body politic in the years that followed. The war seared itself into the memory of a generation, as the country tore itself apart over the conflict. Drafting the nation's youth ensured that the war was unpopular at home. Violent protests and anti-war demonstrations surprised both the Johnson and Nixon administrations, which responded with violence as they

While it has always been believed that the Vietnam War was deeply unpopular in the United States at the time, the election result in 1972 gives lie to that belief. In what became the largest Republican victory in US history, President Richard Nixon, who had escalated the American war effort, introduced a draft lottery and was the target of numerous anti-war rallies, was re-elected with over 60 per cent of the primary vote. This was an overwhelming vote of confidence in his presidency and handling of the Vietnam War.

sought to suppress dissent. The optimism of the Eisenhower and Kennedy years was destroyed by the conflict in Vietnam so that, even today, any mention of Vietnam in the United States still evokes bitter memories of the war. The unpopularity of the war at home affected the morale of American soldiers, and even had an impact on the fighting quality of US soldiers stationed in the steamy jungles half a world away. British author George MacDonald Fraser served in World War II alongside American servicemen and it is his opinion that: '[…] there is no doubt why America lost [for] they didn't have an army. For the soldiers [were] simply not fit to go into action. They [were] brutal, degraded, nasty, hysterical, drug-sodden slobs, without decency or discipline […] The Americans of 1942–45 were not like this; they were good soldiers. [How did] the fine army of Normandy and the Pacific […] degenerate to this extent […]?'

American administrations had great difficulty in accepting the defeat, and all Americans struggled to understand the implications of the failure of America's military machine. Even today, debate continues about whether the American defeat in Vietnam was due to military failure, or whether it was a result of a failure of political will by Congress and, by extension, the American people. What the war did do was demonstrate that in a democracy there is never enough strength or resources to fight a war indefinitely, and that this is true for small nations as well as superpowers. The will of the people, as much as military might and economic wealth, is a vitally important factor in determining the outcome of a modern war, and the US administration can no longer count on blind patriotism to rally the nation, as occurred during World War II and the Korean conflict.

The lesson for democracies was that a war had to be popular, and it had to be short, if it was to be won. In the years that followed the Vietnam War, America was reluctant to pursue an aggressive foreign policy, haunted still by its failure in Vietnam. Administrations also tended to focus on concerns closer to home. Unwilling to commit armed forces, US administrations had to resort to less successful strategies to achieve their ends, such as supplying aid to the Contra rebels to overthrow Nicaragua's Sandinista government, or engaging in brief surgical strikes, such as the invasion of Grenada. It was not until the First Gulf War of 1990–91 that a new government and a new generation felt confident enough to emerge from the shadow of Vietnam and take the lead in a new Allied offensive. In the euphoria of a quick and easy victory in Kuwait, the ghosts of Vietnam were thought to have finally been laid to rest, only to have been reawakened as the second Iraq war dragged on and the inevitable comparisons with Vietnam began to be made.

# ACTING UNDER FALSE PRETENCES

'True glory takes root, and even spreads; all false pretences, like flowers, fall to the ground; nor can any counterfeit last long.'

MARCUS TULLIUS CICERO

An exaggerated seventeenth-century painting of the trial of Galileo.

# CARTHAGE MUST BE DESTROYED! (146 BC)

*'This corn is well grown and Carthage must be destroyed!'*
**Cato the Elder**

*'The military don't start wars. Politicians start wars.'*
**William Westmoreland**

### LIE
Rome was provoked by Carthage to declare war.

### TRUTH
Rome wanted revenge after the Second Punic War, and used a flimsy pretext to declare war!

### CHIEF PARTICIPANTS
Marcus Porcius Cato (Cato the Elder), a leading Roman senator
Scipio Aemilianus, a Roman general
King Masinissa of Numidia

### THE STORY SO FAR
Two rival powers dominated the western Mediterranean in 300 BC—Rome and Carthage. Rome, a land power, had finally succeeded in conquering the entire Italian peninsula, while Carthage, a sea power, had gained control of much of North Africa and the island of Sicily. It was over Sicily that the two states eventually came into conflict, leading to the First Punic War in 264 BC. Rome's armies were victorious, but her inferior navy endured numerous defeats at first until it was eventually able to prevent reinforcements from reaching Sicily, leading to the surrender of Carthaginian forces. The rivalry continued, however, with the Second Punic War breaking out in 218 BC, when the brilliant Carthaginian general Hannibal invaded Italy. Unable to defeat Carthaginian forces in the field, Rome responded by fighting a war of attrition, eventually forcing Hannibal to retreat to Carthage where he was defeated in the Battle of Zama in 202 BC. Carthage sued for peace after the defeat, abandoned its dreams of a military empire and concentrated instead on establishing commercial ties with her neighbours. There were many in Rome, however, who nursed grievances …

The end of Carthaginian military ambitions—the Battle of Zama, 202 BC.

A most unusual event took place in February 1985, when a group of well-dressed diplomats and government officials gathered in a functional government building at the foot of a hill in Tunisia. Ugo Vetere, mayor of Rome and leader of a party from the Senatus Populusque Romanus (SPQR), and Chedly Klibi, mayor of Carthage, signed a symbolic treaty of friendship and cooperation. The unusual feature of this treaty was that it marked the formal end of a series of wars that had begun 2248 years earlier.

The three Punic Wars, fought between 264 and 146 BC, marked the rise of Rome and the fall of Carthage. Officials at the signing ceremony in Tunisia were moved to proclaim the ceremony as 'the last act, sealing symbolically our final reconciliation', but it is interesting to speculate on what the person responsible for engineering Carthage's downfall two millennia earlier might have had to say if he had been present. Would he have congratulated his republican successors? Or would Cato the Censor, whose paranoia resulted in his manipulating the Roman people into a war against a pacified nation that ended in its complete destruction, have declared even now that 'Carthago delenda est'—'Carthage must be destroyed'?

## The Official Story—Carthage Seeks a War

The official Roman view—outlined by the historian Livy—was that the Romans had discovered that the Carthaginians were building up their army and navy, in direct violation of a treaty between the two nations. The Carthaginians protested that they were only preparing for war against King Masinissa of Numidia (in North Africa). In Rome, however, Cato declared that the preparations were directed at Rome herself and envoys were duly despatched to determine the truth of the matter. Once in Carthage, the envoys criticised the Carthaginian senate for making warlike preparations, contrary to their treaty, and proposed to act as arbitrators between the Numidians and the Carthaginians. The Carthaginian senate agreed, but the people rioted, forcing the Roman envoys to flee. This helped to convince the Roman senate that the Carthaginians were resolutely anti-Roman.

When the envoys returned from Africa, accompanied by ambassadors from Carthage and Gulussa, the son of King Masinissa, they reported to the senate on the warlike preparations they had witnessed. Gulussa declared that he had no doubt that the Carthaginians were preparing for war against Rome—why else would they be building warships? The senate debated the question, with Cato demanding that Rome send an army to Africa immediately. However, the senate voted in favour of continued discussions, calling on the Carthaginians to disarm and for Rome to mediate between Numidia and Carthage. If the Carthaginians did not burn their ships and stand down their army, proceedings would be commenced in the Roman senate the following year to issue a declaration of war against Carthage. When the envoys returned to Carthage with these terms, the Carthaginians refused to allow Gulussa into their city and decided to ignore Rome's demands, declaring war against King Masinissa.

When news of this reached the Roman senate, Cato flew into a rage and once again put the case for war. This time he was successful and an army was duly despatched. When it arrived in Africa, envoys were sent to the Carthaginian senate to inform them about the declaration of war, and to demand immediate surrender. The terms of the surrender were that the Carthaginians must hand over 300 hostages and all of the weapons and engines of war they possessed, and further that the city must be torn down and rebuilt on another site at least 15 km (9 miles) from the sea. The Carthaginians rejected these demands outright and prepared for a siege.

It took the Romans three years to capture the city. Because of its size—Carthage was 34 km (21 miles) in circumference—the Romans had to take it section by section, concentrating their attacks on small areas at a time. Carthage finally succumbed in 146, in the seven-hundredth year of its existence.

## The Truth—Origins

If any event could be said to mark the defining moment between when the Republic thrived upon its virtue, and when the acquisition of the overseas provinces corrupted the Republic, beginning its downward slide into chaos and civil war, then the Third Punic War would be it.

The Punic Wars were a series of conflicts fought between two great powers of the ancient world. On the one hand there was the long-standing empire of Carthage, the commercial centre of the western Mediterranean, situated on a fertile strip of land between the barren sands of the Sahara to the south and the warm waters of the Mediterranean to the north. Then there was the rising power of Rome, a city straddling seven hills on the banks of the River Tiber, the people of which had cast out their foreign kings and created a republic. The First Punic War (264 to 241 BC) was fought for control of Sicily. Initially things went in Carthage's favour, because of their experience in naval warfare, but the Romans eventually wore the Carthaginians down, expelling them from Sicily and making the island the first Roman-controlled territory outside of the mainland.

The Carthaginian military vowed revenge, and it was not long in coming, with the second and best-known of the Punic Wars breaking out in 218 BC. The Carthaginians had compensated for their loss in Sicily by expanding their territory into Spain. Rome objected, provoking Hannibal, the Great Carthaginian military commander, into invading Italy. Hannibal took his army of 40,000 men across the Alps in winter, surprising the Romans. During the crossing, the Carthaginian army lost over one-quarter of its men, as well as all but one of its 37 war elephants. Nevertheless, their arrival in Italy marked the beginning of a series of humiliating defeats for the Romans.

In 217 BC, Hannibal marched south, defeating the Romans at the Battle of Lake Trasimene. Bypassing Rome, he advanced into southern Italy, hoping to enlist allies. The Romans appointed Fabius Maximus to lead them, and he decided to avoid direct confrontation, opting instead to try to wear Hannibal down. However, this tactic offended the martial pride of the Romans, and so within a year Fabius Maximus was sacked and replaced by two consuls who, in the time-honoured tradition of all politicians, promised to end the war quickly. They assembled 50,000 men—the largest Roman army seen up until that time—and fought Hannibal at Cannae in 216 BC. Despite the fact that the Romans vastly outnumbered the 30,000 Carthaginians, Hannibal was able to encircle his opponents and completely annihilate them. It is said that less than a hundred Romans escaped. The Romans, chastened, reappointed Fabius Maximus, and eventually won by wearing Hannibal down in Italy and attacking Carthaginian forces in Spain and North Africa. Hannibal was finally defeated in North Africa in 202 BC, ending the war.

In the third and final Punic War, which broke out in 149 BC, the Roman people were manipulated into attacking a beleaguered enemy. In the 50 years between the Second and Third Punic Wars, Rome was very busy with her overseas territorial conquests, including destroying the Greek empires in the east and illiterate Spanish tribes in the west. However, their pride would not let them forget the time when they were humiliated and brought to their knees by Carthage. Surprisingly, for a culture that prided itself on its military prowess and martial discipline, it was not the military that hungered for a chance to subdue and humiliate Carthage. In republican Rome there was no standing army to maintain the frontiers. Armies were assembled as the need arose, drawn from the various peoples living on the Italian peninsula. They may have considered it their patriotic duty to fight for Rome, but they certainly did not want to fight. They would much rather stay at home, looking after their crops and livestock. It was the politicians in Rome, particularly the senatorial elite, who were the main driving force behind the war.

Chief among the voices clamouring for a renewal of the conflict was the esteemed Senator Marcus Porcius Cato, one of a number of politicians who believed that Rome's greatness was due to a continued devotion to the old Roman ideals of self-denial and love of order. Contemptuous of the Hellenistic east, he condemned all extravagance and any foreign customs imported from that part of the Mediterranean. He was especially critical of the decadence and disorder he saw as being linked to luxury. In his view, rural simplicity was the ideal, and he himself consciously imitated the down-to-earth appearance and rustic manners of a farmer. He was proud of the fact that Rome was a tiny, unsophisticated and dilapidated city that could not be compared to the magnificent cities of the East.

Cato the Elder showing figs from Carthage to the Roman Senate.

Cato believed that discipline was essential in both private and public life. He held that the family depended for its strength on each member of the household and that the family was the foundation of the state. Accordingly, he was a hard husband, a strict father and a severe master. He saw affection and softness as having no place in the home, or the state, since in his opinion they would only lead to the destruction of both. It was this patriotic fervour and regard for Roman history and tradition that set him on the path to Carthage's destruction, and the Romans loved him for it.

## The Fate of Carthage

Carthage had learned its lesson after the Second Punic War, and no longer sought to become a military power. Instead, it became a city of traders, and regained much of its prosperity. This caused alarm in Rome, where many felt that a reinvigorated Carthage might once again pose a threat, and over time bitterness and hatred towards Carthage became more intense. Rome, it seemed, would brook no rival, either militarily or financially. Nor had the humiliation experienced by the various aristocratic generals defeated by Hannibal been forgotten by their senatorial descendants. Until the late 150 BCs, the Romans were content to let their Numidian allies, under the leadership of King Masinissa, make regular attacks on Carthage to prevent its resurgence. Under the terms of the treaty signed at the end of the Second Punic War, Carthage had been forced to give up its army. They were therefore unable to resist the Numidian incursions, which meant that Carthaginian territory was lost on a regular basis. When Carthage sent embassies to Rome asking for her help, they were denied justice, with Rome upholding the gains made by Masinissa.

While Scipio Aemilianus watched the flames devour Carthage, he wept and uttered what the Romans of later generations saw as a prophecy: 'Assyria has fallen, Persia and Macedonia have likewise fallen. Carthage is burning. The day of the destruction of sacred Troy will arrive, and the slaughter of Priam and his people.'

It was the increasing number of Numidian raids that brought matters to a head. Four years before the outbreak of the Third Punic War, the Carthaginians made yet another plea to Rome for assistance. The Romans decided to take advantage of this request to assess Carthage's strength, despatching a mission headed by Cato. It was during this trip that Cato became concerned about the wealth of the city and the richness of its surrounding land. Accordingly, on his return he set about turning public opinion against Carthage, even though there was not one shred of evidence that they harboured any hostile intentions towards Rome, and in fact had long since renounced the military expansionism of Hannibal.

The Roman senate now desperately wanted to destroy Carthage, and while waiting for the opportunity to arise, politicians regularly denounced the military aspirations and ambitions of the Carthaginian trading consortium. The manipulation was blatant, with Cato ending every speech, whatever the topic, with the phrase 'Carthago delenda est!'—'Carthage must be destroyed!' The Roman people now believed that the Carthaginians were once again preparing to invade them. There is a story told of how, when making a speech to the senate one day, Cato shook a Libyan fig from the folds of his toga. As the senators admired its size and beauty, Cato reminded them the country where the fig grew was only three day's sailing from Rome, demonstrating that Roman efforts to restrict Carthage's resurgence had failed.

To provoke the war they wanted so badly, the Romans took advantage of a Carthaginian attempt to defend their territory. In 151 BC, King Masinissa invaded Carthage with Rome's tacit assent, but this time the Carthaginians decided that they had had enough. They raised an army of 25,000, but it was no match for Masinissa's battle-hardened Numidians. Roman observers, rather than painting a picture of Carthaginian weakness in the face of Numidian aggression, declared that the Carthaginians had raised an army in obvious violation of their treaty. In response, Rome sent an army to North Africa with the goal of starting a war. They demanded that the Carthaginians abandon their city and move inland. The abandoned city was to be razed to the ground by the Romans to punish Carthaginian disobedience. They declared that Carthaginian refusal would indicate that a military campaign was being planned against Rome. It is hardly surprising that the Carthaginians refused to abandon Carthage, claiming that their ancestors had lived in the city and so would they. Unmoved, the Roman senate used this refusal as an excuse to declare war and promptly laid siege to the city.

The citizens of Carthage withstood the siege for three years, as a series of incompetent Roman generals struggled to take the city. They were eventually replaced by Scipio Aemilianus, who took the city by storm, subduing it after six days of vicious hand-to-hand fighting. The Romans were merciless. By the time the Carthaginians finally surrendered, only some 50,000 people remained out of a total population of 700,000. These pathetic survivors were rounded up and sold into slavery. In a final act of vindictiveness—ignoring Scipio's objections—the senate ordered the city be razed. Taking everything movable, the Romans demolished the harbour, pulled down all of the large buildings and walls and allowed the city to burn for 17 days. As Scipio watched the flames devour the city, he is reported to have wept, foreseeing a similar fate for his own country.

## Legacies

With the final obliteration of the Carthaginian Empire, Rome became mistress of the western Mediterranean. During the course of the Punic Wars, she had seized a number of provinces, and it was these provinces that changed the nature of the Roman republic and ultimately affected the fate of Western Europe.

The acquisition of overseas provinces meant that Rome became intimately concerned with the affairs of foreigners, despite the fact that the republic was not set up to deal with the management of an overseas empire. Rome's initial success and rise to greatness was due principally to the fact that she was a small city-state, with a political system that was able to deal efficiently with local issues. Managing an empire changed all that, and it also changed the way that the Roman elite saw themselves. The provinces became the personal playthings of proconsular governors, who exploited them ruthlessly. Those more martially minded used their domains as bases from which to launch opportunistic military interventions against foreign kings, in actions that rarely had the approval of the senate. These governors found it all too easy to disregard Rome's authority whenever they were threatened by other vested interests from rival senatorial families. With Roman law so bound up with the 'mos majorum', or traditions of the ancestors, there were no guidelines

## SOWING THE FIELDS WITH SALT

There is a story told about the destruction of Carthage that is often repeated, despite its doubtful authenticity. It claims that to make certain that Carthage would never rise again and threaten Rome after her buildings and fortifications had been torn down, the fields were sown with salt to ensure that nothing would ever grow there.

First, the story is not mentioned by any of the ancient sources, only appearing in accounts written by twentieth-century historians. Second, although it may have been possible for the Romans to damage the soil in this manner, such an action would have impeded Rome's continued expansion, which depended on grain imported from North Africa. After all, access to new sources of grain was one of the main economic benefits of the Punic Wars. Finally, salt was an expensive commodity in the ancient world. The amount needed to permanently destroy the fertility of the soil would have been so enormous that the supposed benefit would not have been worth the financial cost. Indeed, as the Roman historian Cassiodorus noted, 'Some seek not gold, but there lives not a man who does not need salt.'

for gubernatorial responsibility or for the punishments of corruption. This dilemma was a new one, and the republic (through the senate) was so constrained by tradition that it could not adapt to manage the situation—especially in cases where the governor was one of their own. Once the republic had acquired an empire, it was only a matter of time before the senate, with its small-town ideas, was replaced by a single ruler.

The vast increase in wealth that came with the acquisition of provinces meant that governors were now able to influence the political process in ways that had never been possible before. Candidates in elections might be murdered and political groups began to use urban mobs to frighten their opponents into doing what they were told. Simply tolerated at first, the use of brute force to 'save' the republic was eventually promoted as desirable. Senators who were unable to use legitimate channels to prevent reformist legislation employed assassins, bribery and false accusations to get their way. Consequently, reformers who found their legislation blocked by conservative forces used the ever-increasing frustration and rage of the Roman plebeians—in the form of a mob—to intimidate the senate. Another method was to seek the intervention of generals who no longer saw any use for a senate that blocked reforms that could help improve the life of a soldier after his service.

The fact that Roman citizens were now being called upon to fight more frequent wars meant that the farmers who were the backbone of most Roman armies were no longer able to manage their farms effectively. Many farms were consequently sold, with the now-wealthy senators buying up these parcels of land. This changed not only the composition of the army, but also the very nature of the republic itself. Whereas previously the soldier-farmers had fought for Rome out of a sense of patriotic duty, the new armies followed their generals for the spoils of war and their soldiers remained permanently employed in the army. Members of this professional army formed a core group loyal only to their commander. Loyalty to the republic was something that had been lost forever.

In the end, it was the senate's failure to put in place new rules for running the provinces, and for controlling the commanders and their armies that caused the downfall of the republic. The senate was prepared to turn a blind eye to even the most brazen crimes, avoiding prosecutions when associates, supporters and fellow senators were involved. It was this corruption of the republic— largely as a result of the Carthaginian and Eastern wars—that turned Roman citizens against it. When a century of civil unrest ended and Augustus became the first emperor of Rome in 27 BC, he subjugated the senate and started dismantling the antiquated machinery of government. He did so with the approval of those in the plebeian classes, who had dreamed of reforms since the end of the Punic Wars. There was therefore a direct connection between the acquisition of overseas provinces and the eventual decline and fall of the Roman republic. The chaos of the civil wars, the rise of the dictators and triumvirs who eventually brought the republic to its knees and the final collapse of the republic under its own contradictions were the most important legacies of the lies told to further Rome's territorial ambitions.

> When the Romans eventually selected Scipio Aemilianus to conclude the siege of Carthage, he was praised by Cato the Censor, who declared, 'He alone has a mind, the rest are but passing shadows.'

It is nevertheless true that while the republic was destroyed, the expansionist phase ushered in by the defeat of Carthage led to the creation of an empire that would last, in one form or another, for 1500 years until the final overthrow of the Eastern Roman Empire in 1453. It was this empire, more than any other institution, that shaped Europe as we see it today. The Roman Empire gave Europe a unity—in language, laws and customs—for the first time in its history. It also gave the citizens of Europe a sense of a shared common destiny, which even the dissolution of the western half of the Roman Empire did little to change. Whether through, for example, Catholicism or the European Union, the echo of the empire has lived on.

The events that led up to the final Punic War also provided another legacy—in the form of a striking example of the way in which a war can easily be provoked by inflaming public opinion. It is evident that Cato was a consummate politician, as demonstrated by his constant appeals to patriotism and the righteousness of the cause, and his deliberate misrepresentation of Carthage as a threat to Rome. Techniques such as these have been used innumerable times through the ages, and are still being used today.

Bust of King Masinissa of Numidia, whose attacks against Carthage were to trigger the Third Punic War.

# THE FIRST HOLY CRUSADE— WHAT'S IN IT FOR ME? (1099)

*'This royal city, however, situated at the centre of the earth, is now held captive by the enemies of Christ and is subjected, by those who do not know God, to the worship of the heathen. She seeks, therefore, and desires to be liberated and ceases not to implore you to come to her aid. From you especially she asks succour, because as we have already said, God has conferred upon you above all other nations, great glory in arms. Accordingly, undertake this journey eagerly for the remission of your sins, with the assurance of the reward of imperishable glory in the kingdom of heaven …'*

**Pope Urban II**

*'Every war results from the struggle for markets and spheres of influence, and every war is sold to the public by professional liars and totally sincere religious maniacs, as a Holy Crusade to save God and Goodness from Satan and Evil.'*

**Robert Anton Wilson**

## LIE

The army of the First Crusade was made up of devout pilgrims wanting only to free the Holy Land.

## TRUTH

The army of the First Crusade was made up of thieves, murderers, rapists and brigands intent on conquering territory and acquiring booty!

## CHIEF PARTICIPANTS

Pope Urban II, leader of the Catholic Church
Emperor Alexius I Comnenus, the Byzantine Emperor
Raymond of Toulouse, leader of the First Crusade

## THE STORY SO FAR

Palestine and the Middle East had been Christian lands for over 300 years before the armies of Islam conquered large areas, removing them from the control of the Eastern Roman (Byzantine) Empire in 634 AD. The Byzantine Empire then spent the following 400 years fighting a rearguard action in an attempt to preserve her territory. By the year 1000, the Byzantines had reclaimed much land lost

Peter Desiderius exhorting the crusaders to begin the assault on Jerusalem, July 1099.

253

in previous centuries. However, a catastrophic military defeat at the Battle of Manzikert (in modern-day Turkey) in 1071 crippled her and opened up the empire to military conquest by the Muslim Turks. The Byzantines appealed to the pope, suggesting that Christians were being persecuted in the Holy Land and that military intervention was required to save the situation. The Byzantines hoped for an army they could use to reclaim territory lost to the Turks, and perhaps to enable them to rule over the Holy Land, as their Roman predecessors had once done. What they got was something else entirely …

The image of noble warriors riding through the sands to liberate the fabled city of Jerusalem has been imprinted in the minds of Western Christians for a thousand years. Stories of knights, their armour gleaming brightly in the sun, their banners fluttering bravely in the breeze, have been passed down through the generations. Tales of their daring deeds have appeared in folk tales and fables recounted by village storytellers, in medieval romances and in historical novels and epic films.

The story presented is one of chivalry and gallantry for a noble cause; of personal sacrifice, honour and glory in the name of Christ. Dig deeper, however, and the reality turns out to be quite different. The army of knights and devout pilgrims turns out to have been one made up of murderers, thieves, arsonists and rapists, the very dregs of society. They were the ones who answered the call of the crusade to purge their sins, and they were the ones who turned the First Crusade into a bloodbath of monstrous proportions. The legacy of the First Crusade has been a climate of distrust between Muslims and Christians that endures to this day.

## The Official Story—To Free the Holy Land

It was a cold spring morning in March 1095 when a party of men, the likes of whom had not been seen in western Europe since the coronation of the Emperor Charlemagne more than 200 years earlier, arrived in the northern Italian city of Piacenza. They were envoys from the Byzantine Emperor Alexius I, and they were there to ask Pope Urban II for aid in defeating the Seljuk Turks. The Seljuks were Muslims who had conquered parts of the Holy Land (modern-day Israel and Palestine), where they were accused of subjecting Christian pilgrims to all manner of indignities.

Urban, seeing an opportunity to heal the 40-year-old Great Schism between Eastern and Western Christians, summoned a council to be held in Clermont, France in November 1095. In front of the assembled nobles and clergy, he urged all devout pilgrims throughout Christendom to take up the sword for Christ and retake the Holy Land from its Muslim occupiers.

The ponderous machinery of the church swung into action in response to this appeal. Priests and monks all over Europe—from Spain to Germany, Sicily to Scotland—preached the need for urgent action to reclaim the holy places from the sacrilegious unbelievers. Wild and extravagant stories—some of them true—told by monks such as Peter the Hermit and Walter the Penniless of countless atrocities committed by Muslims on Christian pilgrims travelling to Jerusalem and other holy sites in the Middle East inflamed the crusading fever.

As an incentive to persuade people to join the fight, the pope offered plenary indulgences to all participants, which meant that their stay in purgatory would be shortened after their death. Thousands from all walks of life responded to the call, from peasants and artisans to priests and minor nobility. Eventually, a total of around 50,000 crusaders, including some 7000 knights, made their way in numerous small bands across Europe to the Byzantine capital of Constantinople.

The army was under the leadership of three great princes. First, there was Count Raymond IV of Toulouse, who, at the age of 56, was the oldest, richest and the most devout of the crusaders, having spent many years fighting the Muslims in Spain. Next was Prince Bohemund I of Otranto, a Norman who was the most able military commander among the princes. Standing over 1.8 m (6 ft) tall, with blond hair and blue eyes, he dwarfed his fellow crusaders. As a veteran of the Byzantine wars of the 1080s, his experience, especially in conducting difficult sieges, was going to be vital in the coming battles. Finally, there was Godfrey of Bouillon, a descendant of the great Charlemagne himself.

These noblemen, the brothers of kings, impressed all as they rode into the imperial city of Constantinople at the head of their mail-clad knights. Their presence meant that, aside from the occasional bouts of pillaging and looting, the army's progress was remarkably trouble-free, considering its size. Upon their arrival, Alexius I arranged for the crusaders to be ferried across the Bosphorus to Asia Minor, where they began their campaign. After capturing Nicaea in 1097, the crusaders moved on to Antioch (in modern-day Turkey), which was taken after a desperate siege that lasted for eight months. In 1099 they started on the road to Jerusalem, their morale at a low point after the hardships experienced during the battle for Antioch.

The army's morale received a much-needed boost when it finally arrived before the walls of Jerusalem in June 1099, and again when a priest named Peter Desiderius announced that he had received a message from Bishop Adhemar of Le Puy, who had died the previous year. Adhemar's ghost told Peter that the crusaders must free themselves from the corruption of the world, discard sin, and march in a barefoot procession around the city walls. He told them that God had promised that Jerusalem would fall in nine days, in the same way that he had made Jericho fall to Joshua, because Joshua had trusted in the word of the Lord. He also told them that if they didn't do as Adhemar's ghost said, God would increase their misfortunes.

So it was that on 8 July 1099, the crusaders began their long march around the walls of Jerusalem as instructed by Peter Desiderius, a distance of nearly 5 km (3 miles). Seven days later, on 15 July, the crusaders ended the siege by breaking down sections of the walls and entering the city. To the crusaders this was a miracle every bit as wondrous as the parting of the Red Sea for the Israelites, and was taken as a sign of God's favour and his approval of their actions. Additional miracles reinforced this belief, such as the finding of the Holy Lance (that had pierced the side of Christ) at Antioch and Latin Patriarch Arnulf of Chocques' discovery of the True Cross (upon which Christ was crucified) in the days following the capture of Jerusalem.

After Jerusalem was taken and all resistance quelled, the crusaders asked Raymond of Toulouse to become King of Jerusalem, but he refused, saying that he couldn't wear a crown of gold where Christ had worn a crown of thorns. Baldwin of Edessa was therefore elected King of Jerusalem in his place. As they celebrated Mass on that first victorious night under the vaulted ceiling of the Church of the Holy Sepulchre, none of the crusaders present could have predicted that they would hold the Holy City for a mere 88 years, until they were finally evicted by the Muslim hero Saladin in 1187.

## The Truth—Priests and Nobles

The reality was quite different from the orthodox version of events outlined above. Regardless of claims made at the time and since, the crusading armies were not made up of devout Christian pilgrims, motivated to free the Holy Land. For the priests, monks and, ultimately, the pope, it was a suspicion of Eastern Orthodox Christianity that motivated them throughout the planning and execution of the First Crusade. They saw their fellow Christians as a greater threat than the Muslim occupiers of Jerusalem.

Pope Urban II, Bishop of Rome, Vicar of Christ, Successor of the Prince of the Apostles, Supreme Pontiff of the Universal Church, Servant of the Servants of God, was a man who possessed great determination, flexibility and diplomatic finesse. At the time, the pope was the supreme head of the European community and the religious successor to the old Roman emperors, and his law was obeyed by all members of the European community, from kings to peasants. Only 20 years earlier, Pope Gregory VII, Urban's predecessor, had excommunicated the Holy Roman Emperor, forcing him to beg forgiveness on bended knee. Urban was a shrewd political operator, seeing the crusades as an opportunity to extend the leadership of the Latin Church into the Greek east.

At the time of his request for help, Emperor Alexius I was a man beset by crises. This was not surprising, since he had inherited an empire on the verge of collapse. He was the ruler of the Christian Eastern Roman Empire (now commonly known as the Byzantine Empire), which for 400 years had been fighting a war against the Muslims.

The situation had not always been so bleak. The political and military situation between the Muslims and the Byzantine Christians had remained relatively balanced until 1071. However, a series of ineffectual Byzantine emperors and a crushing defeat by the Seljuk Turks at the Battle of Manzikert (in modern-day Turkey) meant that large portions of Asia Minor were now lost to the Christians.

After the Turks conquered Jerusalem in 1076, the situation was looking increasingly bleak, and by the time Alexius I ascended the throne, the Byzantine Empire was on the brink of extinction. Desperate times called for desperate measures, and so it was that Alexius sent envoys to the pope to appeal for help in recapturing lost Byzantine territory and reducing the threat posed by the Seljuk Turks. The Latin west—made up of all of Western Europe—had always been contemptuous of the Greek east, and this appeal confirmed their opinion, demonstrating just how weak the Byzantine Empire really was, and how poor the emperor's bargaining position.

The Latin prelates considered the Greeks to be schismatics who threatened the unity and stability of the worldwide church by their obstinate refusal to accept papal primacy. Intolerant of any deviation from their own beliefs—even the most insignificant decision concerning the use of leavened or unleavened bread in the sacrament—the Latin priests were certain that the internal enemy was a greater danger to Christendom than any external foe.

The Great Schism of 1054 had left the Western Church convinced that a concerted attempt to impose Western beliefs upon the East was the best way to ensure uniformity. So, regardless of Urban II's stated intentions of brotherly assistance and rapprochement, the real motive of the religious leaders of the crusades was the imposition of the Latin church on the Greek east.

## THE CRUSADE OF THE POOR

The First Crusade had a disastrous predecessor in the so-called Crusade of the Poor. Pope Urban II was expecting the nobility of Europe to respond to his call, but what he got in the first instance was a force made up of 100,000 peasants and mostly unskilled fighters, including women and children. This group was led by a monk named Peter the Hermit, who rode a donkey and dressed in simple clothing.

This initial campaign got off to a bad start, with members of the crusade pillaging their way through Hungarian and Byzantine territory. When the rag-tag army eventually arrived at Constantinople, Alexius I had no idea what to do with it, so he packed it off to Asia Minor as quickly as possible, advising its members to avoid the Turks at all costs. They ignored his advice and were slaughtered, with only a few thousand returning to Constantinople to join the more carefully organised First Crusade a few months later.

This was made clear when Arnulf of Chocques—chaplain to the Norman crusader army—was elected first Latin patriarch of Jerusalem in 1099, ignoring the claims of the Greek patriarch. Even when the pope declared Arnulf ineligible for office, it was another Latin prelate who replaced him. The Latin patriarch's actions in enforcing the Latin rite among the crusaders and banning non-Roman Catholic Masses at the Holy Sepulchre further alienated the disaffected Greeks. This was the first in a series of attempts to bring Eastern Orthodox churches under the direction of the Roman Church, with the aim of eventually converting all eastern Christians to the Roman rite.

The noblemen who led the crusades also failed to live up to their popular image. Far from being an idealistic royal brotherhood who saw their Christian duty as the liberation of the Holy Land from the tyrannical Muslims, they were, in fact, mercenary opportunists who saw the crusade as an opportunity to create kingdoms for themselves in the East. Raymond of Toulouse was a poor administrator and notorious womaniser who hated Muslims, having lost an eye in single combat against the Moors in Spain. Prince Bohemund of Otranto was cruel and unscrupulous, with an unruly temper. His ambition was to conquer the Byzantine Empire. Godfrey of Bouillon was reputed to have once wrestled a huge bear, and when asked by a Bedouin Arab to kill a camel, had carved off its head with a single stroke of his sword. These were tough and ambitious men, all of them interested only in seeking glory, territory and wealth for themselves, and a kingdom to pass on to their children.

Opportunities to achieve such ambitions were rare in their native Europe. However, there had been precedents. They had all witnessed their Norman compatriots establish kingdoms in southern Italy in 1055 and England in 1066.

Although many members of the lesser nobility may have wanted to return home after the crusade was over, it was inconceivable that these royal warrior princes should make the long journey to Palestine, endure three years of hardship, squander money and troops to defeat the Muslims, and then simply return home after handing the conquered lands to the Byzantines. In fact, the division of the spoils started almost immediately after the taking of Antioch when, in typical crusader style, they spent the next six months bickering over who would hold the city. It eventually ended up being controlled by Bohemund of Otranto, who had himself crowned Prince of Antioch even before the crusader army had pressed on to Jerusalem.

Having finally occupied Jerusalem, the leading French and Norman knights decided not to return any of the conquered land to the Byzantine Emperor, but to create their own tiny kingdoms. Alexius I despatched numerous angry letters, reminding the crusaders of their oaths to return all lands to him, but they ignored him. As far as the priests and nobles of the First Crusade were concerned, the outcome was a stunning success.

Pope Urban II presiding over the Council of Clermont, France.

## Thieves and Criminals

The clergy and nobility only formed a small proportion of the total crusading army, however. Forgotten by history, which tends to focus on the leaders of the crusade, the bulk of the army—the common people who formed more than 80 per cent of the foot soldiers—also differed significantly from the way they are generally portrayed. Thousands of common people answered the call of the crusade, but who were they? An average town in Europe at this time was inhabited by farmers, artisans, shopkeepers and other tradesmen. But is wasn't these people who answered the call to take up arms for their religion, and the blame for that can be placed squarely on Pope Urban II's broad shoulders.

The pope, in summoning the Christian faithful to fight the infidel, promised a plenary indulgence for all participants. In an age when everyone took their salvation seriously, this was a virtual free pass into heaven. It meant that as long as an individual was in a state of repentance and confession, he would not spend any time in purgatory. Who, therefore, was most in need of this holy 'get out of jail free' card? Logically it was those who had sinned in this life, and the greater the sin, the more they were in need of an indulgence. It should therefore come as no surprise that thieves, murderers, arsonists, rapists and other serious sinners answered the call to join the crusade in great numbers. Unlike the wealthy nobles and priests, these individuals brought very little with them, usually just the clothes on their backs and some implement for killing.

> The Al-Aqsa Mosque is the spot where the Prophet Mohammed was said to have ascended to Heaven.

According to Archbishop William of Tyre, who wrote a chronicle of the crusades, there were only a few knights among the groups that made up the army, with the vast majority carrying only the most primitive weapons—axes, daggers and the occasional sword. They had few horses or baggage carts, and in an incredible feat of endurance, walked the entire distance from Western Europe to Palestine. Two characteristics shared by most of the common foot soldiers were a criminal past and a tendency to anti-social behaviour.

The church ignored their misdemeanours, since it was in its interest to attract men of this type, who could be let loose on anyone labelled an enemy by the church. Since these men were the backbone of the crusading armies—numbering in the tens of thousands—it was inevitable that the victorious crusaders massacred almost every inhabitant of Jerusalem. They spared no one—Muslims, Jews and Orthodox Christians were all slaughtered indiscriminately. Although many Muslims sought shelter after a failed defence of the Al-Aqsa Mosque on Temple Mount—and despite the fact that Tancred, the Norman noble, had granted them refuge—other crusaders butchered them the following morning. The many Jews who gathered for safety in the chief synagogue by the Western Wall of Temple Mount were burned to death along with the building that sheltered them. These actions have been excused by some as normal in the context of a medieval war, or as an inevitable consequence of having an army made up mainly of religious fanatics eager to kill in the name of Christ, but this was obviously not the case. They were, in fact, the actions of criminals, and they were to have a profound effect on the course of Middle Eastern and world history.

## Legacies

The First Crusade provided the first real example of the militarisation of the Christian Church, although it is significant that it was in response to the ascendancy of militant Islam. The Church had, for centuries, supported the right of the secular arm of government to fight a 'just war', but this was the first occasion on which the Church itself had become involved in the planning and execution of a war.

The creation of military orders such as the Templars and Hospitallers to defend the Church's interests and halt the rapid expansion of Islam might seem to go against Christ's command to 'love one another as I have loved you'. However, the practical example of Islam, as a religion that combined military ideology and an aggressive theological underpinning, meant that the Christian Church had to follow the example or be destroyed. The Templars were a monastic order drawn from minor nobility throughout Europe. They came into existence after the success of the First Crusade, with their charter being to defend the Holy Land and to protect pilgrims. The Hospitallers were a much older organisation, having been founded in the 600 ADs as a Christian body responsible for running hospitals for the sick and destitute. They were also transformed into a monastic military order in the aftermath of the First Crusade, but they maintained their original function. These orders became the foundations upon which universal papal power was built.

The result was the creation of the medieval papacy, combining in one organisation that which was owed to God and that which was owed to Caesar. This development of the church as a secular power through military means would have enormous consequences, the most disastrous for the Church being the rupture of Christendom in the Reformation, as other voices called for the Christian Church to return to the fundamental teachings of its founder.

In the actions of the crusaders, Protestant critics such as Martin Luther saw the errors of the Catholic Church made manifest. They condemned the fanatical priests and monks who fooled the people with false miracles and relics. They condemned the practice of issuing indulgences as an ignorant and unscriptural superstition. Above all, they condemned the pope in his attempt to use the crusades as a tool for universal dominion throughout Christendom.

Nevertheless, the myth of the noble Christian warrior fighting for God and the true faith still exercises a powerful influence on the minds of Protestants and Catholics alike. While Protestant reformers railed against the papally inspired crusades, they were only too happy to adopt the image of the crusader ideal in order to inspire their followers into doing God's work in cleansing His Church and the world. A clear example of this can be seen in the actions of the Scottish covenanters during the English Civil War (1638–51). Bound together by the notion that they were the true followers of Christ and the true members of the reformed church, they were determined to bring Presbyterianism to the English and overthrow the quasi-Papist Anglican Church. They therefore invaded England on behalf of the Parliamentarians against King Charles and his bishops to further their religious agenda.

Although the covenanters might not have seen themselves as 'crusaders', there is no doubt they believed they were Christian warriors fighting for God and the true faith against Satan's hordes. They had well and truly adopted the myth of the crusading ideal, and it led them to imitate the papal objective of the crusades—imposing religious uniformity through military might. It was this principle that drove the wars of the Protestant and Catholic Reformations, wars that destroyed tens of thousands of lives during the sixteenth, seventeenth and eighteenth centuries.

꙰ ꙮ ꙰

Prince Bohemund hailed from Otranto, a town located on the heel of Italy. It was ironic that he answered the call to help Emperor Alexius I as he had inflicted many defeats on the emperor during the preceding decade.

꙰ ꙮ ꙰

Echoes of the crusades are still audible even today, with this brand of muscular Christianity holding many attractions for fundamentalist Christians of all persuasions. They see in Islam a threat to the western Judaeo-Christian way of life. Their prejudices are reinforced by scenes of terrorism perpetrated by the extremist followers of Islam, and they view the crusades as a patriotic and justifiable defence of the faith of their fathers and the Western way of life.

To quote American author James Atticus Bowden in *Renew America*, the publication of an evangelical conservative organisation: 'The Crusades were strategic counterattacks from the West. "Crusade" was a good word for a noble struggle until very recently. Liberal human secularists and sissy Christians, who hate conservative Christians so much they would rather see the West go under Islam than rise with Evangelical Christianity, push a multi-cultural historical curse on the Crusades [...] Until evangelical Crusades truly roll back Islam, America must face Muslims' implacable hostility and insatiable demands.'

This misrepresentation of the crusades has its greatest impact on Muslim attitudes towards Westerners. The brutality of the First Crusade, and the mistaken belief that the crusader armies were made up of average Christians rather than hardened criminals, has left a lingering distrust of Christians in the minds of many Muslims. Stories of the sack of Jerusalem have been passed down within families right to the present day. The bloody aftermath of the siege reinforced, and continues to reinforce, Muslim attitudes towards Christians and Westerners generally.

Such attitudes are seen clearly in the thinking of Al-Qaeda leader Osama bin Laden. Interviewed by CNN, bin Laden indicated that jihad was a duty. It had many aspects, including the goal to unite against the newest Crusade by the Christians. He emphasised that this was a recurring war; describing Bush's actions as a raising of the cross, continuing the original crusade brought by Richard the Lionhearted, Louis of France and Frederick Barbarossa of Germany.

# GALILEO AND THE JESUITS (1633)

*'And who can doubt that it will lead to the worst disorders when minds created free by God are compelled to submit slavishly to an outside will? When we are told to deny our senses and subject them to the whim of others? When people devoid of whatsoever competence are made judges over experts and are granted authority to treat them as they please? These are the novelties which are apt to bring about the ruin of commonwealths and the subversion of the state.'*
**Galileo Galilei**

*'Great spirits have always encountered violent opposition from mediocre minds.'*
**Albert Einstein**

## LIE
The Church persecuted Galileo because of his theory that the Earth orbits the sun.

## TRUTH
The Church persecuted Galileo because he had annoyed some influential Jesuits!

## CHIEF PARTICIPANTS
Galileo Galilei, an Italian astronomer
Pope Urban VIII, leader of the Catholic Church
Father Horatio Grassi, Jesuit professor of mathematics

## THE STORY SO FAR
By the 1600s, the Catholic Church had drawn in upon itself, hoping to avoid any further Reformation-type disruptions. Having endured the trauma of the Reformation in the 1530s and 1540s, and redressed abuses within the Church with the Council of Trent in 1563, it was now ensuring that dogma would remain intact and unchanging. A symbol of that stability, and the one thing that theologians regarded as unchanging, was the notion that the Earth was the centre of the universe (a theory known as geocentrism and originally proposed by the philosopher Aristotle). It was the geocentric model of the universe, as outlined by the astronomer Ptolemy in around 150 AD, that the church maintained to be the truth. This theory remained unchallenged for over 1000 years, until the Polish astronomer Copernicus published a book in 1543 in which he declared that the Earth was not the centre of the universe. He maintained that the Earth and the other planets travelled around the sun (a theory known as heliocentrism).

Galileo Galilei before members of the Holy Office in the Vatican in 1633.

Although Copernicus' theory encountered some minor criticism from officials at the time, the Church itself took no official action against the teachings of heliocentrism until someone else, almost 60 years later, took up the theories of Copernicus and peered into the night sky with the aid of a telescope …

For those of us in the modern world, it is hard to conceive of a time when people were unaware of the nature of the Earth and its relationship to the solar system. While we take it for granted that the Earth is a rock travelling through the vacuum of space, and that it and the other planets orbit around the sun, for many centuries the celestial dance performed by the sun and the planets was interpreted in a very different way. The apparent solidity of the Earth beneath their feet, coupled with simple observation, once suggested to all rational people that the Earth was an immovable object at the centre of the universe, and that all other bodies in the universe revolved around it. The origins of this belief can still be seen today when people speak of the sun rising in the east, implying that it moves through the heavens, and not our planet. For those who accepted this geocentric view of reality, it was only natural to believe that a deity of some kind was responsible for maintaining our home in its position under the vault of the heavens.

When this view started to be challenged in the 1600s, people reacted in different ways. Some welcomed and accepted the new science, while others rejected it out of hand and sought to discredit or silence it. The most famous of these challenges involved the Italian astronomer Galileo Galilei, and it was his fight with the Catholic Church that came to epitomise the great struggles of the modern age: that between science and superstition; between reason and religion; and between enlightenment and a world where religious authorities sought to silence anyone who dared to challenge their world view.

It is a mistake, however, to suppose that Galileo was persecuted because of his support for the heliocentric theory. In reality, the Church initially supported the new ideas that Galileo was presenting. What doomed him was his contempt for the religious authorities whose job it was to assess his theories. They lost interest in reviewing his ideas, and sought instead to destroy him for his insolence. The myth has persisted however, with the result that the Church was, and still is, presented as the enemy of all seekers after truth.

## The Official Story—Galileo's Heresy

In the early hours of the morning of 7 January 1610, a small 44-year-old university lecturer stumbled excitedly through the narrow winter streets of the Italian town of Padua. Clutched in his hand was a piece of parchment on which was outlined an exciting discovery, one that he hoped would make him famous. His name was Galileo Galilei, and he had just discovered three of Jupiter's moons—Io, Europa and Callisto. But what was really exciting and groundbreaking about his discovery was that the moons appeared and disappeared intermittently, an observation Galileo interpreted as showing that the moons passed behind Jupiter. Galileo therefore theorised that the moons were in fact orbiting Jupiter. Later that week, as he was continuing his observations, he discovered another moon, later named Ganymede, which also behaved in the same way as the first three. The importance of this finding—that a planet had smaller celestial bodies orbiting it—was that it was the first real evidence that Copernicus was correct, and that a belief in an orderly, geocentric universe, in which everything in the heavens revolved around the Earth, was fatally flawed.

Later that year, having moved to Florence, Galileo noted that Venus displayed a full set of phases, similar to those of Earth's moon—crescent, first quarter, waxing gibbous, full moon etc. This was further evidence that Ptolemy's geocentric model had problems. Just as Copernicus had predicted, the orbit of Venus around the sun caused its illuminated face to change, depending on where it was during its journey. Buoyed by his many discoveries, Galileo published a short treatise entitled *Sidereus Nuncius* (*Sidereal Messenger*) announcing his unexpected observations and how they seemed to overturn both Ptolemy's and Aristotle's view of the universe.

Accusations of heresy were not long in coming. Based on their literal reading of the Bible, monks and theologians attacked Galileo's findings and his interpretations. His most determined opponent was Florentine Friar Tommaso Caccini, who went to Rome in 1615 to report Galileo to the Inquisition—the organisation within the Roman Catholic Church responsible for rooting out heresy. It met with Galileo in 1616, with the result that heliocentrism was declared 'foolish and absurd in philosophy, and formally heretical since it explicitly contradicts in many places the sense of Holy Scripture'. Galileo was told to abandon his belief in the Copernican model, which he did.

In the years that followed, Galileo made no further attempt to examine and prove the truth of the Copernican theory of heliocentrism. Around 1630, however, he returned to the controversy, and began writing a book that would provide a balanced comparison between the two competing theories—geocentrism and heliocentrism. The book was published in 1632 under the title *Dialogue Concerning the Two Chief World Systems*. In it, Galileo once again sought to prove the truth of the Copernican system by both praising it and ridiculing the Ptolemaic view of the universe. The Church was outraged, and in 1633 Galileo was directed to appear before the Inquisition again to answer the charge of heresy.

After a short trial, he was found to have held as true 'the false doctrine taught by some that the sun is the centre of the world', and that he had disobeyed the instructions given by the Congregation of the Holy Office in 1616. These were that he would 'abandon this doctrine, not to teach it to others, not to defend it, and not to treat of it; and that if you did not acquiesce in this injunction, you should be imprisoned'. Considering him a lapsed heretic, the Inquisition ordered that he recant his heliocentric theory and sentenced him to be imprisoned (later changed to house arrest) for the remainder of his life. They also declared that the *Dialogue Concerning the Two Chief World Systems* would be banned and placed on the Index of Prohibited Books. Our last view of Galileo is of a sick old man on his knees before the Tribunal of the Holy Office, denying a theory in which he still believed, and publicly cursing and detesting his errors. He never publicly discussed Copernicus or heliocentrism again up until the time of his death in 1642.

## The Truth—Beware the Jesuits

No event in the recorded history of the Catholic Church has been so misconstrued as the condemnation of Galileo. It has been used for centuries as evidence to support the notion that science and theology don't mix; that science had to liberate itself from the blinkered beliefs of the medieval Church. As American author Thomas Woods writes: 'The one-sided version of the Galileo affair with which most people are familiar is very largely to blame for the widespread belief that the church has obstructed the advance of scientific inquiry.' As Woods asserts, the belief that Galileo was persecuted because of his theory should be replaced by the view that he was persecuted because he made some powerful enemies who were determined to bring him down by any means possible. In other words, politics, not religion, was the cause of Galileo's downfall.

Many things could be said of Galileo. He was a genius, a man of quick wit with a marvellous intellect that he was able to apply to understanding the way in which the world and the universe operated. He was also wilful, and disdainful and intolerant of anyone he considered a fool. Obstinate and uncompromising, he ridiculed and mocked numerous people during his career and made himself many enemies. Of these, the most important were the Jesuits. Jesuit astronomer Christoph Grenberger touched on the heart of the matter when he declared: 'If Galileo had only known how to retain the favor of the Jesuits, he would have been spared all his misfortunes, and he could have written what he pleased about everything, even about the motion of the Earth.'

When Galileo's first troubles appeared, he had much good will, and many friends among the Church hierarchy who were keen to help him and who did not see his theories as having any heretical leanings. When Galileo appeared before the Inquisition in 1615–16, it was Cardinal Bellarmine who was asked to provide an opinion on the Copernican theory. He wrote to Galileo after the adverse findings by the Inquisition advising him that while he could not hold or defend the heliocentric theory, he

# THE NOTE OF 26 FEBRUARY 1616

Of all the incidents that occurred during the lengthy debates over the condemnation of Galileo in 1616, one event remains a mystery, one that would have significant ramifications when Galileo faced the Inquisition for a second time in 1633.

When officers of the Inquisition passed down their 1616 verdict—that the Copernican doctrine was 'foolish and absurd, philosophically and formally heretical inasmuch as it expressly contradicts the doctrine of Holy Scripture in many passages'—it was overruled by some of the more cautious cardinals, who agreed with Cardinal Bellarmine that Copernicanism was a valid working hypothesis. A gentler ruling, which removed the word 'heresy', was accordingly released. After a personal appeal by Galileo, Bellarmine provided him with an official document that merely ordered him not to 'hold or defend' the theory.

At some stage, however, a statement was placed in Galileo's Holy Office file stating that he was advised to abandon Copernicanism and directed 'to abstain altogether from teaching or defending this opinion and doctrine, and even from discussing it'. There are still unanswered questions as to whether this statement was authentic, or whether it might not have been a forgery inserted into the file by some corrupt curial official. Historians would also like to know when, exactly, it was placed there.

The supposed verdict in its original form did not surface until 1633, when Galileo's foolishness saw him in trouble again after the release of his *Dialogue on the Two Chief World Systems*. Strictly speaking, the contents of the *Dialogue* did not breach Bellarmine's command. However, it did breach the decree recorded in the questionable statement found in Galileo's file, the contents of which he was apparently entirely unaware of, but which was nevertheless used against him at his second trial in 1633.

was certainly free to present the theory hypothetically, discuss it and continue with his experiments and observations. Further, even though the Inquisition decreed it heretical, their opinion was not binding on the Church.

Galileo, however, was determined to push for acceptance of the Copernican theory and his own findings, whatever the consequences. In doing so, his usual abrasive manner and aggressive tactics annoyed almost everyone who could help him, giving the Church hierarchy no alternative. It either had to acknowledge Copernicanism as the truth—regardless of the fact that it had not yet been proved—with the consequent reinterpretation of scripture, or it had to denounce the theory.

Believing that he was right, Galileo was not prepared to argue with Jesuits who were coming up with some substantial objections to the Copernican theory. However, his disputes with the Jesuits were concerned with more than just heliocentrism. Galileo was already having a disagreement with the Jesuit Christoph Scheiner over the discovery of sunspots and their interpretation. Further, in 1619, Galileo and another Florentine, Mario Guiducci, refuted theories about comets published by Father Horatio Grassi, the professor of mathematics at the Jesuit Collegio Romano. Galileo and Guiducci insulted Christoph Scheiner in their paper and made numerous unflattering remarks about the professors of the Collegio Romano. Galileo then poured more scorn on Grassi when he issued his own rebuttal. By these actions, Galileo had virtually guaranteed that many of the Jesuits who had been considering his ideas would now turn against him.

It was in this environment that the Jesuits began their investigations into the Copernican theory supported by Galileo. Arguments put forward by the ancient Greek philosopher Aristotle were cited, which pointed out that if the Earth did orbit the sun there should be a noticeable shift in the location of a star as seen from

Frontispiece and title page of Galileo Galilei's *Dialogue Concerning the Two Chief World Systems,* published by Giovanni Battista Landini in 1632.

the Earth on one side of the sun, and then six months later on the other side—a phenomenon now known as the stellar parallax. Galileo could find no evidence of this with the crude instruments at his disposal, and such evidence was not forthcoming for another 300 years. Galileo also insisted that the planets orbited the sun in perfect circles, something that even the Jesuit astronomers could see was not correct.

It must be remembered that by the 1630s, even the Catholic Church had been influenced by the Renaissance and the Reformation, however much the Franciscan and Dominican theologians who dominated the Inquisition might have hated it. Though they attacked Galileo on theological grounds, it was the Jesuits who were the intellectual vanguard of the Church, and it was they who had the pope's ear.

Galileo responded to the criticism by launching an anti-Jesuit campaign with a series of pamphlets and letters that were distributed throughout Europe. He answered his Jesuit critics by stating that it was not worth the effort to try to convince fools who were incapable of the most elementary reasoning. Disregarding the advice of his friends in Rome, he persevered in shifting the discussion onto theological grounds. He felt that he had to answer the objection that his theories contradicted Holy Scripture, thus moving the battle from the scientific to the religious arena. This is precisely what the Jesuits wanted, and they used Galileo's misjudgment to humiliate and destroy him as revenge for his scorn and abuse.

## Condemnation

Even after insulting the intellectual capacity of the Jesuits and alienating many leading churchmen, Galileo could still have retrieved the situation. This was because, up until that time, he had the support of the one man who counted more than any other in Catholic Europe—the pope. It provides an insight into the man's mind that Galileo would proceed to alienate the one individual who could have ensured that his work might be accepted, or at least tolerated.

Still resentful of the actions of the Inquisition in prohibiting him from holding or teaching Copernican views, Galileo was presented with an opportunity to have that decision rescinded. In 1623, Galileo's acquaintance and sponsor, Cardinal Barberini, became Pope Urban VIII. Barberini had opposed the condemnation of Galileo, and the astronomer immediately proposed that his friend should lift the decree of 1616. They had meetings to discuss the matter, but Urban was a conceited, short-tempered man who—as a self-styled prince of the Renaissance—believed he was competent to issue declarations covering all aspects of humankind's knowledge. In one meeting, Urban declared that while the Church would never define Copernicanism as heretical, he deemed all arguments over the planets to be irrelevant.

At around this time, Galileo began work on the book that was to cause his downfall, his *Dialogue Concerning the Two Chief World Systems*. Pope Urban himself had asked Galileo to provide arguments both for and against the Copernican world-view, but insisted that he must be balanced and not openly support heliocentrism. Urban also requested that his own perspective on the subject be included. By the time Galileo had finished, in 1630, he had written a book that was an assault on geocentrism and a justification of the Copernican theory. Given the amount of criticism and church opposition he had encountered, it is surprising that officers of the Inquisition who reviewed the book approved its printing. Even a Dominican professor of theology who was asked to review the work was in favour of its publication. With these endorsements and the tacit approval of the pope, the book was published in 1632.

While others may have approved of Galileo's book, the pope himself was furious when he learned of it in detail. Although no one had any issues with the science, Galileo had badly misjudged Urban's lenient attitude by showing his contempt for his opponents in the *Dialogue*. Not only did he make it apparent that he believed supporters of Aristotle and Ptolemy to be intellectually deficient, but he placed Pope Urban's views on cosmology into the mouth of a character in the book named Simplicio. Simplicio's role was as chief defender of the Aristotelian geocentric view, and he was portrayed as an imbecile. Galileo quite clearly seemed to be mocking the only person who was prepared to defend and protect him, and the pope could not allow such insults to escape unpunished.

Galileo's religious enemies now knew that the time was right to strike. They persuaded the pope to summon Galileo to Rome to answer charges about the illegal publication of his book as well as heresy. Appearing before the Inquisition, he was accused principally of publishing his book under false pretences, without the formal approval of the Inquisition. Of the eight charges, the accusation of heresy regarding the movement of the Earth was a smaller charge, third down the list. The principal reason for bringing Galileo before the Inquisition was that he had given offence to the Inquisition itself. The result was a foregone conclusion, with Galileo being found guilty of heresy. However, it is important to realise that whatever the official reason given for Galileo's condemnation, the Church's support for the publication of the *Dialogue* in 1630 demonstrates quite clearly that it was not against his theory. The truth was that Galileo's many enemies within the church had simply used the opportunity presented to exact their revenge.

## Legacies

Galileo's influence on our understanding of the universe was profound and revolutionary. He improved the telescope, making astronomical observations that no one else had been able to achieve. His use of quantitative experiments, the outcomes

Galileo Galilei—brilliant, volatile and arrogant in equal measure.

of which could be scrutinised with mathematical accuracy, was groundbreaking, and he demonstrated a remarkable understanding of the relationship between mathematics, theoretical physics and experimental physics. His work received the highest praise from Sir Isaac Newton, and his contributions to modern science have been recognised by such luminaries as Albert Einstein—who labelled him 'the father of modern science'—and cosmologist Stephen Hawking, who declared that Galileo was the principal figure in the birth of modern science as it is understood today.

It could be argued, however, that Galileo's greatest impact on the world was not the result of his scientific work. In his battle with the Catholic Church over his support for Copernican astronomy, Galileo demonstrated how out of touch the religious authorities of the time were. This dispute is often cited as the crucial defining point in the history of the association between science and religion. Galileo's devotion to experimental outcomes and their analysis led to a questioning of the practice of complete submission to dogmatic authority when considering matters related to science, and is believed to be the spark that began the separation of science from both philosophy and religion. As Winston Churchill wrote:

> This quickening of the human spirit was accompanied by a questioning of long held theories. For the first time [...] men began to refer to the preceding millennium as the Middle Ages. Though much that was medieval survived in their minds, men felt they were living on the brink of a new and modern age. It was an age marked not only by splendid achievements in art and architecture, but also by the beginnings of a revolution in science.

A key legacy of the Church's misunderstood persecution of Galileo was that the Catholic Church's reaction gave credence to the belief that religious authorities were the enemies of all seekers after truth. Galileo's trial was just the latest in a string of events that distanced the Catholic Church from new ideas being debated by some of Europe's greatest minds. The trend had begun with Erasmus and the Reformation, when the Protestant reformers accused the Church of being run by superstitious fakers intent in keeping people in perpetual ignorance and in thrall to clerics.

One of the biblical passages used to denounce heliocentrism was Psalm 104:5, 'You fixed the earth upon its foundation, not to be moved forever.'

The Galileo affair was seen in the context of the post-Reformation world, and as a consequence the Church was judged quite harshly for it. In their attempt to humiliate and repudiate Galileo, the Church was seen as belonging to the bygone era of the Middle Ages, to be swept away, along with magic, superstition and witches. No one was really interested in the reason why the Catholic Church was persecuting Galileo, they only saw these events in the context of a long history of the Church's repression of dissent. They equated Galileo's persecution with attacks on Martin Luther, the denunciation of Calvin, and the persecution and slaughter of Protestants throughout Europe in Catholicism's attempt to reimpose its superstitious barbarism on a free people.

So it was that many of Europe's finest thinkers began to turn away from the Church in their search for knowledge about the nature of the world. They were no longer prepared to accept vague reassurances that the world was created in seven days, or that the heavenly bodies were perfect spheres—they wanted proof. The search for proof began almost immediately in Florence, where the first academy devoted to the new experimental science—the Accademia del Cimento—was established in 1657. It was here that Europe's first controlled experiments were conducted, and numerous other significant scientific innovations were introduced.

The end result of these changes was a steady march towards the Enlightenment, with the aim of raising reason and science to positions of pre-eminence, and of ultimately disentangling religion from the state. The social, political and economic devastation wrought by decades of religious conflict in Europe had convinced many of the inherently destructive nature of a religious state. The only sensible system of government was seen to be one in which Church and state were separated. With an emphasis placed on individual conscience and personal choice about whether or not to observe boundaries placed by state-incorporated religious authorities, such a system provided a fertile ground for nurturing scientists, doctors, mathematicians and other intellectuals. Science and reason were increasingly held to be the way forward, with religion being relegated to a superstitious primitive state from which humankind needed to escape. Religion gradually ceased to be a reason or an excuse for conflict, and the West reverted to more 'reasonable' excuses for warfare, such as economics, power, prestige and ego.

# THE HIDDEN AGENDA OF AMERICA'S FOUNDING FATHERS (1776)

*'Among the natural rights of the colonists are these: First a right to life, secondly to liberty, and thirdly to property; together with the right to defend them in the best manner they can.'*
**Samuel Adams**

*'[The rebels were] ignorant, restless desperadoes, without conscience or principles, who have led a deluded multitude to follow their standard, under pretense of grievances which had no existence but in their imaginations.'*
**Abigail Adams**

## LIE

The founding fathers were morally driven men.

## TRUTH

The founding fathers were interested in making money and wielding power over their fellow colonists!

## CHIEF PARTICIPANTS

Samuel Adams, American revolutionary leader
George Washington, revolutionary general and first President of the United States of America
John Hancock, third president of the Continental Congress

## THE STORY SO FAR

It was in 1607 that the first English colony was established in what was to become the United States of America. From the 1630s onwards, the process of establishing colonies proceeded more rapidly, with the thirteenth and final colony being established in 1733. Although several of the colonies were used as penal settlements, America was seen as the place where puritans and other non-conformists could escape the state-imposed Anglican religion of England, and thus create a land for God's chosen people. A number of the colonies began as enterprises run by private individuals (proprietary colonies), but by the 1700s all had been converted into colonies of the Crown, with governors appointed by the British parliament and all colonists subject to British parliamentary laws. The French and Indian War

America's defining moment: the signing of the Declaration of Independence, 1776.

(1754–63) gave the colonists a shared sense of a common identity as Americans as they fought alongside British troops. The costs of the war were high, however, and as the British people were already quite heavily taxed, the British parliament declared that the cost of the war and of maintaining a military presence in the colonies to prevent French incursions, should be borne by the colonists, who contributed very little in the way of taxes. Naturally this was resented …

---

'We can't all be Washingtons, but we can all be patriots.' Words that echo the foundation myth of the great American republic of ordinary men and women standing up to oppression by a foreign power, under the leadership of a group of individuals who sacrificed life, limb and property to achieve the dream of liberty and justice for all. One cannot read the following lines from the Declaration of Independence without feeling inspired by the idealism of the founding fathers: 'We hold these truths to be self-evident, that all men are created equal, that they are endowed by their Creator with certain unalienable rights, that among these are life, liberty, and the pursuit of happiness.'

However tempting it is to eulogise those who dedicated their lives to the overthrow of non-representational government in the 13 colonies, it is important to remember that the myths constructed about the founding fathers are simply that—myths. The American revolution is yet another case of the victors rewriting history, with less than noble sentiments being masked by myths of freedom, just causes and unprovoked attacks.

The main players set out to construct their preferred version of history: Thomas Jefferson drafted elegant memoirs, others destroyed documents to prevent the truth from escaping. Tobias Lear, George Washington's personal secretary, sorted through his master's presidential papers and wrote to Alexander Hamilton offering to suppress certain documents: 'There are as you well know among the several letters and papers many which every public and private consideration should withhold from further inspection.' Samuel Adams burned many of his letters, claiming that they would have damaged the reputations of men who had trusted him. Charles Thomson, secretary to the Continental Congress from 1774 to 1789, refused to leave eyewitness accounts of the actions and the motives of the founding fathers, both in their relationships with each other and their interaction with the British administration. 'I should contradict all the histories of the great events of the Revolution,' Thomson wrote, 'and show by my account of men, motives, and measures, that we are wholly indebted to the agency of Providence for its successful issue. Let the world admire the supposed wisdom and valour of our great men. Perhaps they may adopt the qualities that have been ascribed to them, and thus good may be done. I shall not undeceive future generations.'

## The Official Story—The Intolerable Acts

Britain had for years issued laws for its American colonies without consulting the colonists who had to obey them. Over time, a group of men—the founding fathers—decided that resistance against such tyranny was the only course left open to them. In 1761, Massachusetts lawyer James Otis argued that the Writs of Assistance—a legal document that served as a general search warrant—violated the constitutional rights of the colonists. In 1762, George III's veto of Virginia's *Two-Penny Act* motivated Patrick Henry, the future governor of Virginia, to declare the king a tyrant. In 1765, the *Stamp Act* united the colonies in protest, with future Pennsylvania governor John Dickinson declaring that taxation passed without representation violated man's earliest and most fundamental rights. Benjamin Franklin also pleaded that the additional taxation of the colonies was unjust after all the blood the colonists had shed during the Seven Years' War against France (1756–63).

However, it was in 1770 that events really began to accelerate, as great men stood up to fight for their liberty. In the aftermath of the Boston Massacre—in which British troops killed some civilians—John Adams spoke of the danger posed in general by standing armies. In 1772, Samuel Adams created the Committees of Correspondence, which joined patriots throughout the 13 colonies under one framework, including such notables as Patrick Henry and Thomas Jefferson. The following year, Samuel Adams led a raid on the ships of British tea merchants to protest against the *Townshend Acts*, which placed a tax on tea, paper and glass. Britain reacted by issuing the so-called *Intolerable Acts*. These included the *Boston Port Act*, which closed the port of Boston until the East India Company had been repaid for the destroyed tea, and the *Administration of Justice Act*, which allowed the governor to change the location where an accused British official would stand trial. The colonists responded by establishing the First Continental Congress in 1774, calling on all colonists to form militias for the defence of their property.

> Washington declined the offer of military dictatorship in 1783 and when King George III was told in 1796 that Washington declined further power and wanted only to return to his farm, the king declared him to be 'the most distinguished character of the age'.

By the time the fighting began at Lexington and Concord in 1775, the leading patriots had grown in stature and earned the people's trust. George Washington, a wealthy landowner and steadfast republican, was elected commander-in-chief of the Continental Army, and it was his vision and determination that led the colonists to victory. But, perhaps the most significant act of the founding fathers was the drafting of the *Declaration of Independence*. Inspired by the writings of French intellectuals, and based in large part on the *British Bill of Rights* of 1689, it gave a vision and a poetic power to the thoughts, words and deeds of the preceding 15 years. It expressed all

that was noble in the fight, justified all that had occurred in the years of conflict, and declared the righteousness of the cause in seeking independence from Britain and her king—whom they labelled a tyrant.

The idealism of the founding fathers inspired subsequent generations of Americans to follow in their footsteps, holding firm to the central tenet of the *Declaration of Independence*. As Abraham Lincoln would say during another crisis in America's history, 'Four score and seven years ago our fathers brought forth on this continent, a new nation, conceived in liberty, and dedicated to the proposition that all men are created equal.'

## The Truth—The Search for Tyranny and Nobility

Regardless of the aura of sanctity that has been spun around the American Revolution, the truth of the matter is that the war of secession was also motivated by a greed for Indian land, a lust for money and a desire for personal power. It was the merchant and landowning classes who promoted the war for reasons connected to their own personal agendas and ambitions.

It is probable that few of the poorer colonists really cared that their taxes were being sent back to the mother country. According to author Frank E. Smitha, 'roughly half of city populations were without property, many of them recent immigrants from Europe. Tax records show that in the cities the bottom 30 percent owned nothing and the wealthiest ten percent owned 60 percent of the wealth. People [...] without property were not allowed to participate in the political life of the community.' These poor colonists were so preoccupied with foraging for the basics that they didn't care that Britain decided to identify specific goods—the most important being lumber—which could only be exported to Britain. Nor did the frontiersmen care to whom the city folk or plantation owners were paying their taxes. It was only the rising wealthy middle class that had a vested interest in where their money was going. In fighting for the principle of 'no taxation without representation' they could see the means by which they could attain power for themselves and their fellow Americans. If they could not be a part of the political process in England, they would be at the forefront of that process in America, regardless of the cost.

By the end of the revolution they had achieved that aim. They had created a state in which people like themselves, who had land and wealth, held supreme power. The common man in the infant United States did not have the right to vote or to stand for office: that right was reserved for those who had reached a certain level of land ownership and personal wealth. In the words of military historian Hugh

Thomas Jefferson, Benjamin Franklin and John Adams meet in Philadelphia to review a draft of the Declaration.

Bicheno: 'They were no less a self-perpetuating oligarchy than the British political establishment, neither elected nor respected by the majority of the people they claimed to represent.'

Three key stories form the backbone of the foundation myth, the first of which was the catchcry that taxation without representation was tyranny. As mentioned above, the seeds of the American revolution lay in the desire of wealthy men to obtain and exercise power over their fellow colonists. This was something they couldn't do while they were under the dominion of the British parliament. Many prominent colonists, such as John Adams, found the idea of local government appealing once they understood that independence had the potential to enhance their social standing beyond what could be achieved within the colonial relationship.

The root cause of their complaint was envy—envy that 'foreigners' had the power to raise taxes and pass laws in their land whereas they could not. The main agitators for the revolution were individuals from wealthy backgrounds, many of them plantation and slave owners, such as George Washington, who owned large areas of land but were not of great wealth. The other major group of agitators were wealthy merchants from Boston, who resented the restrictions Britain had placed on trade. These two groups also resented the restrictions that Britain had placed upon further westward expansion and the acquisition of land at the expense of the American Indians.

When their interests were threatened, this local wealthy elite was far more ruthless in protecting its power than the British had ever been. The first test came during Shays' Rebellion of 1786–87, when the small farmers of Massachusetts rose up under the banner of no taxation without representation, just as the Boston merchants had done. They were ruthlessly suppressed, not by the British this time, but by rulers of the newly emerged American nation fearful of losing their privileges. So disturbed were the ruling classes that Abigail Adams—the wife of John Adams—was moved to write a furious letter from London to Thomas Jefferson, railing against these 'ignorant, restless desperadoes, without conscience or principles'. It was irrelevant that the farmers had a justifiable complaint and were merely echoing the patriotic calls of a decade before. The fact that her criticisms could equally have been directed against the founding fathers seemed to have escaped Abigail's notice.

Finally, despite being separated by the Atlantic Ocean, the colonists and their British counterparts shared some things in common, such as the threat of French and Spanish expansionism. It is important to remember that taxes derived from the colonies helped to pay for the defence of the colonies against French and Spanish territorial ambitions. Keeping troops on foreign soil is expensive, as the United States discovered in Iraq after its 2003 invasion.

The second myth of the American Revolution centres on the nobility of the founding fathers. As a whole, the founding fathers were ordinary men, rather than heroes and saints. Some, such as Dr Joseph Warren, were indeed noble men, motivated by dreams of a better tomorrow. He was one of the few revolutionaries who was genuinely worried that a war with Britain would weaken her in the far greater conflict against France. He was also morally and physically courageous, taking his place with the common soldiers at Breed's Hill in 1775, where he gave his life for the future he believed in.

It is safe to say, however, that many of Warren's fellow leaders fought for the opportunity to exercise power without having to bow to the wishes of a mother country. Many were like John Hancock: men who had inherited wealth, not earned it. Much like the aristocracy across the sea, the founding fathers were men who demanded leadership positions commensurate with their elevated status in the colonies.

Of the principal agitators for war, the main driver was the Boston-born Samuel Adams. Severely puritanical, Adams developed a political ideology that was driven by the bitterness he felt after his father's banking venture failed. Adams' father lost most of his wealth because of the failure of an investment venture in paper currency, which the British government had outlawed in 1744. Adams' parents were puritans, and thus already predisposed to distrust the British government. They were forced to watch, impotent, as an interfering central government on the other side of the world, caring little about the needs of the colonists, destroyed their livelihood at the stroke of a pen.

## THE CHERRY TREE

One of the most famous anecdotes told about young George Washington concerns a cherry tree that was chopped down in his father's orchard. When asked by his father who had done this deed, little George is supposed to have responded by saying, 'I cannot tell a lie, father, you know I cannot tell a lie! I did cut it with my little hatchet.' Charming and instructive though the story may be, it is entirely untrue.

It was invented by a parson named Mason Locke Weems, who wrote and published a biography of Washington after the great man's death. Seeking to identify those attributes possessed by Washington that could be held up as a beacon to guide and instruct new generations of Americans, Weems created numerous fictitious stories which were published in his books *A History of the Life and Death, Virtues and Exploits, of General George Washington* (1800) and *The Life of George Washington, with Curious Anecdotes Laudable to Himself and Exemplary to his Countrymen* (1806).

These engaging tales were presented to the American people as true, and helped to shape American perceptions of their first president. Although the authenticity of the story about the cherry tree has long been questioned, the fact that it is still quoted speaks volumes for a need that people have for a virtuous leader capable of embodying all that is just in the fight for freedom.

Adams advocated violent confrontation with Britain, believing the worst about the British elite. He incited riots, opposed parliament and shamefully distorted events. At the time of the Boston Massacre, Adams described the killing of five people who were part of a drunken mob confronting armed and edgy British soldiers as a 'massacre', hoping that the use of the term would trigger a larger revolt. He was also a principal organiser of the infamous 'Boston Tea Party', during which 342 chests of tea were dumped into Boston harbour in protest against a tea tax ordered by the British government. Adams wrote vast numbers of seditious letters to editors, often succeeding in inflaming public opinion by creating fake debates in which he would write in defence of both sides under different aliases. Despite the fact that he was a devout Protestant, Adams was quite prepared to ally himself with Catholic France and its monarch to achieve his ends.

Adams was not alone, since many of the founding fathers orchestrated acts aimed at provoking Britain into war. In 1772, for example, patriots under the leadership of the future Rhode Island statesman John Brown burned the British naval ship HMS *Gaspée*, prompting a crack down on anti-British activities. Then, in the aftermath of the *Intolerable Acts*, the First Continental Congress declared the Acts to be unconstitutional, urging the people to form militias, and, in a highly provocative act, called for Massachusetts to form a patriot government.

There were numerous occasions when the founding fathers could have ended the war early and still gained virtually all the freedoms they were asking for. Britain was ready to concede sovereignty by 1778, but the patriots' ambitions kept the war going for another five years, hoping that their alliance with France would allow them to obtain the British portions of Canada as well. By the end of the conflict, some 70,000 Americans and 31,000 British had died.

Once the war was over, the victors proceeded to write its history to emphasise their heroic role. The official version barely mentioned patriot preparations, intelligence gathering, warning signals and uncertainty about the first shot; the histories had to show that the war began due to unprovoked British aggression against defenceless farmers. Despite all the myth making, however, there were those among the founding fathers who deserved to be regarded as true heroes. George Washington, for example, is one of few men in history who was able to resist the lure of absolute power when it was his for the taking. He only wanted to be a one-term president, and had to be pushed by Thomas Jefferson into accepting a second term against his better judgment. Many in the newly created Federalist Party were keen for him to continue acting in that role, but he had no desire for the kind of power that was being offered.

## Unity of the Few

The third and final myth to emerge from the saga of America's foundation is that of the allegedly unprovoked aggressive acts committed by British Redcoats against simple farmers, which led to the formation of militias when the British presence became intolerable. There is no doubt that the militias were made up of simple farmers, but they were manipulated into acting against their best interests by those in positions of wealth, power and influence.

The militias were already in existence before the war broke out, with men such as Samuel Adams preparing them for the conflict that he and others were inciting. This was the case with the first battle of the revolutionary war—the Battle of Lexington, and the British advance on Concord in April 1775. The official view is that the Redcoats fired on a group of innocent farmers who were just minding their own business, but the alternative explanation is rather different.

Samuel Adams and John Hancock had prepared the militias to gather at Lexington that day, and had persuaded the leader of the troop to confront the British. The Redcoats were there because they had heard that weapons that were to be used against them had been hidden at Concord. The weapons in question were three siege cannons, not the sort of hardware that ordinary farmers would have in eighteenth-century America. Cannons of that type have no defensive role, and are only of use when laying siege to a fortified town or blockading a harbour. Concord is a mere 32 km (20 miles) from Boston harbour, and cannons such as these were used after March 1776 to threaten ships approaching the Boston peninsula. It was therefore not unreasonable for the British to assume that the militias were planning to use these weapons against them, otherwise why bury them in the courtyard of Concord jail before the outbreak of hostilities? This indicates that the militias were not simple farmers defending their way of life, but well-armed soldiers planning to fight a war that hadn't yet begun.

The *Two-Penny Act* was a law that allowed debts in tobacco to be paid out for two pennies a pound, which was one-third the market price.

The fact that the British did not, during the first stages of the revolution, make any serious attempt to bring the colonies back under the authority of the Crown also supports the argument that they were not overly aggressive or heavy-handed. They certainly wanted to retain the colonies, but crushing the revolution ruthlessly would have meant that the British could only hope to retain the colonies by keeping a substantial armed force in place for an indefinite period of time. They attempted to beat the militias and the Continental Army in the field, but then allowed them to move away, hoping that they would become demoralised and the revolution would fizzle out. They misjudged the determination of the founding fathers, however, as they pushed the British into a fully fledged war by signing the *Declaration of Independence* and then by siding with France. It was, in fact, the entry of the French that forced the British to take the war seriously, although their principal concern was never about the colonists, but always about ensuring that the French did not increase their influence in North America.

This war, like most wars, was both ruthless and brutal, particularly in the case of battles fought between loyalists and the patriots. At the Battle of King's Mountain in 1780, for example, loyalist American troops were massacred after they had surrendered, with others being given a show trial, and then slowly strangled to death. The corpse of Major Patrick Ferguson, the leader of the loyalists, was mutilated and urinated upon. The truth is that the leaders in this war fought for the same reasons as all leaders have done in the past—for power, wealth and ego. Stories of American liberty, oppression by the British and the noble cause of democracy were just a mask to conceal more basic human drives.

## Legacies

The passions, invective and propaganda involved in the foundation of the American republic marked one of the major turning points in history, effectively ushering in the modern world. The immediate legacy of the revolution was a change in status for many who lived in North America and had survived the war. Both during and after the war, loyalists were forced to escape to Canada or Britain. Many native Americans also fought against the revolution, believing—rightly, as it turned out—that they were more likely to lose their lands to the colonialists than the British. An estimated 15 per cent of colonists were loyalists, and about one-third of them left the United States during and after the war. Approximately 70,000 loyalists escaped, along with 2000 native Americans. The majority moved to Canada, where they aided in the creation of New Brunswick and Ontario. Some African-American loyalists fled to Sierra Leone.

Those who remained in the United States were those who actively supported the break with Britain and who regarded their former relations as enemies. They saw themselves as a new class of men, one that had broken free of the old order in Europe, independent and not at all concerned with the affairs of the old world.

Even with this perceived indifference to the affairs of the world, the United States soon began to advocate spreading democracy throughout the world. With that in mind, perhaps the most interesting irony of the revolutionary war was how the founding fathers used flaws in Britain's democracy to aid their cause. One of

A French print showing buildings on fire and citizens being beaten by Redcoats on 19 September 1776.

the main factors holding Britain back from total war during the conflict was a vocal parliamentary opposition to the war. The founding fathers used the opposition's political aims to achieve their revolutionary ends. They pushed as hard as they did because they were aware that a lengthy war was what the opposition parties wanted in order to achieve government, and this is precisely what happened. Had Britain not been a parliamentary democracy, but an absolute monarchy like France, the war would have been fought quite differently, and Britain would not have given in so easily.

Another, and far more deadly, legacy of the revolutionary war was the apparent division of the 13 colonies into distinct northern and southern identities. George Washington himself identified this problem in his farewell address:

> In contemplating the causes, which may disturb our Union, it occurs as a matter of serious concern, that any ground should have been furnished for characterizing parties by Geographical discriminations [of] Northern and Southern [...] whence designing men may endeavor to excite a belief, that there is a real difference of local interests and views [...] to misrepresent the opinions and aims of other districts.

The divisions were real enough, of course. The war had begun in the north, and for some years the south showed little interest. Northern claims of liberty and mercantile independence from parliament's laws were never taken very seriously in the south, certainly not until 1780. The southern frontiersmen were much more concerned with their independence from a central government, and little concerned with distant England.

What caused them to become involved was the British attempt to open a front on the Indian frontier to force the rebels to fight a war on two fronts. This alienated the frontier settlers, who had rejected the call to arms in 1775 precisely because they were afraid that they would be exposed to Indian attacks while otherwise occupied. Thus, they finally joined the wealthy coastal slave traders who had been in the forefront of the southern rebellion up until that point. However, what the south fought for was not quite what the northerners fought for. The south may have fought for liberty and property; but in their case the property was slaves, and the liberty was something that the slaves must be denied at all costs. These very different views would fester for 70 years, until a bloody civil war engulfed the land in 1861.

After the war was over and democracy established in the former colonies, further consequences were felt, both at home and abroad. The new nation continued with its belligerent stance towards Britain, while the mother country quietly supported and protected its former colonies in the Atlantic Ocean and Canada. A continued British presence in Canada ensured that France could not once again extend its power into the New World, posing a threat to American interests, and American trade was able to expand due to the Royal Navy's suppression of piracy in the Atlantic. President James Monroe might have outlined his doctrine declaring the Americas off-limits to the old European powers, but it was the British who enforced it, preventing any of her rivals from gaining territory in the New World, where they would threaten British interests.

But by far greater was the effect the war had on France. The French had supported the rebels with both money and arms, in an attempt to limit British power in the New World. The effect was to bankrupt the French economy, and was one of the main causes of the French Revolution. However, it wasn't just the cost of the American Revolution that brought about the French Revolution 13 years later. It was the successful creation of a republic and the overthrow of a monarchy perceived to be tyrannical and oppressive that reverberated throughout French society. Men who actively fought for freedom in the North American campaigns—such as the Marquis of Lafayette—were impossible to silence when they returned to their native France, where they inspired their fellow aristocrats to seek to reshape the French political system. And it was not only the French who absorbed this lesson. The revolution also had a great effect on the United States' immediate neighbours in Latin America. Living under the imperial power of distant Spanish and Portuguese governments, the American experience profoundly influenced local struggles for independence.

# THE ANNEXATION OF MEXICO BY THE UNITED STATES (1846)

*'The world has nothing to fear from military ambition in our Government.'*
**President James Polk**

*'Xenophobia manifests itself especially against civilizations and cultures that are weak because they lack economic resources, means of subsistence or land. So [they] are the first targets of [...] aggression.'*
**Antonio Tabucchi**

### LIE

American blood has been shed on American soil.

### TRUTH

After the illegal annexation of the Republic of Texas, the US Government pushed Mexico into a war that she had no chance of winning in order to validate the annexation!

### CHIEF PARTICIPANTS

James Polk, 11th President of the United States
Zachary Taylor, military leader and later 12th President of the United States
Santa Anna, general and former President of Mexico

### THE STORY SO FAR

In 1821, after an 11-year struggle, Mexico finally won her independence from Spain, ending three centuries of colonial rule. Mexico at that time was made up of modern-day Mexico, as well as land that is now California, New Mexico and Texas. Finding it difficult to control the borders of the country from the capital in Mexico City, the government allowed US immigrants to settle in the sparsely populated land. These immigrants, calling themselves Texans, became disillusioned with the Mexican government because, first, it insisted on Catholicism being the state religion, second, it had a policy of settling Spanish peoples in Texas and, third, it abolished slavery. When the United States offered to buy Texas from Mexico, the Mexican authorities refused, and white settlers, now in the majority, revolted in 1836. This resulted in Texas breaking

Columbia, the female personification of America, leads pioneers westward.

away, although Mexico never formally recognised the treaty granting Texas its independence. Texas then sought admission into the United States, something the US government eagerly agreed to …

The Mexican-American War of 1846–48 was a conflict that pitted the might and power of the United States against an impoverished Mexico, which had inherited its land from the former Spanish Empire. While the actual fighting posed no problems for the far more powerful US army, it took considerable effort to manipulate the Mexicans into a war they could not hope to win. The eventual trigger that was to send American troops into war was the lie that American blood had been shed on American soil. This was entirely untrue, but the lure of new territory and the temptation to realise what many felt to be America's Manifest Destiny were too strong a temptation for the government of President James Polk to resist.

## The Official Story—American Blood, American Soil

It was not an inviting prospect for the men of Captain Seth Thornton's small troop of US Dragoons. In April 1846, they had been sent to patrol an area of south Texas bordered by two rivers—the Nueces to the north and the Rio Grande to the south. There they were greeted by a vast brown plain, sparsely covered with grass, mesquite, thorny shrubs and cacti, that stretched away into the distance as far as the eye could see. The prospect may have seemed boring, but it turned out to be far from that.

This was a tense time for the region. The state of Texas had been admitted into the Union over objections from Mexico, and President James Polk, eager to defend American interests, sent armed troops under General Zachary Taylor to the Rio Grande to defend America's latest acquisition. General Taylor brushed off Mexican demands to remove his troops to the Nueces and proceeded to build a fort on the banks of the Rio Grande, opposite the town of Matamoros. On the Mexican side of the border, General Mariano Arista had been appointed to take overall command of the situation, with orders to prepare for war.

It was at this point that General Taylor decided to despatch the scouting party of 70 Dragoons commanded by Captain Thornton to investigate an area some 32 km (20 miles) northwest of the present site of the Texas town of Brownville, within the disputed territory. The Mexicans had also despatched an army to the same region, consisting of 2000 cavalry under the command of Colonel Anastasio Torrejón. As the small US scouting party was investigating an abandoned hacienda at Rancho de Carricitos on 25 April, they encountered the superior Mexican force that was camped nearby. Both sides started firing, and although the Dragoons fought bravely, they were forced to surrender after 16 men had been killed during several hours of fighting. Thornton himself was severely wounded during the engagement, and although he and many of his officers were captured and held in Matamoros, a few men managed to escape and return to the newly constructed fort on the Rio Grande with the news of their defeat.

A week later, Mexican cannons at Matamoros began to bombard the American fort, which returned fire with its own artillery. Two US soldiers were killed during the battle which lasted for five days as Mexican troops slowly encircled the fort. Relief came with the arrival of 2400 troops, who would be under the command of Zachary Taylor, who had inflicted two crushing defeats on the Mexicans during his journey—at Palo Alto and Resaca de la Palma. Public opinion in the US was outraged, and there were demands for retribution. Accordingly, on 11 May 1846, President Polk addressed the Congress declaring:

> *The cup of forbearance had been exhausted even before the recent information from the frontier of the Del Norte [Rio Grande]. But now, after reiterated menaces, Mexico has passed the boundary of the United States, has invaded our territory and shed American blood upon the American soil. She has proclaimed that hostilities have commenced, and that the two nations are now at war.*

A joint session of Congress ratified the declaration of war, with only 14 members of the Whig Party voting against the president's wishes, including Abraham Lincoln and John Quincy Adams. The United States officially declared war on Mexico on 13 May 1846.

## The Truth—The Problem with Texas

The origins of the Mexican-American War stretch back to 1821, when Mexico, inspired by her American neighbour's War of Independence, broke away from the Spanish Empire and in the process inherited the province of Texas. Politically and financially weakened in the aftermath of independence, Mexico allowed a few hundred American settlers to move into Texas, which was sparsely populated. This opened up the floodgates, and thousands of American settlers swarmed across the border in search of land on which to settle and raise a family. The United States then sought to buy Texas from the Mexican government, but this suggestion was fiercely rejected by the Mexicans, who began to encourage Spanish-speaking settlers to make their homes in the new province.

Things came to a head in 1835 when Mexico declared slavery illegal. Many Texans were slave owners who had moved from the southern states, and they objected to the laws. Their fears increased when the Mexican government enacted legislation to additionally centralise its power. Texas erupted into violence, with its inhabitants declaring independence from Mexico. Victory came swiftly in the conflict that followed, with the Texan rebels defeating the Mexican army and capturing their leading general, Antonio de Padua María Severino López de Santa Anna y Pérez de Lebrón—more succinctly known as Santa Anna.

Santa Anna had risen to fame following a number of victories against Spain during Mexico's war of independence, but time would show that he did not have the military talents to take on either the Texans or the Americans when their turn came. Under duress, Santa Anna agreed to acknowledge the independence of the Republic of Texas and signed the Treaty of Velasco, which identified the Rio Grande as the border between Texas and Mexico. There was a problem, however. Although Santa Anna had previously been President of Mexico, he had relinquished that office before embarking on his ill-fated campaign. The new Mexican government consequently refused to recognise the negotiations and declined to ratify the Treaty of Velasco. A confrontation followed between Texas and Mexico over the location of the border, with the Mexican government rejecting the Rio Grande and maintaining that the Nueces River was the recognised border with Texas.

The US army's superior weaponry in the Mexican-American War included the latest US-manufactured breech-loading flintlock 'Hall's' rifles and Percussion cap Model 1841 rifles.

In the United States, meanwhile, there was increasing debate about how to acquire new territories in the west. Texan independence was naturally considered in that context, since it was common knowledge that the majority of its slave-owning, English-speaking settlers were in favour of joining the Union. Eager for Texan natural resources, the United States was willing to shed blood and money to make this a reality. The US government therefore decided that Texan independence really meant its becoming part of the United States, and they consequently decided to annex Texas in 1845. This was done, knowing full well that it would push Mexico into a declaration of war, given that the Mexicans had never officially recognised Texan independence in the first place. It was also done over the strenuous objections of the non-white citizens of now-independent Texas. The United States also made its expansionist ambitions clear when the government offered to settle the outstanding debt owed by Mexico to American settlers, provided Mexico allowed the United States to purchase the Mexican territories of New Mexico and California.

President John Tyler eventually offered Texas admission to the Union as a territory in 1844, but his bill was rejected by the senate, which did not support Tyler's expansionist tendencies. Undeterred, Tyler then pushed through a bill to acquire

Antonio López de Santa Anna.

Texas as a State of the Union, which only needed ratification by a joint sitting of the Congress. The bill was enacted on 1 March 1845, and was endorsed by Texas on 4 July, at which point it became the 28th State of the Union. From this point on, all the US government needed was an excuse to launch an assault on Mexico. As Ulysses S. Grant recalled, 'We were sent to provoke a fight, but it was essential that Mexico should commence it.'

With Texas now claimed as American territory, the next US President, James Polk, sent an army into disputed Texan land that had been settled by Mexicans. The United States adopted the Texan position that the Rio Grande was the boundary, as laid down in the 1836 Treaty of Velasco. Even though the Mexicans rejected the treaty's legality, the Americans nevertheless used it to advance their claim, seeking any pretext for war. The subsequent battle between Captain Thornton's troops and Mexican forces, and the deaths of the Dragoons was just the excuse the US administration was looking for. The US government took the moral high ground, President Polk claiming that the Mexicans had started the war, and that 'American blood had been shed on American soil'.

A joint sitting of Congress endorsed the declaration of war, with southern democrats expressing enthusiastic support because they saw the defeat of Mexico and the acquisition of much of her territory as a chance to increase the number of slave-owning states. Despite opposition to the intervention from the Whig Party, Congress declared war on 13 May 1846, with Mexico following suit on 7 July.

## End Game

It was obvious from the outset that the Mexicans were no match for the United States. That fact had been established when they failed to hold on to Texas 10 years earlier. One of the major reasons Mexico lost the war was because their weapons were inadequate. The Mexican army was equipped with British muskets dating from the time of the Napoleonic Wars, some 30 years earlier, while US troops were equipped with much more up-to-date rifles. Superior US artillery was also important, cancelling out any advantages the Mexicans might have had in sheer numbers.

Mexico was crushed within 12 months. California was lost to the Mexicans in January 1847, with the US army linking up with colonists who had declared independence. Santa Anna attempted to revive his military career, fighting the armies of Zachary Taylor in the northeast of the country, although without success. A second US army, which made a thrust directly into the heart of Mexico, was despatched under the command of General Winfield Scott. The war reached its inevitable conclusion with the capture of Mexico City on 13 September 1847.

Like any other war, this was a violent and ugly affair. Invading American troops were supplemented by large numbers of volunteers who were responsible in large part for the great number of war crimes committed against civilians. Soldiers' journals tell of the scalping of innocent civilians, the rape and murder of women, the murder of children, the looting and destruction of homes and the desecration of churches.

The scale and magnitude of the defeat left Mexico with little choice but to accept the US government's outrageous demands—or risk the entire country being annexed. The Treaty of Guadalupe Hidalgo, signed on 2 February 1848 by the interim government of an occupied country, was virtually dictated to Mexico by the United States. Under the terms of the treaty, Mexico turned the entire northwest of the country over to the United States in exchange for the sum of $15 million—less than half the amount the US had originally proposed before the war started. The contested area between the River Nueces and the Rio Grande became a part of the State of Texas and was lost to Mexico forever. Victory and the acquisition of the long sought-after western territories brought an outpouring of patriotism and optimism throughout much of America. The lie that American blood had been shed on American soil had given the United States everything it had wanted.

> Many of the US officers who took part in the war would find themselves on opposing sides when the American Civil War began in 1861.

## Legacies

The immediate legacy of the war was huge and long lasting. By using patriotic fervour to manipulate the American public into supporting the war, the United States had acquired the present-day states of California, Nevada and Utah, together with parts of Colorado, Arizona, New Mexico and Wyoming. The border along the Rio Grande had also been settled in the victor's favour. This windfall, which established the contours of the United States more or less as they are recognised today, has since been referred to as the Mexican Cession. Apart from the Louisiana Purchase, this was the largest single piece of territory ever added to the expanding United States. It was directly responsible for ushering in a new period of growth and development that would fuel much of America's prosperity in the late nineteenth and early twentieth centuries. It was especially important in promoting economic growth in the years following the Civil War.

Mexico, on the other hand, had lost more than 1.3 million square km (500,000 square miles) of land—almost half of its territory—leaving it weaker both economically and militarily. The Mexican government responded by endorsing a strategy aimed at settling colonists in its northern territories in an attempt to prevent further land from annexation, as had happened with Texas.

Within the United States, one immediate effect of this rapid increase in territory was to upset the delicate balance between the slave-owning states of the south and the free states of the north. Concerned that admitting California as a free state would diminish their power, the slave-owning states threatened to secede from the Union. To avoid this catastrophic outcome, a number of measures were adopted in what is known as the 'Compromise of 1850'. It was agreed that California would be admitted to the Union as a free state; that slave trading would be abolished in the District of Columbia; that the territories of New Mexico—including present-day Arizona— and Utah would be handed over to popularly elected territorial governments; that a *Fugitive Slave Act* would be passed, requiring all US citizens to assist in the return of runaway slaves; and finally that Texas would give up much of the western land that it claimed, receiving $10 million in compensation to pay off its debts.

Even though the compromise was initially successful in staving off a looming war, the forces unleashed by the acquisition of new territory as a result of the Mexican-American War would trigger a series of increasingly bitter debates about the institution of slavery that would ultimately lead to the Civil War just 10 years later.

There were other concerns about the acquisition of land following the war. To justify it, many influential people began using the term 'Manifest Destiny' to explain their support for what was in essence a war of conquest. They maintained that the United States was justified in its actions as she had a mission to expand, spreading her particular brand of democracy and freedom to all areas of the continent. Proponents of this view took pride in the fact that the United States was extending the sphere of freedom to other areas, and promoted the idea that the American people were 'destined' to establish a single great, homogeneous and God-fearing nation across the entire North American continent, from the Atlantic to the Pacific. The easy victories against the inferior Mexicans seemed to validate this view of American expansionism, and it became a popular belief among many Americans, as expressed in the words of poet Walt Whitman:

> *What has Mexico, inefficient Mexico—with her superstition, her burlesque upon freedom, her actual tyranny by the few over the many—what has she to do with the great mission of peopling the new world with a noble race? Be it ours to achieve that mission [...] For our part, we look upon the increase of territory and power, not as a doubter looks, but with the faith the Christian has in God's mystery.*

This vision of America was one of the major influences in starting the war, and it remains a powerful and potent factor in America's relationship with the rest of the world. The idea of a Manifest Destiny in its original form may have run its course by the end of the Mexican conflict, but its legacy shaped American foreign policy for

# THE ORIGINS OF MANIFEST DESTINY

Manifest Destiny—the belief that the United States had a God-given right to spread across the continent and implement a liberated and federated self-government—was first put forward formally in the 1840s to support the appropriation of much of what is now the western United States. However, the origin of the belief itself goes back much further.

The idea that God had a grand destiny for America arose from religious beliefs held by the majority of America's first settlers, many of whom were 'Puritans', and later Presbyterians of Scots-Irish descent. Out of the numerous upheavals that shook western Christendom from the sixteenth century on, a notion was born that the Catholic Church was decadent, and did not reflect the true Christian faith. This led to the emergence of a number of sects that believed that they were the true Christians; the ones favoured by God because of their adherence to His Truth. Since they believed that everyone had been preordained by God Himself to be either saved or damned—and that only a select few would be saved—they were convinced that they were the 'elect, God's chosen few'.

Anxious to escape the wicked of the world, the 'elect' decided to leave the mother country and create God's promised kingdom on earth. The site chosen for this new kingdom was North America, where these first Puritans were later joined by the Scots-Irish, many of whom were devout Presbyterians. Originally from Scotland, the great grandparents of these newest immigrants had originally settled in Ireland, believing that they were destined to build the New Jerusalem on earth. This New Jerusalem was originally to have been in Scotland, but with immigrants flooding to the New World, the chosen location was shifted to America instead. America was to be a great Christian Land, favoured by God, destined to be a leading light among nations, and therefore clearly a nation with a Manifest Destiny.

many years to come, as, for example, when it intervened in Cuba in the 1890s and in the Philippines in the 1900s.

It has been argued that belief in America's 'mission' to promote and defend democracy has continued to influence American political thinking, although it did wane during the period of the two world wars. However, a revised Manifest Destiny doctrine began to be articulated in reaction to the threat that communism seemed to represent to the American way of life. It was seen as America's mission to defend democratic governments, such as those in Korea and Vietnam, from the communist threat. Even with communism vanquished, the desire to promote 'American democracy' throughout the world did not disappear. It has resurfaced most recently as George W. Bush, in his

second term as president, declared that it was his country's mission to promote and establish democracies throughout the Middle East, by force if necessary.

Supporters of the idea of a Manifest Destiny may have had no qualms about provoking Mexico in order to achieve their aims, but the use of a lie to start the war did concern some. A month before the war with Mexico ended, James Polk was censured for 'a war unnecessarily and unconstitutionally begun by the President of the United States' in a House of Representatives revision to a bill acclaiming the achievements of Major General Zachary Taylor. Years later, former President Ulysses S. Grant, who as a youthful army officer had served in Mexico under General Taylor, recollected:

> *Generally, the officers of the army were indifferent whether the annexation was consummated or not; but not so all of them. For myself, I was bitterly opposed to the measure, and to this day regard the war, which resulted, as one of the most unjust ever waged by a stronger against a weaker nation. It was an instance of a republic following the bad example of European monarchies, in not considering justice in their desire to acquire additional territory.*

Despite condemnation by some within the United States, victory against Mexico did open up the western portion of the country, and it was fortuitous that the end of the war coincided with the discovery of gold in California in January 1848. This sparked a rush, with an estimated 300,000 immigrants changing California from a sleepy, little-known backwater to a flourishing centre of enterprise and industry. Roads, schools, churches and civic organisations followed swiftly. Railroads were built, with the first transcontinental railroad being completed in 1869, uniting California with the central and eastern United States. A journey of six days by train whisked travellers from Chicago to San Francisco, compared to six months by ship. All of these monumental changes were a direct legacy of the Mexican-American War.

President James Polk.

# CHAIRMAN MAO'S GREATEST TRIUMPH— THANKS TO CHIANG KAI-SHEK (1937–1949)

*'We call on the people of the whole country to throw all their strength behind the sacred war of self-defence against Japan [...] defend our homeland to the last drop of our blood! Let the people of the whole country, the government, and the armed forces unite and build up the national united front as our solid Great Wall of resistance to Japanese aggression! Let the [Nationalists] and the Communist Party closely cooperate and resist the new attacks of the Japanese aggressors! Drive the Japanese aggressors out of China!'*
**Mao Zedong**

*'The world is divided into people who do things and people who get the credit.'*
**Dwight Whitney Morrow**

### LIE

Mao and the Chinese communists fought against and helped to defeat the Japanese.

### TRUTH

It was the Nationalists under Chiang Kai-shek who fought and defeated the Japanese, while Mao either refused to engage the Japanese or actively fought against the Nationalists!

### CHIEF PARTICIPANTS

Mao Zedong, leader of the Chinese communists
Chiang Kai-shek, head of the Chinese government and leader of the Nationalists

### THE STORY SO FAR

Emperors had ruled China for over 2000 years. This began to change during the final years of the Qing Dynasty due to civil unrest and foreign invasions. By 1912, the Qing Dynasty had been abolished and replaced by the Republic of China, headed by a democratically elected government, with the socialist Nationalists becoming a major party. The republic had a difficult history— with Yuan Shikai, head of the Beiyang army, overthrowing the republic and appointing himself emperor in 1915. After Yuan's death, the era of the warlords began, during which numerous ephemeral republican governments came under the control of various warlords who gained control of Beijing.

Chinese propaganda poster showing soldiers and people united, led by the benevolent Mao Zedong.

The Nationalists, after first joining forces with some of the warlords, decided that gaining the support of Soviet Russia was more likely to achieve their goal of stabilising China and reintroducing a democratic republic. The Russians began to provide support to the Nationalists, as well as the newly formed Chinese Communist Party. By 1925, a new figure had emerged from the ranks of the Nationalists, one who was to lead the party and end the era of the warlords—Chiang Kai-shek. By 1927, the Nationalists had fallen out with the communists, who established the Soviet Republic of China in 1931, the same year that Japan invaded Manchuria. The chairman of the Soviet Republic of China was a man who would eventually become Chiang Kai-shek's nemesis—Mao Zedong ...

The Great Wall—one of the world's most famous landmarks—stretches across China's heartland for 6760 km (4200 miles). Instantly recognisable, it is now an object of pride for the Chinese people, a symbol of an illustrious history that stretches back for millennia. For centuries, however, the Chinese had disparaged the Great Wall, considering it a useless and ineffectual barrier against the barbarian hordes that descended upon the civilised cities of the Middle Kingdom. They saw it as a monument to the folly and imperial delusions of the Chinese emperors, who sacrificed their people's wealth and blood in a futile exercise—as demonstrated by the fact that China was often ruled by foreigners, such as the Manchu Dynasty from Manchuria (1644–1912).

This was the generally held view of the Great Wall until Mao Zedong, leader of the Chinese Communist Party, decided that it would make the perfect symbol to represent China's greatness. He accordingly rewrote history, turning the Great Wall into a triumph of Chinese ingenuity, iconic of China's distrust of foreign ideas and thought. The historical truth about the wall—its age, purpose and varying appearance, as well as the blunders and catastrophes connected with it—was erased, to be replaced by an authorised history eulogising its longevity.

Mao practised similar deceptions on many occasions during the course of his long career, but his greatest triumph was to rewrite the history of China's conflict with Japan before and during World War II. He declared that the communists had been the principal opponent of the Japanese in the Sino-Japanese War, personally taking all the credit for driving them out. The reality was rather different, since Mao's account completely ignored the contribution of the one man to whom victory in the war truly belonged—the leader of the Nationalist Party, Chiang Kai-shek.

## The Official Story—Victory Over the Japanese

In China it is known as the War of Resistance against Japan, an heroic, eight-year struggle against the predatory forces of the militaristic Japanese, whose brutal occupation caused untold suffering for millions of Chinese. During the war, the Chinese Communist Party, under the inspired leadership of Mao Zedong, led the armed resistance against the foreign invaders, sought national unity with the Nationalists, and placed itself in the front line of the struggle for national liberation.

The war began in July 1937, when Japanese troops attacked Chinese forces at the Marco Polo Bridge, just outside Beijing. By the end of the month, the northern cities of Beijing and Tianjin had fallen, and in August 350,000 Japanese troops attacked Shanghai, Nanjing and Shanxi further south. In response, Mao and the other communist leaders began to direct the war effort, instructing all Chinese forces to battle the enemy, wherever they were, and to get ready for a lengthy and brutal war.

Seeking to tie down the invading Japanese, Mao directed the communist armies to position themselves behind the enemy's front line. There they mobilised the common people—especially the peasants—in a campaign of guerrilla warfare, luring the greater part of the Japanese forces into an expensive and demoralising campaign they could never hope to win.

Mao set up secure anti-Japanese areas containing both troops and civilians, which became central points from which counter-offensives could be launched. His own headquarters in Yan'an—the capital of the Shaanxi-Gansu-Ningxia border region—became the nerve centre in the fight against the Japanese.

---

Once Chiang Kai-shek and the Nationalists were forced out of mainland China, they fled to Taiwan where they re-established the Republic of China. Chiang was President in Taiwan from 1949 until 1975.

---

The hot war ground to a halt in 1940, with the Chinese no longer able to match the Japanese armies in conventional military terms. By this time, Japan held most of the eastern coastal areas of China, with guerrilla fighting continuing in the conquered areas. To prevent further advances, the Communist Party abandoned any idea of fighting the Japanese directly. Instead the struggle moved underground with the communists coordinating Chinese resistance in Japanese-occupied areas.

Mao also tried to maintain a united front with the Nationalists in the fight against Japan, all the while trying to restrain those Nationalists intent on fighting the communists and appeasing Japan. The success of the united front was a testament to his determination and leadership.

Mao's strategy frustrated a Japanese military unable to combat the guerrilla tactics, despite adopting a 'Kill all, Loot all, Burn all' policy as they sought to lure the Chinese troops out into the open. Mao refused to take the bait, instead consolidating his position by moving industry from coastal areas to inland cities. This, and the increase in armaments production that followed, laid the foundation for victory in the war.

In the final months before the Japanese were forced out of China, Mao chaired the Seventh National Congress of the Chinese Communist Party. He set out an agenda during the proceedings that included driving out the invaders, rebuilding China and uniting the country on the basis of Mao Zedong Thought. When the war ended in 1945, after a bitter, eight-year struggle, not only had the Chinese people won a great victory, but so had Mao.

## The Truth—What Mao Really Did

As inspiring as the official communist history of the war is, it is vague in many places. How, exactly, did the communists force the Japanese out of China? Without full-scale battles and Japanese defeats, how did the communists win? And what about the role played by Nationalist leader Chiang Kai-shek? It is difficult to find even a mention of his contribution to the war against Japan.

At the time of the initial Japanese invasion of Manchuria in 1931, the communists under Mao were engaged in a life-or-death struggle with the Nationalists under Chiang Kai-shek. Mao was a cold-blooded bully who joined the communists as a means of achieving power. By 1928, he was already organising public execution rallies where local landlords were butchered. It was compulsory for local residents to view such executions, as a way of instilling fear into them.

Chiang was a corrupt and ambitious general looking to unite China under his rule. He was infamous for transferring millions of dollars of US aid into family coffers, being known in some Washington circles as 'Cash My-check'. President Harry Truman reportedly declared: 'They're all thieves, every damn one of them. They stole 750 million out of the billions that we sent to Chiang.' Although originally quite low in the Nationalist Party's hierarchy, Chiang successfully manoeuvred himself into the leader's position when founder Sun Yat-sen died in 1925.

The Nationalists and the communists had not always been at each other's throats. Both were parties of the left and had worked together for years to establish a unified government. Both had also received Soviet support, though the Soviet Union provided the largest monetary and military aid to the Nationalists up until the later stages of World War II.

Chiang Kai-shek, Franklin D. Roosevelt and Winston Churchill during the Cairo conference, 1943.

What, then, did Mao really do when the Japanese invaded in 1931? The answer is nothing. He was busy establishing the Soviet Republic of China in the mountainous areas of Jiangxi province. He hoped this would be his power base, where he could avoid annihilation by the Nationalists and hatch plans for fulfilling his ambitions.

The Japanese invasion did interrupt Chiang's advances against the communists, but his adoption of a policy of 'first internal pacification, then external resistance', meant that he came close to destroying Mao, who was forced to flee to Shaanxi Province in the northwest of China. It was there, surrounded by snow-capped mountains to the south and a desert to the north, that Mao established a base at Yan'an. It was far enough away from both the Nationalists and the invading Japanese forces to make it even harder for the communists to directly engage with the enemy.

The civil war in China made at least one foreign power nervous—the Soviet Union. Japan's speedy occupation of northern China in July 1937 alarmed Soviet leader Joseph Stalin, who saw Japan's large, well-trained armies as a threat to his country's border with China. Disgusted by the struggle for supremacy between the Nationalists and communists, and Chiang's approach of northern containment, he sent word to a compromised general on Chiang's staff to trigger a war with Japan in Shanghai. Neither Japan nor Chiang Kai-shek wanted a full-scale war. Japan did not want to extend the war front beyond northern China, and Chiang was happy to keep the invaders there while he dealt with the communists. Mao, on the other hand, was very happy with this turn of events and took full advantage of it.

The escalation of the war meant that Mao could keep control of the Chinese Red Army because Chiang Kai-shek was no longer in a position to fight both the Japanese and the communists. Mao also insisted that the Red Army would only participate in the struggle if he retained direct authority over it, a stipulation he used to keep his forces, as far as possible, out of the war. From 1937 to 1939, Chiang bore the brunt of the defensive war, which saw the Chinese army trying to delay a Japanese advance into the northeastern cities. This allowed key personnel and support industries to move from the areas under threat to Chongqing in the southwest. It was this area that became Chiang's operational base during the war.

Mao, meanwhile, had no intention of taking on the Japanese. His plan was to preserve his forces at all cost, expand the areas under communist control and attack Nationalist troops where possible. Mao had Chiang agree that the Red Army would not engage the Japanese directly, and would instead act as support troops for Nationalist forces.

For the next six years, Chiang's wartime policy was to employ indirect defensive strategies, with the Chinese army luring advancing Japanese troops into locations where they could be ambushed or attacked. Chiang still offered the most effective resistance to the Japanese. In 1937, for example, his best German-trained divisions delayed the advancing Japanese, forcing them into a three-month battle to take Shanghai, instead of the three days the Japanese had boasted would be all the time they needed. Fierce engagements such as this came at a cost, however, with the Nationalists suffering 3.2 million casualties by the end of the war.

Mao concentrated on building up his strength and taking territory from the Nationalists during this same period. His efforts against the Japanese were limited to conducting a guerrilla-style war of attrition against them, which was far less costly in terms of men and munitions. It was also very popular with peasants in the occupied regions, who saw first-hand the communist resistance at work. Tales of distant battles between armies they had never seen meant nothing to them. This helped the communists to recruit new soldiers, enabling them to increase their forces enormously.

Mao's strategy was opposed by the Soviet Union and the United States, with both countries wanting more direct confrontation with the Japanese. Under pressure from them, Mao did occasionally order his troops into battle, but major encounters were the exception rather than the norm. Of the 22 principal engagements of the war, the communists did not participate in a single one. The Soviet Union also put pressure on Chiang to reach an agreement with his opponent after Mao, instead of attacking the Japanese, made territorial gains near Nanjing and Shanghai. Mao's strategy enabled the communists to increase their membership from 100,000 to 1.2 million. By 1945, the ratio of Nationalist to communist forces in China had been reduced from 60:1 to 3:1.

As the war drew to a close in 1944–45, the Nationalists still bore the brunt of the fighting as they drove the Japanese out of northern Burma and retook Guangxi and other southwestern regions. When the war ended it was in spite of, not because

## EDGAR SNOW AND MAO ZEDONG

America's early love affair with Mao, as someone who was dynamic, determined, and more importantly, sympathetic to the United States, had its origins in a 1937 book entitled *Red Star Over China*. It was written by American journalist Edgar Snow, a sympathetic and trusting individual, who served Mao well in his efforts to concoct a preferred version of his life story. The book described Mao as a kind and gentle man, who was committed to fighting the Japanese, and it was this depiction that began the myth that the Chinese communists were the most committed of the anti-Japanese forces. Snow declared that Mao was 'direct, frank, simple, undevious', and that he never imposed any form of censorship on him when he was writing his books.

Snow's several books helped to rewrite history, avoiding any mention of Mao's bloody rise to power, inventing battles and acts of bravery, and creating the legend of the Long March—the year-long, 13,000-km (8000-mile) forced retreat of the first Red Army and the communist leadership in 1934–35—which occupied pride of place in the new, sanitised history of Mao and the communists. Regardless of subsequent claims, Mao checked everything that Snow wrote, and rewrote some parts to his satisfaction.

Snow was made to feel unwelcome in the United States in the aftermath of the communist victory in 1949, so he moved to Switzerland. After his death in 1972, to honour the service he had provided to Mao, half of Snow's remains were buried in Beijing, alongside the Unnamed Lake.

of, the communists. In Manchuria, for example, it was Soviet troops who pushed back the Japanese. The Chinese communists simply followed in their wake, helping themselves to abandoned arsenals, and freeing Chinese prisoners, who helped to swell their ranks. It was these opportunistic tactics that placed Mao in a winning position as the war came to an end and the two antagonists—Mao and Chiang—faced each other in a final struggle for supremacy.

## Chiang Kai-shek's Poor Reputation

If it is true that Chiang Kai-shek led Chinese military resistance to the Japanese, why has his reputation been so overshadowed by that of Mao? Communist propaganda and Mao's subsequent victory were obviously important factors, but during the war it was the American advisers who were instrumental in turning American opinion—in particular that of President Franklin Roosevelt—against Chiang and in favour of Mao.

Mao and the communist leadership had for years been seeking to influence opinion in the West by misleading official and unofficial American visitors. Their efforts began with reports about the massacre of the New Fourth Army in 1941. Mao deliberately sent this army across the Yangtze River, using a route that Chiang had prohibited, meaning it ended up in the middle of a Nationalist army. The two sides fought and the communist army was wiped out. Mao claimed that it was a deliberate attack and that it showed that Chiang was more interested in killing Chinese communists than in stopping the Japanese. Reports that came back to Roosevelt praised the communists for their efforts and repeated the communist version of events verbatim.

> As a result of the Cultural Revolution of the 1960s, many people in China still worship Mao in temples or at their family altars.

It was at about this time that chief White House economic advisor Lauchlin Currie was visiting China. In his reports to Roosevelt, he criticised Chiang and praised Mao, painting a comforting picture of the latter's intentions. He prevented Chiang from making direct and independent contact with Roosevelt, and ensured that much of Roosevelt's information about the situation in China came through him.

Chiang's reputation suffered even further damage when the Allies appointed General Joseph Stilwell as Chiang's chief of staff in 1942. Their relationship deteriorated rapidly, with Stilwell claiming the corruption and inefficiency of Chiang's administration was destroying the war effort, criticism that he took straight to Roosevelt and the American media. Chiang saw matters differently and had opposed Stilwell's request to assume operational control of the Chinese troops.

Stilwell's inability to appreciate Chiang's dilemma in facing both the communists and the Japanese simultaneously hindered Nationalist efforts. He also accepted Mao's protestations of innocence. Most importantly, Stilwell had his reputation to consider when the Japanese took the Hunan, Henan and Guangxi provinces in 1944. The failure of Chinese forces to defend these areas led to Stilwell being replaced by Major General Albert Wedemeyer, but Stilwell sought to shift the blame for the debacle onto Chiang. All this negative publicity lowered Allied confidence in China's ability to conduct offensive operations from the Asian mainland. As a consequence, they began to focus their efforts against the Japanese in the Pacific Ocean.

There were others, however, who were not so quick to accept Mao's interpretation of his own role in the war. Ernest Hemingway—who was not unsympathetic to the communists—reportedly said that, 'Due to [the Chinese communists'] excellent publicity, America has an exaggerated idea of the part they have played in the war against Japan. Their part has been very considerable but that of the Central Government troops has been a hundred times greater.' Hemingway also noted that in his experience in Spain, the communists always claimed that they were the ones doing the lion's share of the fighting.

There is no denying that some of the criticisms of Chiang Kai-shek were deserved. His government was corrupt and did attempt to hinder communist expansion at a time when Chiang should have been focusing all of his attention on the struggle against the Japanese. He was surrounded by incompetent and compromised generals who limited his ability to successfully prosecute the war. Nevertheless, his achievements were considerable. After his destruction of the warlords in the late 1920s he tried very hard—and twice almost succeeded—in uniting China under his leadership. Chiang also tied down hundreds of thousands of Japanese troops from 1938 through to 1944, slowing the Japanese advance through the Pacific, and ensuring that they were not able to launch a ground assault on the Australian mainland in 1942. It was Chiang who forced America and Britain to return their nineteenth-century territorial acquisitions to China (excluding Hong Kong). Chiang's achievements in World War II earned him a place at the 'Big Four' table—alongside America, Britain and the Soviet Union—and also ensured that China was eventually able to get a permanent seat on the UN Security Council.

# Legacies

By the time the war ended, the Nationalists were exhausted militarily and damaged economically by years of occupation. Yet, less than six months after the ceasefire with Japan, Chiang Kai-shek again came close to crushing Mao and eliminating the communist threat. He was thwarted by the wartime myth of Mao's heroic struggle, which convinced the United States to withdraw support from Chiang, forcing him to negotiate with Mao at a time just when the communists were on the point of capitulating.

President Truman sent General George C. Marshall to China in December 1945 to force Chiang to come to terms with Mao, thereby halting the civil war that was sending the country spiralling into disorder. Marshall reported to Truman that the communists were much more cooperative than the corrupt Nationalists, that the Soviet Union did not support Mao, and that forces on the loose in Manchuria were not organised communist armies, but 'little more than loosely organised bands'. Marshall was swayed by communist propaganda that insisted that they had been the principal force involved in defeating the Japanese during the invasion. He accordingly requested that Chiang 'immediately issue an order terminating advances, attacks, or pursuits by government troops', just as Nationalist forces threatened the last major communist-held city in Manchuria. Chiang complied, and Mao was able to regroup and fight another day, having gained a base in northern Manchuria that was within easy reach of assistance from the Soviet Union.

Intervention by the United States in China in 1945–46 was a disastrous miscalculation. It was US assistance, when added to the crippling effects of the fight against the Japanese occupation and the preservation of the communist forces, that was a key factor in Mao's eventual victory and the creation of the People's Republic of China. The United States eventually realised its mistake and supplied the Nationalists with money and weapons, but by then it was too late.

The legacy of Mao's eventual victory in the Chinese civil war was enormous. Had Chiang Kai-shek defeated the communists, America would have had a powerful ally in the Far East, one that would have acted as a deterrent against Soviet ambitions in Europe. Chiang had shown himself to be sympathetic to American interests during the war, and the threat of a second front against the Soviets during the Cold War would probably have forced the Soviet Union to proceed cautiously in Europe, forcing them to be more conciliatory and less belligerent.

Instead, the Soviet Union gained in the short-term an ally who would tie down American resources in the Far East, leaving Stalin free to turn his attention to Europe and his long-term objective of seizing European countries not already under his control, starting with West Germany.

As it was, actions by Mao and the Chinese communists were to trigger the Korean War, plunging the United States and its allies into a complex struggle that would occupy America's attention for more than two decades, ending only when it abandoned South Vietnam 25 years later. Regardless of Stalin's motives in wanting the war and being involved in its planning stage, it was Mao's decision to supply tens of thousands of troops from the Chinese People's Liberation Army that gave the North Koreans the strength they needed to launch an invasion of South Korea. Mao was reported to have advised North Korean leader Kim Il-sung that, 'It would be much better if the North Korean government launched an all-out attack against the South in 1950 […] if necessary, we can stealthily put in Chinese soldiers for you.'

When the North Korean advance had been halted and its soldiers pushed back almost to the Chinese border, Chinese troops crossed the border in enormous numbers and inflicted great harm causing heavy losses on United Nations' forces, giving the world a taste of what a formidable fighting force the Chinese had become after the 20 years of internal and external conflict. Two decades later, Chinese assistance given to North Vietnam was crucial in its victory over the United States.

For many people living within China, Mao's victory was catastrophic. The Chinese invasion of Tibet resulted in a humanitarian crisis that persists to this day. His attempts at land reform and the suppression of counter-revolutionaries—real and imagined—resulted in the deaths of some 2 to 5 million people. When Mao instituted the 'Great Leap Forward', which created farming communes and promoted the expansion of heavy industry, the result was the greatest famine in human history, during which an estimated 38 million people died. His attempted 'Cultural Revolution' resulted in the destruction of much of China's pre-Communist heritage, and the imprisonment and torture of thousands of individuals.

Although Mao died in 1976, his legacy is still cherished by those in the Chinese leadership who consider themselves his heirs and successors. They continue to perpetuate the myths surrounding Mao and his achievements—among them that it was Mao, not Chiang Kai-shek, who was responsible for China's victory over the Japanese.

# FURTHER READING, PRINCIPAL SOURCES AND SPECIAL ACKNOWLEDGMENTS

A number of works have been indispensable to the writing of this book, and for several chapters I am deeply indebted to the research and publications of writers, journalists and specialist historians. These are acknowledged in the following list, alongside other books and articles in which readers can find further information about the events recounted in every chapter.

## SECTION 1—SPIN & DOUBLESPEAK

### The Victor's Version of the Battle of Kadesh

Matthews, Roger & Roemer, Cornelia, (eds.), *Ancient Perspectives on Egypt* (Routledge Cavendish, London, 2003)

Stanley, Arthur Penrhyn, *Sinai and Palestine in Connection with Their History* (Redfield, New York, 1856)

### The Little Lie that Built the Roman Empire

For this essay, I am deeply indebted to Richard Holland's excellent overview of the reign of Augustus, *Augustus: Godfather of Europe*, which provided many of the details of the events leading to the fake abdication in 27 BC.

Holland, Richard, *Augustus: Godfather of Europe* (Sutton Publishing, Gloucestershire, 2005)

Suetonius, *The Twelve Caesars* (Penguin Books, London, 1979)

### The Hijacking of the Fourth Crusade

Many of the details for this essay have come from John Julius Norwich's excellent account of the events leading to the Fourth Crusade, *Byzantium: The Decline and Fall*.

Norwich, John Julius, *A History of Venice* (Penguin Books, London, 1983)

Norwich, John Julius, *Byzantium: The Decline and Fall* (Penguin Books, London, 1996)

Payne, Robert, *The Crusades: A History* (Wordsworth Editions Ltd, Hertfordshire, 1998)

## When Merry England was a Police State

Hogge, Alice, *God's Secret Agents: Queen Elizabeth's Forbidden Priests and the Hatching of the Gunpowder Plot* (HarperCollins, New York, 2005)

Hutchinson, Robert, *Elizabeth's Spymaster: Francis Walsingham and the Secret War that Saved England* (Macmillan, London, 2007)

Maxwell-Stuart, P.G., *The Archbishops of Canterbury* (Tempus Publishing Ltd, Gloucestershire, 2006)

Thomas, Jane Resh, *Behind the Mask: The Life of Queen Elizabeth I* (Clarion Books, New York, 1998)

## What Happened to the Prisoners of the Bastille?

For this essay, I am deeply indebted to Simon Schama's masterwork on the French Revolution, *Citizens: A Chronicle of the French Revolution*, which provided many of the details about life in the Bastille as well as the events leading to its overthrow.

Schama, Simon, *Citizens: A Chronicle of the French Revolution* (Penguin Books, London, 2004)

## The Forced Migration of the American Indians

Banner, Stuart, *How the Indians Lost Their Land: Law and Power on the Frontier* (Harvard University Press, Cambridge, 2005)

Horsman, Reginald, *Race and Manifest Destiny: The Origins of American Racial Anglo-Saxonism* (Harvard University Press, Cambridge, 1981)

Remini, Robert V., *Andrew Jackson and his Indian Wars* (Viking, New York, 2001)

## France's Legitimate Wartime Government

For this essay, I am deeply indebted to both Alfred Cobban's *A History of Modern France, Volume 3*, and to Erna Paris' *Long Shadows: Truth, Lies and History*, which was used extensively, especially in the details involving the trial of Maurice Papon and the creation of the post war fiction of Vichy's illegitimacy.

Cobban, A., *A History of Modern France, Volume 3* (Penguin Books, London, 1990)

Curtis, Michael, *Verdict on Vichy: Power and Prejudice in the Vichy France Regime* (Arcade Publishing, New York, 2003)

Jackson, Julian, *France: The Dark Years, 1940–1944* (Oxford University Press, New York, 2001)

Paris, Erna, *Long Shadows: Truth, Lies and History* (Bloomsbury, London, 2002)

Tourunoux, Jean Raymond, *Sons of France: Pétain and De Gaulle* (Viking Press, New York, 1966)

## SECTION 2—PASSING THE BUCK

### Rome Burns and Nero Points the Finger

Bowman, Alan K., et al. (ed.), *The Cambridge Ancient History XI: The High Empire*, (Oxford University Press, Cambridge, 2002)

Chadwick, Henry, *The Early Church* (Penguin Books, London, 1993)

Suetonius, *The Twelve Caesars* (Penguin Books, London, 1979)

### King Richard III—Victim of a Smear Campaign

For this essay, I am deeply indebted to John Julius Norwich's insightful analysis of the reign of Richard III, *Shakespeare's Kings*.

Churchill, Winston, *A History of the English-Speaking Peoples*, abridged (Cassell & Co., London, 2000)

Gairdner, James, *History of the Life and Reign of Richard the Third to Which Is Added the Story of Perkin Warbeck from Original Documents* (Kessinger Publishing, Whitefish, Montana, 2004)

Norwich, John Julius, *Shakespeare's Kings* (Penguin Books, London, 2000)

### The Forgery that 'Proved' a Jewish Conspiracy

Evans, Richard J., *The Coming of the Third Reich*, (Penguin Books, London, 2004)

Johnson, Paul, *A History of the Jews* (Phoenix, London, 1995)

Keren, Dr. Daniel, 'Commentary on The Protocols of the Elders of Zion', (2002) <http://www.nizkor.org/ftp.cgi?documents/protocols/protocols.zion>

Marsden, Victor E., 'The Protocols of the Learned Elders of Zion', (2002) <http://ddickerson.igc.org/The_Protocols_of_the_Learned_Elders_of_Zion.pdf>

### Passing the Blame for World War I

For this essay, in particular the legacies portion of the chapter with its emphasis on the devastation wrought on Germany, I am deeply indebted to Richard J. Evans' *The Coming of the Third Reich*.

Abrams, Lynn, *Bismarck and the German Empire, 1871–1918* (Routledge, New York, 1995)

Evans, Richard J., *The Coming of the Third Reich*, (Penguin Books, London, 2004)

Mahajan, Sneh, *British Foreign Policy, 1874–1914: The Role of India* (Routledge, London, 2002)

Röhl, John C. G., *Wilhelm II: The Kaiser's Personal Monarchy, 1888–1900* (Cambridge University Press, Cambridge, 2004)

### Russian Peasants and Stalin's Paranoia

For this essay, I am deeply indebted to Simon Sebag Montefiore's *Stalin: The Court of the Red Tsar*.

Montefiore, Simon Sebag, *Stalin: The Court of the Red Tsar* (Phoenix, London, 2004)

Neville, Peter, *Russia – A Complete History in One Volume* (The Windrush Press, Gloucestershire, 2000)

Wood, Alan, *Stalin and Stalinism* (Routledge, New York, 2005)

### Pointing the Way to Pearl Harbor

Best, Antony, *Britain, Japan and Pearl Harbor: Avoiding War in East Asia, 1936–41* (Routledge, London, 1995)

Kimmel, Husband E., *Admiral Kimmel's Story* (Henry Regnery Company, Chicago, 1955)

Schmidt, Donald E., *The Folly Of War: American Foreign Policy, 1898–2005* (Algora Publishing, New York, 2005)

Stinnet, Robert B., *Day of Deceit: The Truth about FDR and Pearl Harbor* (Simon and Schuster, New York, 2000)

# PART 3—OFFICIAL DECEPTIONS & COVER-UPS

### The Pharaoh Erased from History

For this essay, especially for the details about the pharaohs, I am deeply indebted to Ian Shaw's *The Oxford History of Ancient Egypt*.

Mehler, Stephen S., *From Light Into Darkness: The Evolution of Religion in Ancient Egypt* (Adventures Unlimited Press, Kempton, 2005)

Montserrat, Dominic, *Akhenaten: History, Fantasy and Ancient Egypt* (Routledge, London, 2003)

Shaw, Ian, *The Oxford History of Ancient Egypt* (Oxford University Press, Oxford, 2000)

### The Forgery that Gave Wordly Power to the Popes

Pearse, Roger, 'The Donation of Constantine and the critique of Lorenzo Valla', (2001) <http://www.tertullian.org/rpearse/donation/donation_of_constantine.htm>

Southern, R.W., *Western Society and the Church in the Middle Ages* (Penguin Books, London, 1990)

### The Betrayal of the Knights Templar

For this essay, I am deeply indebted to Piers Paul Read's *The Templars*, especially the events leading to the fall of the Knights Templar.

Barber, Malcolm, *The Trial of the Templars* (Cambridge University Press, New York, 1993)

Menache, Sophia, *Clement V* (Cambridge University Press, Cambridge, 1998)

Read, Piers Paul, *The Templars* (Phoenix Press, London, 2001)

### The Fiction that Justified D-Day

Carlton, David, *Churchill and the Soviet Union* (Manchester University Press, Manchester, 2000)

Dallek, Robert, *Franklin D. Roosevelt and American Foreign Policy, 1932–1945* (Oxford University Press, New York, 1979)

### Politics and the Partition of India

Ali, Tariq, *The Clash of Fundamentalisms—Crusades, Jihads and Modernity* (Verso, London, 2003)

Kamra, Sukeshi, *Bearing Witness: Partition, Independence, End of the Raj* (University of Calgary Press, Calgary, 2002)

Khan, Adeel, *Politics of Identity: Ethnic Nationalism and the State in Pakistan* (Sage Publications, New Delhi, 2005)

Panigrahi, D. N., *India's Partition: The Story of Imperialism in Retreat* (Routledge, New York, 2004)

Richards, John F., *The Mughal Empire* (Cambridge University Press, Cambridge, 1993)

### Send Troops—The North Vietnamese are Attacking!

For the retelling of the events surrounding the incident at the Gulf of Tonkin, I am deeply indebted to Edwin E. Moise's *Tonkin Gulf and the Escalation of the Vietnam War*.

Goulden, Joseph C., *Truth is the First Casualty: The Gulf of Tonkin Affair: Illusion and Reality* (Rand McNally, New York, 1969)

McMaster, H. R., *Dereliction of Duty: Johnson, McNamara, the Joint Chiefs of Staff, and the Lies That Led to Vietnam* (HarperCollins, New York, 1997)

Moise, Edwin E., *Tonkin Gulf and the Escalation of the Vietnam War* (UNC Press, Chapel Hill, 1996)

Prados, John, 'Essay: 40th Anniversary of the Gulf of Tonkin Incident', National Security Archive (2004) www.gwu.edu/~nsarchiv/NSAEBB/NSAEBB132/essay.htm

# PART 4—ACTING UNDER FALSE PRETENCES

### Carthage Must Be Destroyed!

For this essay, especially the section dealing with the causes of the fall of the Roman Republic, I am heavily indebted to Tom Holland's excellent work on the subject, *Rubicon: The Triumph and Tragedy of the Roman Republic*.

Goldsworthy, Adrian, *The Fall of Carthage: The Punic Wars 265–146BC* (Cassell Military, London, 2004)

Holland, Tom, *Rubicon: The Triumph and Tragedy of the Roman Republic* (Abacus, 2004)

McDonnell, Myles Anthony, *Roman Manliness:* Virtus *and the Roman Republic* (Cambridge University Press, New York, 2006)

Plutarch, *The Parallel Lives, Vol. II* (Loeb Classical Library edition, Cambridge, 1914)

## The First Holy Crusade—What's in it for Me?

For this essay, I am deeply indebted to Robert Payne's excellent overview, *The Crusades: A History*.

Madden, Thomas F., *The New Concise History of the Crusades* (Rowman & Littlefield, Lanham, 2005)

Payne, Rober, *The Crusades: A History* (Wordsworth Editions Ltd, Hertfordshire, 1998)

## Galileo and the Jesuits

For this essay, I am deeply indebted to the arguments mounted in Edward Burman's challenging review of the condemnation of Galileo in *The Inquisition: The Hammer of Heresy*, pages 169-177.

Burman, Edward, *The Inquisition: The Hammer of Heresy* (Sutton Publishing, Gloucestershire, 2004)

De Santillana, Giorgio, *The Crime of Galileo* (University of Chicago Press, Chicago, 1955)

Reston, James, *Galileo: A Life* (Beard Books, Washington, 2000)

Woods, Thomas, *How the Catholic Church Built Western Civilization* (Regnery Publishing, Washington, 2005)

## The Hidden Agenda of America's Founding Fathers

For this essay, I am heavily indebted to Hugh Bicheno's book *Rebels & Redcoats: The American Revolutionary War* for its critical analysis of the reasons for the start of the war.

Alexander, John K., *Samuel Adams: America's Revolutionary Politician* (Rowman & Littlefield, Lanham, 2002)

Bicheno, Hugh, *Rebels & Redcoats: The American Revolutionary War* (HarperCollins, London, 2003)

Churchill, Winston, *A History of the English-Speaking Peoples*, abridged (Cassell & Co., London, 2000)

Galvin, John R., *The Minute Men: The First Fight: Myths and Realities of the American Revolution* (Brassey's, Dulles, 1996)

Szatmary, David P., *Shays' Rebellion: The Making of an Agrarian Insurrection* (University of Massachusetts Press, Amherst, 1980)

## The Annexation of Mexico by the United States

Fantina, Robert, *Desertion and the American Soldier, 1776–2005* (Algora Publishing, New York, 2006)

Grant, U.S., *Personal memoirs of U.S. Grant, Volume I. Chapter IV* (C.L. Webster & Co., New York, 1885)

Hamilton, Holman, *Prologue to Conflict: The Crisis and Compromise of 1850* (University Press of Kentucky, Lexington, 2005)

Jones, Howard, *Crucible of Power: A History of American Foreign Relations to 1913* (Rowman & Littlefield, Wilmington, 2002)

## Chairman Mao's Greatest Triumph—Thanks to Chiang Kai-shek

For this essay, I am deeply indebted to Jung Chang and Jon Halliday's book, *Mao: The Unknown Story*, especially in relating how Mao outmanoeuvred Chiang and how he manipulated the United States.

Chang, Jung & Halliday, Jon, *Mao: The Unknown Story* (Vintage Books, London, 2006)

Lynch, Michael, *Mao* (Routledge Press, New York, 2004)

Romanus, Charles F. & Sunderland, Riley, *The China-Burma-India Theater: Stilwell's Command Problems* (Bernan Assoc, Blue Ridge Summit, Pennsylvania, 1956)

# ADDITIONAL SOURCES

Adams, Samuel, 'The Rights of the Colonists', Hanover Historical Texts Project,
 <http://history.hanover.edu/texts/adamss.html>

Adams, William Howard, *The Paris Years of Thomas Jefferson* (Yale University, New Haven, 1997)

Alighieri, Dante, *Dante's Divina Commedia*, Translated by Ramsay, C.H. (Tinsley
 Brothers, London, 1862)

Allsopp, Michelle, 'Achieving Zero Dioxin', Greenpeace International, September
 1994, <http://archive.greenpeace.org/toxics/reports/azd/azd.html>

Alouni, Tayseer & Bin Laden, Osama, 'Transcript of Bin Laden's October interview', CNN
 <http://archives.cnn.com/2002/WORLD/asiapcf/south/02/05/binladen.transcript/>

American Almanac, The, 'Churchill's Plans For WWIII', from *Executive Intelligence Review*,
 *The New Federalist*, October 1998, <http://american_almanac.tripod.com/church.htm>

Anouilh, Jean, *L'alouette* (Appleton-Century-Crofts, New York, 1956)

Ancient Egypt Online, 'Abydos Kings List', <http://www.ancientegyptonline.
 co.uk/abydoskl.html>

Anti-Defamation League, 'The Protocols of the Elders of Zion: The Renaissance of anti-
 Semitic Hate Literature in the Arab and Islamic World', Anti-Defamation League
 <http://www.adl.org/css/proto_intro.asp>

Appian, *The Foreign Wars* (Loeb Classical Library edition, Cambridge, 1913)

Assmann, Jan, 'Theological Responses to Amarna', PennState University (2001)
 <http://www.scribd.com/doc/40000/Ass-Mann>

Associated Press, The, 'French Nazi-era collaborator Maurice Papon dies' in *USA Today*,
 17 February 2007, <http://www.usatoday.com/news/world/2007-02-17-
 papon-obit_x.htm?csp=34>. Used with permission of The Associated Press © 2009

Associated Press, The, 'Reagan's memorable D-Day speech 20 years ago', msnbc
 <http://www.msnbc.msn.com/id/5146000/>

Austin, Anthony, *The President's War: The Story of the Tonkin Gulf Resolution and how the Nation
 was Trapped in Vietnam* (Lippincott, New York, 1971)

Barnes, Harry Elmer, (ed.), *Perpetual War for Perpetual Peace: A Critical Examination of the
 Foreign Policy on Franklin Delano Roosevelt* (Institute for Historical Review, Newport
 Beach, 1982)

Basset, Bernard, *The English Jesuits from Campion to Martindale* (Gracewing Publishing,
 Herefordshire, 2004)

Benton, Thomas Hart, *Abridgment of the Debates of Congress from 1789 to 1856*
 (D. Appleton & Co, New York, 1858)

Black, Hugo L, 'New York Times Co v United States', 403 U.S. 713, 717 (1971)
 <http://www.bc.edu/bc_org/avp/cas/comm/free_speech/nytvus.html>

Bloch, Robert, *Murphy's Law, and Other Reasons why Things Go Wrong* (Price Stern Sloan,
 Los Angeles, 1980)

Bosworth, R. J. B., *Explaining Auschwitz and Hiroshima: History Writing and the Second World
 War: 1945–1990* (Routledge, London, 1993)

Bowden, James Atticus, 'Jihads and Crusades', Renew America
    <http://www.renewamerica.us/columns/bowden/050521>

Boztas, Senay, 'Letters show Picasso was no collaborator', in *The Independent*, 23 September
    2007 <http://news.independent.co.uk/europe/article2990165.ece>

Breasted, James Henry, *Ancient Records of Egypt: Historical Documents from the Earliest Times to
    the Persian Conquest, Vol. III* (University of Chicago Press, Chicago, 1906)

Brighton, Ray, *The Checkered Career of Tobias Lear* (Portsmouth Marine Society,
    Portsmouth, 1985)

Browne, Charles Farrar, 'Famous Patriotic Quotes by Other Notable Americans 03',
    USA Patriotism, <http://www.usa-patriotism.com/quotes/others-03.htm>

Bush, George W, Press Conference, 19 September 2002, YouTube
    <www.youtube.com/watch?v=eKgPY1adc0A>

Bush, George W, Press Conference, 1 May 2003, YouTube
    <http://www.youtube.com/watch?v=Frlwtz2oOnM&feature=related>

Campbell, G. A., *Knights Templar: Their Rise and Fall* (Kessinger Publishing, Whitefish,
    Montana, 2003)

Cassiodorus, 'The Letters of Cassiodorus', Project Guttenberg
    <http://www.gutenberg.org/ebooks/18590>

Center of Religious Freedom, 'Saudi Arabia's Curriculum of Intolerance', Freedom
    House <http://www.npr.org/documents/2006/may/sauditexts/textbooks.pdf>

Chiang Kai-shek, Madame, *Daily Telegraph*, October 2003 <http://www.telegraph.
    co.uk/news/main.jhtml?xml=/news/2003/10/25/db2501.xml&page=2>

China Internet Information Center, 'An Illustrated History of the Communist Party
    of China', <http://www.china.org.cn/english/features/45956.htm>

Chirot, Daniel, *Modern Tyrants: The Power and Prevalence of Evil in Our Age* (Princeton
    University Press, Princeton, 1996)

Churchill, Winston, 'Churchill & Statesmanship', The Churchill Centre
    <http://www.winstonchurchill.org/i4a/pages/index.cfm?pageid=398>

Cicero, *The Orations of Marcus Tullius Cicero, Volume 4*, FullBooks,
    <http://www.fullbooks.com/The-Orations-of-Marcus-Tullius-Cicero-Volume4.html>

Cicero, Marcus Tullius, *Cicero: The Orations* (J. & J. Harper, New York, 1833)

Cicero, Marcus Tullius, Quoteworld, <http://www.quoteworld.org/quotes/2876>

Clinton, Bill, Grand Jury Deposition, 17 January 1998, YouTube
    <www.youtube.com/watch?v=j4XT-l-_3y0>

Cobban, Alfred, *A History of Modern France, Volume 1: 1715–1799* (Penguin Books,
    London, 1990)

Cobban, Alfred, *A History of Modern France, Volume 3* (Penguin Books, London, 1990)

Cohen, Roger, 'Trial of Vichy Official Lifts Veil on Killing of Algerians' in *New
    York Times*, 18 October 1997 <http://query.nytimes.com/gst/fullpage.html?res=
    9C05E1DF113FF93BA25753C1A961958260>

Colson, Charles, quoted in Becker, Thomas W., *A Season Of Madness: Life and Death
    in the 1960s* (AuthorHouse, Bloomington, Indiana, 2007)

Conan, Eric, Rousso, Henry & Bracher, Nathan, *Vichy: An Ever-present Past* (UPNE,
    Hanover, 1998)

Conquest, Robert, *V. I. Lenin* (Viking Press, New York, 1972)

Craik, Dinah Maria Mulock, *A Woman's Thoughts About Women* (Hurst & Blackett Publishers, London, 1859)

*Daily Mirror*, 'The Declaration of War', 4 August 1914, <http://www.bbc.co.uk/history/worldwars/wwone/mirror01_01.shtml>

Daniels, Robert Vincent, *A Documentary History of Communism in Russia: From Lenin to Gorbachev* (University Press of New England, Lebanon, New Hampshire, 1993)

Davies, Norman, *Europe: A History* (Oxford University Press, Oxford, 1996)

Davis, J. Madison (ed.), *Conversations with Robertson Davies* (University Press of Mississippi, Jackson, 1990)

de Latude, Henry Maserts, quoted in *Museum of Foreign Literature, Science and Art* by Robert Walsh, Eliakim Littell & John Jay Smith (E. Littell, Philadelphia, 1834)

de Lisle, Leanda, *After Elizabeth* (Harper Perennial, London, 2006)

de Villehardouin, Geoffrey, 'Memoirs or Chronicle of The Fourth Crusade and The Conquest of Constantinople', *Medieval Sourcebook* <http://www.fordham.edu/halsall/basis/villehardouin.html>

Deats, Richard L. & Jegen, M., *Mahatma Gandhi: Nonviolent Liberator; A Biography* (New City Press, Hyde Park, New York, 2005)

Descendants of Mexican War Veterans, 'Historic Sites of the U.S.–Mexican War', <http://www.dmwv.org/mexwar/mwsites/cameron.htm#carricitos>

Dio, Cassius, *Roman History Vol. VIII* (Harvard University Press, Cambridge, 1925)

Donovan, Lieutenant Colonel Michael J., 'Strategic Deception: Operation Fortitude', U.S. Army War College <http://www.dtic.mil/cgi-bin/GetTRDoc?AD=ADA404434&Location=U2&doc=GetTRDoc.pdf>

Duckett, Eleanor Shipley, *Death and Life in the Tenth Century* (University of Michigan Press, qMichigan, 1967)

Duncan, Louis, *Medical Men in the American Revolution* (Medical Field Service School, Carlisle Barracks, 1931)

Dunn, Jimmy, 'Amenhotep II, 7th Pharaoh of Egypt's 18th Dynasty', Tour Egypt <http://touregypt.net/featurestories/amenhotep2.htm>

Edwardes, Michael, *The Last Years of British India* (The World Publishing Company, Cleveland, 1964)

Einstein, Albert, Quoteworld <http://www.quoteworld.org/quotes/4160>

Eisenhower, Dwight D., 'General Dwight D. Eisenhower's Order of the Day (1944)', Historical Documents in United States History, <http://www. historicaldocuments.com/GeneralEisenhower'sOrderoftheDay.htm>

Elizabeth I, 'Elizabeth I Quotes' <http://www.elizabethi.org/us/quotes/>

Ellenblum, Ronnie, *Crusader Castles and Modern Histories* (Cambridge University Press, New York, 2007)

*Encyclopaedia of the Orient*, 'The Great Hymn to the Aten', <http://looklex.com/e.o/texts/religion/egypt_hymn_aten.htm>

Erasmus, Desiderius, *The Praise of Folly and Other Writings* (Norton Critical Edition, New York, 1989)

Evans, Hugh E., *The Hidden Campaign: FDR's Health and the 1944 Election* (M.E. Sharpe, Armonk, New York, 2002)

Evans, Richard J., *The Third Reich in Power* (Allen Lane, London, 2005)

Fagan, Garrett G., Pennsylvania State University, 'Augustus (31 BC–14 AD)', Online Encyclopedia of Roman Rulers <http://www.roman-emperors.org/auggie.htm>

Fears, J. Rufus, 'The Lessons of the Roman Empire for America Today', Heritage Foundation <http://www.heritage.org/Research/PoliticalPhilosophy/hl917.cfm>

Fingerson, R., 'Manetho's King List', Egyptian Journey (2003) <http://www.phouka.com/pharaoh/egypt/history/KLManetho.html>

Finocchiaro, Maurice A., (ed.), texts from 'The Galileo Affair: A Documentary History', Mark Gagné, West Chester University <http://astro.wcupa.edu/mgagne/ess362/resources/finocchiaro.html#conreport>

Fischer, Hannah, Klarman, Kim & Oboroceanu, Mari-Jana "M-J", 'American War and Military Operations Casualties: Lists and Statistics', Congressional Research Service (June 2007) <http://www.fas.org/sgp/crs/natsec/RL32492.pdf>

Fraser, George MacDonald, *The Hollywood History of the World* (The Harvill Press, London, 1996)

Galilei, Galileo, quoted in Newman, J.R., *The World of Mathematics* (Simon and Schuster, New York, 1956)

Ghandi, 1947, quoted in 'Commemorating 125th Anniversary of the Birth of Mahatma Ghandi,' United Nations Educational, Scientific and Cultural Organization, 1995, p. 144 <http://unesdoc.unesco.org/images/0011/001145/114536eo.pdf>

Gibbon, Edward, *The Decline and Fall of the Roman Empire, Volume I* (The Modern Library, New York, 1988)

Gilbert, G. M., *Nuremberg Diary* (Da Capo Press, Cambridge, 1995)

Goldstein, Donald M., Dillon, Katherine V. & Wenger, J. Michael, *The Vietnam War: The Story and Photographs* (Brassey's, Herndon, Virginia, 1999)

Goubert, Pierre, *The Course of French History* (Routledge, London, 1991)

Goy-Blanquet, Dominique, *Shakespeare's Early History Plays: From Chronicle to Stage* (Oxford University Press, New York, 2003)

Grant, U.S., 'Ulysses S. Grant's reflections on the war', Smithsonian Source <http://www.smithsoniansource.org/display/primarysource/viewdetails.aspx?PrimarySourceId=1047>

Grasso, June, Corrin, Jay & Kort, Michael, *Modernization And Revolution In China: From the Opium Wars to World Power* (M.E. Sharpe, Armonk, New York, 2004)

Griffith Institute, Oxford, 'Tutankhamun: Anatomy of an Excavation. Howard Carter's diaries. The first excavation season in the tomb of Tutankhamun. Part 1: October 28 to December 31, 1922' <http://www.ashmolean.org/gri/4sea1not.html>

Grobschmidt, Steven, 'Religious Orders: The Rule of St. Benedict Compared with the Rule of the Templars', On-line Reference Books for Medieval Study, <http://www.the-orb.net/encyclop/religion/monastic/comprule.html>

Half, Robert, 'Robert Half Quotes', Brainy Quote, <http://www.brainyquote.com/quotes/authors/r/robert_half.html>

Hallam, Elizabeth M. & Everard, Judith, *Capetian France, 987–1328* (Longman, Harlow, Essex, 2001)

Halliley, Mark (prod.), 'Secrets of the Dead', Educational Broadcasting Corporation, Thirteen/WNET New York. (2002) <http://www.pbs.org/wnet/secrets/previous_seasons/case_rome/clues.html>

Hamas Covenant, 'The Covenant of the Islamic Resistance Movement, 18 August 1988',
    The Avalon Project at Yale Law School
        <http://www.yale.edu/lawweb/avalon/mideast/hamas.htm>
Hamblin, William & Madden, Thomas, 'Cross Purposes: The Crusades', Hoover Institution
        <http://www.hoover.org/multimedia/uk/2994821.html>
Harkins, David, 'Picasso In Paris During World War 2', in *The Daily Telegraph*, May 2007
    (retrieved 29/12/2007)
        <http://my.telegraph.co.uk/david_harkins/may_2007/picasso_in_paris_during_ww2.htm>
Harris, Jonathan, 'Byzantines in Renaissance Italy', On-line Reference Books for Medieval
    Study <http://www.the-orb.net/encyclop/late/laterbyz/harris-ren.html>
Hawking, Stephen, *A Brief History of Time* (Bantam Books, London, 1998)
Henderson, Ernest F., *Select Historical Documents of the Middle Ages* (George Bell, London, 1910)
Hickman, Kennedy, 'World War II Pacific: New Guinea, Burma, & China',
    About.com: Military History,
        <http://militaryhistory.about.com/od/worldwarii/a/wwiipacngburmch_2.htm>
Hitler, Adolf, *Mein Kampf* (Houghton Mifflin, Boston, 1998)
Holland, Tom, *Rubicon: The Triumph and Tragedy of the Roman Republic*
    (Abacus, London, 2004)
Horton, Scott, 'Novus Ordo Seclorum', *Harpers Magazine*, September 2007,
        <http://www.harpers.org/archive/2007/09/hbc-90001205>
Ingram, Edward, *In Defence of British India: Great Britain in the Middle East, 1775–1842*
    (Routledge, London, 1984)
Jackson, Andrew, 'First Annual Message, 1829', The eJournal website
        <http://www.synaptic.bc.ca/ejournal/JacksonFirstAnnualMessage.htm>
Jackson, Andrew, 'State of The Union Address 1830', USA Presidents
        <http://www.usa-presidents.info/union/jackson-2.html>
Jansohn, Christa (ed.), *Queen Elizabeth I: Past and Present* (LIT-Verlag, Berlin, 2005)
Jenkins, Elizabeth, *Elizabeth & Leicester* (Phoenix Press, London, 2002)
Jinnah, Muhammad Ali, 'Presidential address by Muhammad Ali Jinnah to the Muslim League
    Lahore, 1940', Prof. Frances Pritchett, Columbia University
<http://www.columbia.edu/itc/mealac/pritchett/00islamlinks/txt_jinnah_lahore_1940.html>
Johnston, George Sim, 'The Galileo Affair'
        <http://www.catholic.net/rcc/Periodicals/Issues/GalileoAffair.html>
Joshi, Lt Gen. Ashok & Athale, Col. (Dr) Anil, 'Pakistan: Towards democracy?', Rediff News
        <http://www.rediff.com/news/2007/nov/26guest.htm>
Keen, Shirin, 'The Partition of India', Postcolonial Studies at Emory
        <http://www.english.emory.edu/Bahri/Part.html>
Keogh, James, *This is Nixon* (Putnam's Sons, New York, 1956)
Ketchum, Richard M., *The Borrowed Years, 1938–1941: America on the Way to War*
    (Random House, New York, 1989)
Khrushchev, N. S., *Khrushchev Remembers* (Little, Brown & Co., Boston, 1970)
Latner, Richard B., 'Andrew Jackson', Profiles of U.S. Presidents,
        <http://www.presidentprofiles.com/Washington-Johnson/Jackson-Andrew.html>
Lawrence, Mark Atwood & Longevall, Fredrik, *The First Vietnam War: Colonial Conflict and
    Cold War Crisis* (Harvard University Press, Cambridge, 2007)

Lawton, John, 'The Carthage Treaty', Saudi Aramco World, May/June 1985
    <http://www.saudiaramcoworld.com/issue/198503/delenda.est.carthago.htm>
Leliw, Tony, 'Vilified, slandered and abused for telling the truth about
    Communism', Brama News and Community Press
    <http://www.brama.com/news/press/2003/10/031001leliw_muggeridge.html>
Lincoln, Abraham, 'Abraham Lincoln Quotes' <http://thinkexist.com/quotation/
    you_may_fool_all_the_people_some_of_the_time-you/145518.html>
Lincoln, Abraham, 'The Gettysburg Address', Abraham Lincoln Online
    <http://showcase.netins.net/web/creative/lincoln/speeches/gettysburg.htm>
Livy, 'Periochae', Livius
    <http://www.livius.org/li-ln/livy/periochae/periochae048.html>
Livy, *The War With Hannibal* (Penguin Books, London, 1988)
Lopez, Asbel, 'Antonio Tabucchi: A Commited Doubter', UNESCO Courier
    <http://www.unesco.org/courier/1999_11/uk/dires/txt1.htm>
Lovell, Julia, *The Great Wall—China Against The World 1000 BC–2000 AD* (Picador,
    Sydney, 2006)
MacCaffrey, Rev. James, S.J, 'History of the Catholic Church From the Renaissance to the
    French Revolution, Volume II, Chapter IV',
    <http://catholicity.elcore.net/MacCaffrey/HCCRFR2_Chapter04.html>
MacCulloch, Diarmaid, *Reformation: Europe's House Divided 1490–1700* (Penguin Books,
    London, 2004)
Mackintosh, James, *The History of England from the Earliest Times to the Final Establishment of the
    Reformation* (Longman, Brown, Green and Longmans, London, 1853)
Mann, Horace K., *Lives Of The Popes In The Middle Ages, Volume 1 Part 2* (Kegan Paul, Trench,
    Trubner, & Co, London, 1903)
Mann, Horace K., *Lives Of The Popes In The Middle Ages, Volume 8* (Kegan Paul, Trench,
    Trubner, & Co, London, 1915)
Mann, Horace K., *Lives Of The Popes In The Middle Ages, Volume 9* (Kegan Paul, Trench,
    Trubner, & Co, London, 1925)
Marrin, Albert, *Sir Norman Angell* (Twayne Publishers, Boston, 1979)
Marshall, Thomas Maitland, 'The Southwestern Boundary Of Texas, 1821–1840' in
    *Southwestern Historical Quarterly Online*, Vol. 14, No. 4, pp. 271–293
    <http://www.tshaonline.org/shqonline/apager.php?vol=014&pag=281>
*Medieval Sourcebook*, 'Donation of Constantine',
    <http://www.fordham.edu/halsall/source/donatconst.html>
Middlekauff, Robert, *The Glorious Cause: The American Revolution, 1763–1789* (Oxford
    University Press, New York, 2007)
Mill, John Stuart, *On Liberty* (Longmans, Green & Co, London, 1865)
More, Thomas, 'History of King Richard III' (1557)
    <http://www.r3.org/rnt1991/royaltree.html>
Morris, Benny, *The Birth of the Palestinian Refugee Problem Revisited* (Cambridge University
    Press, Cambridge, 2004)
Morris, James & Morris, Jan, *The World of Venice* (Harcourt Brace Jovanovich, New York, 1974)
Morrow, Dwight Whitney, quoted in Nicolson, Harold, *Dwight Morrow* (Harcourt, Brace,
    New York, 1935)

Mountbatten, Louis, quoted in Collins, Larry & Lapierre, Dominique, *Freedom at Midnight* (Simon and Schuster, New York, 1978)

Moyers, Bill, 'In the Kingdom of the Half-Blind', National Security Archive, <http://www.gwu.edu/~nsarchiv/anniversary/moyers.htm>

Mueller, John, 'Pearl Harbor: Military Inconvenience, Political Disaster' in *International Security*, Vol. 16, No. 3 (Winter, 1991–1992), pp. 172–203

Murphy, Gerald, 'George Washington's Farewell Address, 1796', (The Cleveland Free-Net - aa300), distributed by the Cybercasting Services Division of the National Public Telecomputing Network (NPTN)<http://www.historian.org/ushist/washingt.htm>

Murray, Margaret A., *Egyptian Temples* (Courier Dover Publications, Mineola, New York, 2002)

Naimark, Norman M., *The Russians in Germany; A History of the Soviet Zone of Occupation, 1945–1949* (Harvard University Press, Cambridge, 1995)

Nasser, Gamal Abdel, *President Gamal Abdel Nasser's Speeches and Press Interviews during the year 1958* (Cairo, UAR, Information Department, 1959)

National Indian Law Library, *Landmark Indian Law Cases* (Wm. S. Hein Publishing, New York, 2002)

National Park Service, 'Permanent Indian Frontier' <http://www.nps.gov/archive/fosc/pif.htm>

NationMaster Encyclopedia, 'James A. Rhodes', <http://www.nationmaster.com/encyclopedia/James-A.-Rhodes>

*New York Times*, 'Behind Angelo Donghia's Gray Flannel Success', 20 January 1983, < spiderbites.nytimes.com/pay_1983/articles_1983_01_00001.html>

Norman, Geoffrey, 'R.I.P., Mighty O', *Smithsonian Magazine*, November 2006 <http://www.smithsonianmag.com/history-archaeology/points-nov06.html>

Norwich, John Julius, *Byzantium: The Early Centuries* (Penguin Books, London, 1990)

O'Donovan, Oliver & Lockwood, Joan, *From Irenaeus to Grotius: A Sourcebook in Christian Political Thought 100–1625* (Wm. B. Eerdmans Publishing, Grand Rapids, Michigan, 1999)

Office of the Press Secretary, The White House, 'President Delivers "State of the Union"', 28 January 2003, <http://www.whitehouse.gov/news/releases/2003/01/20030128-19.html>

Office of the Press Secretary, The White House, 'President Names Envoy to Iraq', 6 May 2003, <http://www.whitehouse.gov/news/releases/2003/05/20030506-3.html>

Office of the Press Secretary, The White House, 'Vice President Speaks at VFW 103rd National Convention', 26 August 2002, <http://www.whitehouse.gov/news/releases/2002/08/20020826.html>

O'Reilly, Bill, 'The O'Reilly Factor, Transcript 11-30-2001' <http://www.oreilly-sucks.com/transcripts/pressvoreilly.htm>

Pastor, Ludwig, *The History Of The Popes From The Close Of The Middle Ages, Volume 1* (Kegan Paul, Trench, Trubner, & Co, London, 1899).

Pastor, Ludwig, *The History Of The Popes From The Close Of The Middle Ages, Volume 27* (Routledge & Kegan Paul Ltd, London, 1952).

Pencak, Professor William, 'Representing the Eighteenth-Century World: Benjamin Franklin, Trickster', Penn State University, <http://www.trinity.edu/org/tricksters/TrixWay/current/Vol%203/Vol3_1/Pencak2.htm>

Perrie, Maureen, Lieven, D. C. B. & Suny, Ronald Grigor, *The Cambridge History of Russia* (Cambridge University Press, New York, 2006)

Philip IV, quoted in Leinart, Mary Adelle, 'The Iconography of the Knights Templar' (2002)
< http://www.skjaere.me.uk/dissertation/introduction.html>

Pipes, Daniel, 'Conspiracy: How the Paranoid Style Flourishes and Where It Comes From' (1997) <http://www.danielpipes.org/article/2890>

Polk, James K., 'Inaugural Address, Tuesday, March 4, 1845', The Avalon Project, Yale Law School <http://avalon.law.yale.edu/19th_century/polk.asp>

Polk, James K., 'Message of President Polk, May 11, 1846', The Avalon Project, Yale Law School <http://www.yale.edu/lawweb/avalon/presiden/messages/polk01.htm>

Polk, James K., quoted in *Encyclopaedia Britannica*, 'The Age of Santa Anna Texas and the Mexican-American War', <http://www.britannica.com/EBchecked/topic/379167/Mexico/27359/The-age-of-Santa-Anna-Texas-and-the-Mexican-American-War>

Prescott, William Hickling, *History of the reign of Ferdinand and Isabella the Catholic* (George Routledge & Sons, London, 1854)

Priestly, Jospeh, quoted in *The Theological and Miscellaneous Works of Joseph Priestly, Vol II* by Joseph Priestly & John Towill Rutt (G. Smallfield, Hackney, 1782)

Rawnsley, H. D., *Idylls and Lyrics of the Nile* (D. Nutt, London, 1894)

Rayner, Ed, Stapley, Ron, *Debunking History* (Sutton Publishing, Gloucestershire, 2006)

Reagan, Ronald, 'Annual Republican Senate-House Dinner April 7, 1981' <http://www.reagan.utexas.edu/archives/speeches/1981/40781b.htm>

Roberts, J.M., *The Pelican History of the World* (Pelican Books, Harmondsworth, UK, 1980)

Rogers, Nicholas, *Crowds, Culture, and Politics in Georgian Britain* (Oxford University Press, New York, 1998)

Roosevelt, Franklin D., 'Address to Congress Requesting a Declaration of War with Japan December 8, 1941', Franklin D. Roosevelt Presidential Library and Museum, <http://www.fdrlibrary.marist.edu/real/decwarsp.rm>

Rosman, Doreen, *The Evolution of the English Churches 1500–2000* (Cambridge University Press, Cambridge, 2003)

Rous, John, 'Historia Regum Angliae', Richard III Society <http://www.r3.org/rnt1991/royaltree.html>

Rous, John, 'Rous Roll 1483–85', Richard III Society <http://www.r3.org/rnt1991/royaltree.html>

Rumsfeld, Donald, ABC Interview, 'This Week with George Stephanopoulos', 30 March 2003, <http://www.usembassy.it/file2003_03/alia/A3032803.htm>

Schulte, Regina (ed.), *The Body of the Queen: Gender and Rule in the Courtly World, 1500–2000*, (Berghahn Books, Oxford, 2006)

Scott, Sir Walter, *Ivanhoe*, The Free Library <http://scott.thefreelibrary.com/Ivanhoe>

Serling, Rod, *The Twilight Zone*, 'The Monsters Are Due On Maple Street', CBS, 1960

Seybert, Tony, 'Slavery and Native Americans in British North America and the United States: 1600 to 1865', Slavery in America <http://www.slaveryinamerica.org/history/hs_es_indians_slavery.htm>

Shakespeare, William, *The Complete Works of William Shakespeare* (Avenel Books, New York, 1975)

Sicker, Ted (prod.), 'Indian removal 1814 – 1858', *Africans in America*, Public Broadcasting Service <http://www.pbs.org/wgbh/aia/part4/4p2959.html>

Smitha, Frank E., 'The American Revolution' (2002) <http://www.fsmitha.com/h3/h32-rv.htm>

Solzhenitsyn, Alexander, *One Word of Truth …: The Nobel Speech on Literature* (Bodley Head, London, 1970)

Spencer, Robert, 'The Galileo Myth', *Taki's Magazine*, January 2008 <http://www.takimag.com/site/article/the_galileo_myth/>

Stalin, Josef, 'Michael Moncur's (Cynical) Quotations', The Quotations Page, <http://www.quotationspage.com/quote/198.html>

Stevenson, David, *The Scottish Revolution 1637–44* (John Donald Publishers, Edinburgh, 2003)

Stewart, Mark & Stewart, Paul, *The Indian Removal Act: Forced Relocation* (Compass Point Books, Mankato, Minnesota, 2006)

Stinnett, Robert B., 'December 7, 1941: A Setup from the Beginning', *Honolulu Advertiser*, 7 December 2000

Stoler, Mark A., *George C. Marshall: Soldier-statesman of the American Century* (Twayne Publishers, Woodbridge, 1989)

Tacitus, Annals Book XV, Translated by Church, Alfred John & Brodribb, William Jackson <http://classics.mit.edu/Tacitus/annals.11.xv.html>

Teed, Paul E., *John Quincy Adams: Yankee Nationalist* (Nova Publishers, Hauppauge, New York, 2006)

The Library of Congress Country Studies, 'Soviet Union (former) Stalin's Legacy', CIA World Factbook <http://www.photius.com/countries/soviet_union_former/government/soviet_union_former_government_stalins_legacy.html>

The Nizkor Project, 'The "Protocols of the Elders of Zion"', Jewish Virtual Library <http://www.jewishvirtuallibrary.org/jsource/anti-semitism/protocols.html>

Thornton, John Wingate & Mayhew, Jonathan, *The Pulpit of the American Revolution: Or, The Political Sermons of the Period of 1776: With a Historical Introduction, Notes, and Illustrations* (Sheldon and Company, New York, 1860)

*Time Magazine*, 'The Guns of August 4' 1 March 1968 <http://www.time.com/time/magazine/article/0,9171,941198-2,00.html>

Twain, Mark, 'Advice to Youth', 1882, About.com: Grammar & Composition <http://grammar.about.com/od/classicessays/a/adviceyouth.htm>

United States Congress, 'Investigation of the Pearl Harbor Attack, Report of the Joint Committee on the Investigation of the Pearl Harbor Attack', The Minority Pearl Harbor Report <http://www.ibiblio.org/pha/pha/congress/minority.html>

Urban II, 'Speech at Clermont 1095 (Robert the Monk version)', *Medieval Sourcebook* <http://www.fordham.edu/halsall/source/urban2a.html>

Wallis Budge, E. A., *A Short History of the Egyptian People* (Kessinger Publishing, Whitefish, Montana, 2003)

War and Game, Weapons of the Mexican War 1846–1847 <http://warandgame.wordpress.com/2008/03/05/weapons-of-the-mexican-war-1846%e2%80%931847/>

Ware, Timothy, *The Orthodox Church* (Penguin Books, London, 1997)

Washington, George, quoted in Olcott, Frances Jenkins, 'Good Stories for Holidays', Project Guttenberg <http://www.gutenberg.org/etext/359>

Washington, George, 'Washington's Farewell Address', The Avalon Project at Yale Law School <http://avalon.law.yale.edu/18th_century/washing.asp>

Weir, Alison, *Lancaster & York: The Wars Of The Roses* (Pimlico, London, 1998)

Westmoreland, William, quoted in Singh, M. P., *Quote Unquote: A Handbook of Quotations* (Lotus Press, Twin Lakes, Wisconsin, 2007)

Wilde, Oscar, 'Oscar Wilde Quotes', <http://thinkexist.com/quotation/it-s_not_whether_you_win_or_lose-it-s_how_you/153865.html>

Wilson, Robert Anton, *Reality Is What You Can Get Away With* (New Falcon Publications, Reno, Nevada, 1996)

Windchy, Eugene G., *Tonkin Gulf* (Doubleday, Garden City, New York, 1971)

Wires, Richard, *The Cicero Affair: German Access to British Secrets in World War II*, (Praeger Publishers, Westport, Connecticut, 1999)

Wood, Charles T., *The Deposition of Edward V* (Traditio, 31, 1975)

Woodhead, Linda, *An Introduction to Christianity* (Cambridge University Press, Cambridge, 2004)

World War I Document Archive, 'The *Daily Telegraph* Affair' <http://wwi.lib.byu.edu/index.php/The_Daily_Telegraph_Affair>

Woytinsky, Wladimir S., *Employment and Wages in the United States* (Twentieth Century Fund, New York, 1953)

Yeadon, Glen, 'Gold Fillings, Auschwitz & George Bush', The White Rose <http://www.spiritone.com/~gdy52150/bushies.htm>

Zedong, Mao, 'Policies, Measures And Perspectives For Resisting The Japanese Invasion, July 23, 1937', Selected Works of Mao Tse-tung, Marxists Internet Archive <http://www.marxists.org/reference/archive/mao/selected-works/volume-2/mswv2_01.htm>

Zoch, Paul A., *Ancient Rome: An Introductory History* (University of Oklahoma Press, Norman, Oklahoma, 2000)

Zweig, Stefan, *Marie Antoinette* (Cassell, London, 1988)

# PHOTO CREDITS

AKG images: pages 167, 184, 187, 190

Australpress / Topfoto: page 250

Corbis: pages 29, 60, 84, 142, 146, 154, 164, 194, 202, 208, 214, 219, 226, 230, 273, 307

Getty images: cover, pages 11, 20, 41, 67, 92, 97

Library of Congress (The): pages 72, 77, 80, 280, 287, 290, 295, 300

Photolibrary: pages 6, 17, 24, 35, 36, 44, 48, 52, 58, 65, 98, 104, 108, 113, 118, 120, 136, 149, 168, 173, 239, 240, 245, 252, 259, 264, 276, 302

Picture Desk / Art Archive: pages 12, 30, 178

# INDEX

(page numbers in *italics* indicate illustrations)

Published in 2009 by Pier 9, an imprint of Murdoch Books Pty Limited

Murdoch Books Australia
Pier 8/9
23 Hickson Road
Millers Point NSW 2000
Phone: +61 (0) 2 8220 2000
Fax: +61 (0) 2 8220 2558
www.murdochbooks.com.au

Murdoch Books UK Limited
Erico House, 6th Floor
93–99 Upper Richmond Road
Putney, London SW15 2TG
Phone: +44 (0) 20 8785 5995
Fax: +44 (0) 20 8785 5985
www.murdochbooks.co.uk

Publisher: Diana Hill
Project Editor: Sophia Oravecz
Designer: Hugh Ford
Photo Researcher: Amanda McKittrick

National Library of Australia Cataloguing-in-Publication entry
Author:      Canduci, Alexander.
Title:        The greatest lies in history / Alexander Canduci.
ISBN:        9781741964790 (pbk.)
Notes:       Includes index.
Subjects:   Deception--History.
               Deception--History--Case studies.
Dewey Number:  001.95
A catalogue record for this book is available from the British Library.

Printed in 2009. PRINTED IN CHINA.
Reprinted 2009.